Uncommon Sense

UNCOMMON SENSE

IAN SHAPIRO

Yale
UNIVERSITY PRESS
New Haven and London

Published with assistance from the foundation established in memory of Amasa Stone Mather of the Class of 1907, Yale College.

Copyright © 2024 by Ian Shapiro.
All rights reserved.
This book may not be reproduced, in whole or in part, including illustrations, in any form (beyond that copying permitted by Sections 107 and 108 of the U.S. Copyright Law and except by reviewers for the public press), without written permission from the publishers.

Yale University Press books may be purchased in quantity for educational, business, or promotional use. For information, please e-mail sales.press@yale.edu (U.S. office) or sales@yaleup.co.uk (U.K. office).

Set in Gotham and Adobe Garamond types by IDS Infotech Ltd.

Library of Congress Control Number: 2023944620
ISBN: 978-0-300-27256-7 (hardcover); 978-0-300-27257-4 (paperback)

A catalogue record for this book is available from the British Library.

Contents

Introduction: Misdiagnosing the Enlightenment's Failures   1

PART ONE
RENOVATING THE ENLIGHTENMENT

1   Against Impartiality   27
2   On Sen versus Rawls on Justice   50
3   On Nondomination   73

PART TWO
FORTIFYING DEMOCRACY

4   The New Authoritarianism in Public Choice (with David Froomkin)   123
5   Collusion in Restraint of Democracy: Against Political Deliberation   151
6   On Political Parties   169

CONTENTS

PART THREE
POLITICS IN DARK TIMES

7 Negative Liberty and the Cold War (with Alicia Steinmetz)   197
8 Transforming Power Relations: Leadership, Risk, and Hope (with James Read)   234

Notes   271
Acknowledgments   325
Index   327

INTRODUCTION
Misdiagnosing the Enlightenment's Failures

Intellectuals are often prone to the self-defeating impulse to discard proverbial babies with their bathwater. Preoccupied with unsuccessful ways in which arguments play out or unattractive destinations to which they seem to lead, we mistake local failures for more global ones, insisting on the need for new theories. Or even for new paradigms. Or sometimes for resuscitating old ones. The result can be lost insights and ill-conceived remedies.

Abandoning the Enlightenment Project, as Richard Rorty and Alasdair MacIntyre dubbed it four decades ago, has followed this pattern.[1] The project they had in mind was the centuries-long effort to deploy the tools of reason and science to improve the human condition. For different reasons, they thought the project both self-defeating and subversive of better traditions and practices. MacIntyre lamented that we cannot turn the clock back, proposing instead that we withdraw to local communities until the new dark age he believed was already upon us had passed. Other backward-looking reactions came from Leo Strauss and his followers.[2] Their diagnosis was comparable to MacIntyre's: that Enlightenment-inspired efforts to improve the human condition had spawned rampant relativism and nihilism. By designating each individual the sovereign source of moral judgments and political legitimacy, they gave Friedrich Nietzsche the last laugh—however unwittingly. Although these commentators didn't all agree on what to do instead, they were confident that the Enlightenment Project was dangerously misguided.

But most critics of the Enlightenment followed Rorty's recommendation that we should get beyond it. Postmodernists, post-Marxists, deconstructionists, and poststructuralists of various stripes—often strongly influenced by the linguistic turn in philosophy and the humanities—identified the basic problem as the search for objective knowledge itself. This quest was portrayed as ill-advised in various ways, but recurring themes were that objectivity is impossible because all observation is theory-laden; that we cannot escape "the prison house of language," in Frederick Jameson's colorful phrase; that there is no such thing as impartiality, neutrality, or a "view from nowhere," as Tom Nagel once called it; and that since the rot set in with the Cartesian and Kantian agendas to provide indisputable foundations for knowledge, henceforth we should proceed "without foundations."[3]

The metaphor exemplifies the overreach. Yes, there is no foundation that will support any building of any size constructed from any materials built on any terrain such that it will last forever. But to conclude from this that henceforth we should build them without foundations would result in buildings that would constantly be falling over. At most, the antifoundational critique was applicable to early Enlightenment views that focused on apodictic certainty as the hallmark of genuine knowledge. At least since the time of John Stuart Mill, however, Enlightenment thinkers have recognized that all knowledge claims are corrigible without abandoning the idea that adding to the stock of knowledge is both possible and desirable for improving human well-being. Indeed, specifying what would count as disconfirming evidence for a hypothesis is widely seen as vital to its scientific status. And as Max Weber noted over a century ago, whereas artists and musicians might aspire to create works that will stand unrivaled forever, even the greatest scientists know that eventually their findings will be superseded.[4]

INTRODUCTION

The turn against objectivity is no less politically menacing than it is philosophically misguided. Identifying causal connections in politics is notoriously difficult, but it is hard not to worry about elective affinities between a world in which significant swaths of the intelligentsia deny that there is objective knowledge and the existence of friendly terrain for charlatans to push claims about alternative facts and fake news when faced with discordant evidence; and which helps them score political points by impugning science and expertise about pandemics, climate change, and trade wars.[5] Michael Gove's soundbite that went viral during the Brexit campaign that "the people of this country have had enough of experts" underscores this phenomenon. At the very least, it makes such claims harder to debunk.

What bathwater should be thrown out? In this book, I agree with anti-Enlightenment critics that there is no neutral ground in politics. Closely related, I also agree that there is no general principle of justice—the most frequent candidates being some variant of impartiality, equality, or freedom—that will win the philosophical high ground once someone comes up with the killer argument that vanquishes the alternatives and commands assent from all clearheaded people. Nonetheless, I argue that if you dig through the detritus of unconvincing arguments and failed architectonic endeavors, there is plenty of convergence on the thought that domination is bad for people and that most of us have good reasons to mitigate it when we cannot escape it. Some variant of this commitment animates many Enlightenment authors and shapes their most convincing arguments. There are some hard-boiled Nietzscheans who will never agree, but they are few and far between and might as well be ignored since no argument will convince them anyway. If ever they become a real threat, forcible resistance is the appropriate response.

What should be kept from the Enlightenment Project? Though certainty is unavailable, knowledge is possible and the best way of

INTRODUCTION

adding to it is by deploying reason and the methods of science to good effect. This matters because knowledge is helpful—if not vital—to understanding what fosters domination and how best to manage and mitigate it. Improving knowledge does not guarantee advances in human well-being; knowledge can be pressed into the service of domination as well as into its mitigation. Knowledge is power as Bacon said. How people end up using that power is another matter. That is where politics comes in.

There are three connected reasons for embracing democracy. One has to do with its historical rationale and legitimation. Modern democratic movements emerged to oppose domination, sometimes by centralizing monarchs, sometimes by imperial overseers, sometimes by exclusionary elites. This needs emphasis because too many theorists of democracy are ignorant of this rationale or lose sight of it. This leads them to focus on contrived problems and mount spurious attacks on democracy. Efforts to combat domination by democratic means always have mixed results and sometimes spawn new kinds of domination. Life has more imagination than us. But no political institutions yet devised have done better, so that fostering, defending, and improving democracy remain central to resisting domination.

Democratic institutions are also needed because they are friendly to fallibilist views of knowledge. Since all knowledge claims are corrigible and subject to revision, it never makes sense to turn decisions over to vanguards who claim privileged access to indisputable truth. But this does not mean that experts should be ignored. They should be consulted, but always within a framework of institutions in which their claims can be aired but also contested, often by other experts, without turning the experts into the decision makers. This is standard practice in well-functioning democracies. Experts give testimony in legislative hearings, but the legislators make the decisions. They decide when to revise them in light of what has been learned, knowing

INTRODUCTION

that they will be held accountable at the ballot box by voters whose interests are at stake.

Democracy matters also for the related reason that there are no neutral outcomes in politics. There are winners and losers, and those who lose need avenues to mitigate the harmful effects of policies they oppose and try to get them changed. Even policies that bring gains for everyone benefit some more than others, and there are always other possible policies that would distribute benefits and burdens differently. If there are no avenues for loyal opposition, eventually there will be disloyal opposition. Effective democracy depends on making loyal opposition possible.

The chastened Enlightenment outlook just sketched motivates the chapters that follow. They magnify it in ways that I hope will render it plausible and alluring. Part I deals with the hunt for an Archimedean point of view in arguments about justice, and more importantly with what remains once we understand why that quest fails. Much of this endeavor has been informed by a version of Kant's ethics, and in particular by his search for imperatives that can be affirmed from all reasonable points of view.[6] John Rawls's *Theory of Justice* was the catalyst for this effort, but many others continued pursuing it long after Rawls gave up trying to provide incontrovertible foundations for his theory.[7] To the extent that the impulse is Kantian it is a bastardized Kantianism, since Kant himself was skeptical that propositions about politics and human welfare would ever rise to the level of categorical imperatives.[8] I am with the historical Kant here. Political philosophy rests on hypothetical imperatives all the way down. This means abandoning more extravagant expectations about what it can deliver.

At the heart of what must be abandoned is the aspiration to come up with impartial principles of justice that are beyond democratic political battles. Neo-Kantians think of these as shaping what Rawls once described as the basic structure of political institutions: the constitutive rules that are immune from the hurly-burly of everyday politics. By this they don't only mean procedural rules like legal due process or insisting on democratic elections, but also principles governing the nature and distribution of rights, opportunities, income, and wealth. There are about as many accounts of what these should be as there are neo-Kantian theorists, a clue to the reality that they are a bit like a group of people debating whether the number seven is yellow, blue, or red. Rather than proffer my own such account, I argue in chapter 1 that the enterprise itself is hopeless. I do this by considering the case for impartiality put forward by Brian Barry, the most consistent and thoroughgoing neo-Kantian and the most formidable partisan of justice as impartiality. I show that Barry's argument fails on its own terms, and that insofar as his substantive claims are appealing, this is because they implicitly invoke hostility to domination. Moreover, I argue that Barry's defense of impartiality lives in considerable tension with his earlier—compelling—work on democracy and majority rule. He would have done better to stick with it rather than chase the mirage of impartiality over the horizon.

Maybe we shouldn't give up on the idea of impartiality so easily. Perhaps it can be detached from the paraphernalia of neo-Kantian theorizing, yet still generate viable principles for deciding what justice requires independently of democratic politics. I explore this possibility in chapter 2 by taking up Amartya Sen's alternative to neo-Kantian theory, based on his less ambitious approach to political theorizing and an Aristotelian view of human psychology. Sen has been developing different components of this view in a variety of forums for decades, but in 2009 he synthesized them into a programmatic statement in *The Idea of Justice* that has widely been billed as a major alternative to the neo-Kantian venture.[9] I argue that Sen is right to abjure the search for principles that can be affirmed from all reasonable points of view, but that his rejection of what he describes as Rawls's transcendental theory amounts to a typical instance of throwing the baby out with the bathwater. Moreover, Sen's defense of impartiality is even less convincing than Barry's. It leaves him with arguments that are so underspecified that they yield no serviceable conclusions at all. As with Barry, his convincing claims depend for their appeal on hostility to domination. His other positions will not likely persuade anyone other than those who already share his priors about justice. He is preaching to his choir.

If Sen's critique of Rawls misses the mark, what of Rawls's theory? I pursue that question in chapter 3. Rawls's theory of justice was built on a bedrock commitment to equality that much subsequent literature has embraced, even if there is notorious disagreement over the question "equality of what?" Indeed, many protagonists in that literature—including Sen—maintain that the bedrock commitment to equality is so universal that it stands in no need of defense. I think they are wrong about that. Perhaps there is some ultimate sense in which we are all moral equals, though I am skeptical even of this. Long before reaching questions like whether Hitler, Stalin, and Pol Pot are moral equals of the rest of us, it would not be unreasonable to maintain that some people are morally superior to others. But this is not worth pursuing here because protagonists in the "equality of what?" debates all the way back to Rawls are trying to get a lot more blood out of this particular stone than that. From a bedrock postulate of moral equality, they want to derive substantive principles governing the distribution of society's rights, resources, and obligations. As with Barry and Sen, close inspection reveals Rawls's arguments either as unconvincing or to be stalking horses for appeals to nondomination.

Perhaps most roads lead to nondomination, but what is it? There are multiple accounts on offer, some complementary and some competing. A second goal of chapter 3 is to explain the advantages of my conception over the alternatives, and to spell out its political implications. I portray domination as a particular kind of deprivation of human freedom that can be changed if those responsible for it behave differently. Domination need not be conscious, but it is only domination—as distinct from a legitimate exercise of power—if it serves an illicit purpose. This account shares some common features with those of Jürgen Habermas, Michael Foucault, Quentin Skinner, Michael Walzer, and Philip Pettit. But I differ from them on some conceptual matters, and more importantly on the political implications of embracing nondomination. All these authors except Foucault discern connections between combating domination and democratic politics, as do implicit invokers of nondomination like Rawls and Barry. This is the right way to go. Unfortunately, however, preoccupations with republican institutions, participation, and deliberation lead many of them and their followers down blind alleys, with the result that the kinds of democracy they advocate are not up to the job. At best, they amount to attractive nuisances, diverting attention from what matters. In some cases, they make things worse.

What is the best kind of democracy to combat domination? Addressing that question is my focus in part II. Before dealing with the friendly fire from blinkered allies, I take up the hostile fire that has been directed at democracy's normative and conceptual foundations for decades. By attacking the desirability and even rationality of majority rule, these attacks have made it easier to push alternatives that put heavy reliance on courts, and more recently on executive power. As David Froomkin and I argue in chapter 4, these attacks have taken especially virulent forms in recent decades, making the world more receptive to authoritarian populism.

This matters because democratic institutions are far from secure. In 1979, John Dunn observed that, despite widespread disagreement about what democracy is and what it requires, most people embraced some variant of it.[10] When communism began collapsing a decade later, Francis Fukuyama argued in the pages of the *National Interest* that the world was approaching a liberal-democratic end to history.[11] Few informed observers would countenance such assertions today. Confidence in public institutions has been declining in most democracies for decades.[12] Even in older democracies like the United States, large sectors of the public have diminished confidence in democratic institutions, parties, and politicians. Many even reveal willingness to sacrifice democracy to achieve their preferred political outcomes.[13]

There are many economic and political causes of voter dissatisfaction.[14] Here my focus is on the intellectual sources: the failure of scholars and other intellectuals to articulate and defend robust accounts of democratic institutions that can effectively combat domination. It is hard to assign precise causal weight to such factors, but only the most thoroughgoing reductionist would read ideas and ideology right out of the equation. If the resources poured in recent decades into think tanks like the Heritage Foundation, the Cato Institute, and the American Enterprise Institute that are committed to limiting democracy via constitutional and other constraints are anything to go by, hostile critics don't doubt the efficacy of investing in public ideology.[15] In this case, the ideas have been especially destructive: intellectuals not only have failed to supply robust defenses of majoritarian democracy, too many of them have actively subverted it.

The attacks are traceable to the 1950s assault on majority rule in the wake of Kenneth Arrow's Nobel Prize–winning impossibility theorem, which purported to establish that no democratic decision rule can amalgamate individual preferences into a collective expression of the people's will.[16] As Froomkin and I explain, this entire exercise was predicated on faulting majority rule for failing to clear an unnecessary hurdle: to come up with something approximating Rousseau's account of the general will. They ignored the many reasons for endorsing majority rule that have been around for centuries and have nothing to do with solving this problem, but everything to do with minimizing the potential for domination.

The early public choice theorists ignored these other reasons. Instead, they mounted frontal assaults based on the alleged irrationality of majority rule to buttress the case for strong constitutional checks on legislatures to be enforced by courts. This was a reasonable bet for them, given their agenda to limit the reach of democratic politics and the historical behavior of courts in the United States. From antebellum America through the Civil War, Reconstruction, Jim Crow, and Lochner eras, courts have frustrated Congress much more often than they have deferred to it. They were dependable allies for limiting congressional power.

In recent decades, however, a new generation of analytically minded critics of Congress has shifted the focus. People like Eric Posner, Adrian Vermeule, William Howell, Terry Moe, and Francis Fukuyama continue with much the same diagnosis of majoritarian legislatures as the 1950s public choice theorists, and they enumerate familiar alleged consequences like excessive rent-seeking, pork-barrel politics, and ever-increasing public spending. But instead of courts, they have identified strong executive power as the appropriate remedy.

Why this change? In retrospect, it looks like the critics overreacted to a huge historical outlier: the Warren Court. Chief Justice Earl Warren, appointed by President Eisenhower in 1953, ushered in the most progressive Court in American history. By the time Warren Burger replaced him in 1969, the political, legal, and economic landscape had been transformed to entrench core elements of the New Deal, civil rights, and the Great Society. Liberal jurists like John Hart Ely, Ronald Dworkin, and Laurence Tribe welcomed these developments as way stations on a secular path to a better future.

INTRODUCTION

In such a world, it is not surprising that opponents of big government would lose faith in the courts and look elsewhere for instruments to limit congressional power. Their arguments for strengthening executives dovetailed with "unitary" theories of the executive that, since the 1980s, had been gaining currency among conservative legal theorists and presidents who sought end-runs around recalcitrant blocking coalitions in Congress.[17] As we show, however, while these critics identify genuine problems in Congress, their remedies can and do make them worse.

Nor is it surprising that some of these commentators have been getting cold feet lately, as the prospect of minimally constrained executive power has stopped being an academic conceit or something that happens in faraway places like Russia, Hungary, and Turkey. Be careful what you wish for. Moreover, they needn't have worried. Much to the chagrin of liberals who put great faith in the Warren Court, the Burger, Rehnquist, and Roberts Courts have reverted to type, so that today liberals can do little more than remember the Warren era nostalgically as the Court's "heroic age."[18] Judges tend to be conservative by disposition, and the appointing process makes it scarcely credible that another Warren Court is anywhere on the horizon. From 1968 through 2022, Republican presidents appointed nineteen justices to the Supreme Court while Democrats appointed five. The combination of lifetime appointments with structural advantages for Republicans in the Senate and the Electoral College has tilted things strongly in their favor.

Faulting majoritarian democracy for failing Rousseau's test is not restricted to the ideological right. Many who count themselves on the left have been equally unimpressed by the ways in which the political system aggregates—or fails to aggregate—people's preferences. In the 1970s and 1980s this dissatisfaction produced the turn to participatory democratic theory, as theorists sought mechanisms to relocate decisions to local venues in which people could decide things for themselves.[19] More recently, theorists interested in enhancing participation have turned to deliberation, the motivating impulse being that if majoritarian procedures cannot discover a general will, perhaps deliberative processes can manufacture one. Whether it is random samples of the population engaging in in-depth discussion of issues much as juries do or taking advantage of new possibilities opened up by the internet, the goal is to engage citizens directly in public decisions issue by issue. The expectation is that this will enhance the prospects for agreement, or at least that it will produce better-informed and perhaps even better decisions.[20]

Will it? Should it? I take up these questions in chapter 5. The more or less explicit assumption behind almost all of this literature is that, when attainable, agreement is a good thing in politics. Yet this is far from self-evident, as can be gleaned by reflecting on the fact that in the economy we often outlaw the search for agreement as collusion in restraint of trade. This is because it undermines efficiency-enhancing competition. This, I argue, is a good analog for thinking about the political system. Structured competition over public policy is the most democracy-enhancing way yet discovered to institutionalize Mill's contention that competition over ideas is the path to advancing knowledge. The deliberative theorists miss this, embracing institutional choices that undermine efficacious political competition. Worse, institutional rules designed to promote deliberation are easily hijacked by clientelist representatives who condition their agreement on the provision of local private goods at the expense of good public policy—the opposite of what deliberativists say they are after.

The underlying difficulty with writing shaped by the neo-Rousseauist quest for convergence on a general will, its alleged failures, and proposed remedies for those failures, is that it starts in the wrong place. Rather than begin by asking when and under what conditions the people should delegate decisions to politicians, we should start the analysis with the central subject matter of politics: power. Power, as I argue in chapter 6 and has been recognized by political philosophers since the seventeenth century, is a natural monopoly. The fundamental challenge is to design institutions to manage it both democratically and in the public interest, so as to prevent it from being used for domination. Rather than make it difficult to wield power without compromise as the American system was designed to do and as multiparty systems do, the better course is to foster programmatic competition between strong political parties that are then held to account by voters based on their performance in office.

Viewed from this perspective, responding to the flaws in Congress with an agenda to relocate power elsewhere—to courts, the executive, deliberative bodies, social movements, ballot initiatives, behind the next tree—is yet another instance of throwing the baby out with the bathwater. So is a diagnosis that results in efforts further to weaken America's already weak legislative parties by decentralizing control over them. I have written elsewhere about why strong, disciplined parties produce better public policy.[21] Here, my goal is to explain why they are not a necessary evil to be traded off against what, ideally, we should want from democracy. Rather, they offer the best possible way to realize the Enlightenment's promise in politics. This turns on the unique properties of majority rule, and the best ways to institutionalize it.

Useful insights here can be garnered from the seventeenth-century social contract theorists. This might seem surprising, as they are often associated with stylized accounts of presocial individuals coming together and then delegating authority to governments. However, for both Hobbes and Locke, the social contract did not embody any act of delegation. The contract was among the governed

INTRODUCTION

to submit to governments that govern in their interests. They would never have taken seriously the libertarian conceit—even as a heuristic—that people like Robert Nozick indulge to the effect that a modern society and economy ever did or could function without government.[22] Having lived through the execution of one king, the flight of another, and a debilitating civil war, they knew better. They had no doubt that power is a natural monopoly and that this reality makes effective government essential to human well-being.

More importantly, they saw good reasons to embrace majority rule that are unrelated to whether there is any such thing as a general will. Instead, they flow from understanding that the natural monopoly character of power makes collective action ubiquitous to human interaction. Something must determine the form it takes; the question is what? Hobbes maintained that majority rule should prevail when a new state is founded by representatives, as it does when the government is a representative assembly. Locke went further, grounding all political legitimacy in majority rule. Demanding supermajorities or other devices to make change difficult protects the status quo and minority tyranny. Hence their presumption in favor of majority rule.

If seventeenth-century theorists recognized that majority rule can—and in some formulations must—be the ultimate source of legitimate government, they lacked accounts of institutions by which people could prevent governments from abusing their power monopoly. They really answered only the first of two challenges that would subsequently be summarized by Madison in Federalist 51: that in designing a government "to be administered by men over men," it is necessary not only to "enable the government to control the governed," but also to "oblige it to control itself."[23] Hobbes offered no mechanism at all, and Locke insisted on obedience unless there was a long train of abuses that was sufficiently egregious to warrant the risks of revolution.

INTRODUCTION

Madison came up with a solution that would form the basis of modern theories of pluralist democracy. Tyranny would result, he feared, if a faction representing a subset of the population controlled the government. But because factional divisions could be eradicated—if this was possible at all—only by tyrannical means, his answer was instead to multiply them. This led him to reject the then-conventional wisdom that republican government could operate only in small homogeneous polities such as ancient Athens or the Italian civic republics, and argue instead for expansion. "Extend the sphere," he declared, "and you take in a greater variety of parties and interests; you make it less probable that a majority of the whole will have a common motive to invade the rights of other citizens; or if such a common motive exists, it will be more difficult for all who feel it to discover their own strength, and to act in unison with each other."[24] Robert Dahl would relabel this insight as the theory of cross-cutting cleavages.[25]

But Madison lost his nerve. Acknowledging dependence on the people as "the primary control on the government," he nonetheless insisted that "experience has taught mankind the necessity of auxiliary precautions." Asserting without evidence that in republican governments "the legislative authority necessarily predominates," he insisted on hobbling it with a bicameral system in which the two chambers would be governed by "different modes of election and different principles of action, as little connected with each other as the nature of their common functions and their common dependence on the society will admit." Not content with that, he celebrated the robust constraints that the states place on the national government in America's "compound republic," and got behind strong separation of powers with particular attention to fortifying the executive. "Ambition must be made to counteract ambition" was his slogan to justify the sclerotic web of institutions that the founders bequeathed to subsequent generations.[26]

15

Among the things they got wrong is that far from being the strongest branch, the legislature would turn out to be the weakest. The judiciary is more consequential than they expected, and there has been a steady migration of power to the executive. A major reason for this is that it is inherently difficult for hundreds of legislators representing diverse interests to agree on preventing encroachment from other branches. Indeed, some might have interests that are better aligned with the president's than with their leaders in Congress—belying Madison's admonition that "the interest of the man must be connected with the constitutional rights of the place."[27] Republican institutions are often praised in the nondomination literature, but their advocates seldom study them. If they did, perhaps they would see how self-defeating they can be.

Parliamentary systems come closer to institutionalizing the pluralist model in which cross-cutting cleavages do the important work that Dahl took from Madison, but only if they include large, strong parties that engage in programmatic competition that empower them as governments to implement policies that serve most voters well over time. In separation-of-powers systems, the best reforms are those that get those systems to operate more like parliamentary ones by strengthening legislatures and the parties within them at the expense of the other branches and centers of government.[28] It is not surprising that democracy's enemies are trying to weaken legislatures and parties in all these systems. More distressing, I argue, is how many who see themselves as its friends work for changes that amount to little more than bloodletting.

This is a gloomy conclusion, but my message in part III is that there can be good grounds for hope even in dispiriting political circumstances. I begin making this case with Alicia Steinmetz in chapter 7 by considering Isaiah Berlin's pessimistic assessment of the prospects for human freedom during the Cold War. He distinguished negative

INTRODUCTION

libertarians, committed to protecting—and in some formulations expanding—the zone within which people are free to do as they please, from positive libertarians who champion the capacity to achieve such things as escaping exploitation, a certain standard of living, or some more abstract good like happiness or well-being. Berlin's famous lecture romped through the history of ideas classifying the likes of Hobbes, Locke, Constant, Spencer, and Mill as negative libertarians, to be distinguished from positive libertarians like Rousseau, Kant, Hegel, Marx, and Fichte.

Berlin and the other Cold War liberals like Karl Popper and George Kennan, who endorsed his argument, were champions of negative freedom. They saw it as threatened by a particularly virulent instance of positive freedom embodied in Soviet communism. But whereas people like Kennan believed that negative freedom would blossom once the communist threat disappeared, Berlin was less sanguine. He believed insecurity to be endemic to the human condition. This darker view of human psychology led him to posit an almost fatal human attraction to positive libertarian promises, snake oil as they might invariably be, that makes it hard to get people to embrace negative freedom—let alone fight for it.

From our post–Cold War and post-2016 vantage point, the verdict at first sight appears mixed. On the one hand, Berlin's claim seems vindicated by the resurgence of virulent identity politics and ethno-nationalism, and many people's willingness to cede democratic freedoms for promises from authoritarian seducers. That hardly seems like evidence of a groundswell of support for negative freedom. On the other hand, much politics in the older democracies seems like negative freedom on steroids. The antitax, antiregulatory, and gun lobby movements; extensive hostility to public health measures in the face of a catastrophic pandemic; climate change denialism by people who affirm rights to believe in alternative facts that verge on rights to inhabit alternative realities: these all suggest that "Don't tread on me!" ideologies are alive and kicking. The January 6, 2021, assault on the U.S. Capitol was a potent illustration of this politics.

This conflicting evidence points to what should have been evident all along: here is another instance of discarding the proverbial baby. The question never should have been: "Should we reject negative liberty?" or "Should we reject positive liberty?" No one is free or unfree simpliciter, if only one can arrive at the right definition of freedom. As Gerald MacCallum, Jr., pointed out half a century ago, assertions about human freedom invariably involve reference to agents, restraints or enabling conditions, and actions. Some of this reference is often implicit; restraints and enabling conditions can easily be redescribed as one another, as when a prisoner is said to be unfree because of the presence of a lock or the absence of a key. Negative libertarians tend to focus on the agents and deploy the language of restraints, whereas positive libertarians emphasize what the agents seek to do and what they need to do it.[29]

The debate over "kinds" of freedom diverts attention from what really matters: identifying who is free or unfree, from what constraints or because of what enabling conditions, to do—or not do—what? Making these things explicit draws attention to the ways in which claims about freedom are often incomplete, misleading, or hypocritical—as in Anatole France's quip that "the law forbids rich and poor alike from sleeping under bridges, begging in the streets and stealing loaves of bread."[30] Comparable issues arise in debates about domination, diverting attention from differences between trivial and consequential variants of it and the ways in which the costs of avoiding domination by some can be imposed on others.

Seen in this light, while post–Cold War triumphalism was ill-considered, and there is indeed no spontaneous flowering of Enlightenment values in the wake of communism's disappearance, that is not a reason to throw in the towel. Berlin was convincing that people are more easily mobilized in support of illiberal and antidemocratic causes when they feel insecure, and it is plausible to trace the recent advent of populist and authoritarian politics in the older democracies to significant increases in insecurity for many people.[31] But rather than search for the causes of these developments in armchair prognostications about human psychology, it makes better sense to look for them in the declining capacity of many democracies to meet the basic interests of large numbers of their populations, who have consequently become alienated. Stagnant or falling real wages, employment insecurity, and downward mobility have made them frightened and resentful—easy fodder for populist demagogues. Why has this happened?

One major reason is the disappearance of industrial jobs due to globalization and, increasingly, technological innovation. People who once had well-founded expectations of lifetime employment in occupations that brought them meaning and status as well as economic security must now change jobs multiple times over their work lives, often from one low-paying and low-status occupation to another. Many of them also believe, plausibly, that their children are unlikely to face better prospects—forcing them to remain dependent for income and shelter well into adulthood.[32] In addition to long-term maintenance of adult children, these people might well also have to support aging parents who are living in or on the verge of poverty.

In all of the older democracies these developments have been compounded by growing fiscal stress on welfare states as aging populations are supported by shrinking working-age populations, leading to diminished health coverage and anxiety over the reliability of Social Security and similar pension systems elsewhere.[33] In the United States, this is happening in a context of the virtual disappearance of defined benefit pensions in the private sector and their replacement by 401Ks and other programs that are subject to the unpredictable gyrations of financial markets. The result: increasingly widespread fear of poverty in old age.[34]

These vulnerabilities are easily exploited by populists who stoke the politics of resentment. Ever since Ronald Reagan illustrated the political efficacy of attacking Cadillac-driving "welfare queens," it has become easy political sport to fuel this resentment by telling voters that undeserving others are "cutting in line," so that voters increasingly feel, as Arlie Hochschild's study of oil workers in Louisiana has shown, that they are strangers in their own land.[35] Blaming foreigners for stealing their jobs is a more recent additive to this populist mix, accompanied by purported remedies that are unlikely to address the underlying insecurity.[36]

It might seem like thin gruel to be told that our baleful situation results from historical contingencies rather than inescapable features of human psychology, but giving up is neither productive nor warranted. The 1930s and early 1940s surely must have been at least as dispiriting for people with democratic sensibilities who aspired to leave their children a better world than they had inherited. The Great Depression ushered in extraordinary levels of unemployment and inequality, widespread insecurity, fascism, the Holocaust, and the most devastating war in history that, by conservative estimates, killed at least 60 million people and had shattering effects for many millions more.[37] Few, then, would have predicted the economic and political renaissance that subsequent decades would bring: unprecedented levels of wealth and inclusive growth; the Great Society in the United States and democratic welfare states in so many countries devastating by the war; and international peace—at least compared to the first half of the century.[38] There were continuing tensions to be sure, but the superpowers limited themselves to proxy conflicts in the developing world and avoided nuclear catastrophe. The Cold War ended

INTRODUCTION

peacefully and by century's end there were more democracies than nondemocracies in the world for the first time, a circumstance that has persisted into the 2020s.[39]

Except that "the decades" didn't bring these changes. It took sustained imagination and focused effort to design, fund, and implement the Marshall Plan in Europe and the economic revitalization of Japan; to create and then sustain the United Nations where previously the League of Nations had floundered and failed; and to negotiate arms reduction treaties and a peaceful exit from communism where globally devastating war had been an ever-present threat. This took effective leadership, to be sure, but leaders also had to mobilize public support for what they were doing. As Albert Hirschman once noted—supporting a better Rousseauist contention than his general will—it is when people believe that the government is creating a better world that they start seeing participation as a benefit rather than a cost.[40] The resulting positive feedback loops that sustained postwar Western democracies have atrophied, but that does not mean that they cannot be restored.

My final chapter supplies ballast for the impulse that even in dark political times, refusing to give up hope can be reasonable and efficacious—as well as inspiring. In the 1980s the great majority of informed observers believed that South Africa was heading for a calamitous political outcome. The African National Congress had abandoned nonviolence in favor of armed resistance in 1960, following decades of increasingly violent repression by the white minority government. The conflict had escalated as their military wing, uMkhonto we Sizwe, became better trained and organized and a new, more militant generation of black youth came of age. Apartheid as it then existed was obviously doomed, but that did not mean that its demise would be peaceful or that it would be followed by a transition to democracy.

Few people would have bet on either of those outcomes in 1985. Facing ostracism, divestment, and sanctions abroad, and increasingly confident and assertive opposition at home, the beleaguered government had responded by doubling down on its intransigence without achieving a hint of capitulation from the liberation movement. Ever-increasing repression, a coup, autocoup, protracted civil war, or some combination of these all seemed more likely than a negotiated transition to a majority-rule democracy.[41] Yet that is what happened in significant part, as James Read and I argue, because Nelson Mandela and F. W. de Klerk managed to infuse their hopes for a better future into negotiations, reinforcing one another's commitments to a peaceful democratic outcome and making it easier to convince skeptics in both camps that the agreement was worth embracing and investing in. It also enabled leaders to build support for the new dispensation among communities that had been riven by the most destructive kinds of identity politics for decades, fostering legitimacy for the nascent democratic order. Three decades later, South Africa remains one of the developing world's better-performing democracies.

Stunning as this outcome has been, South Africa's subsequent history underscores the perils of triumphalism. As in many other democracies, support for political parties, leaders, and institutions has been at or near record lows for the past decade.[42] Political transformation was not matched by economic transformation; so, despite the emergence of a small black middle class and a tiny black millionaire class, South Africa remains the most unequal country for which we have data. The richest 10 percent own over half the country's wealth while the poorest 40 percent own just 7.2 percent. A quarter of the population lives in poverty.[43] Thirty-five percent of the workforce and two-thirds of young workers are unemployed—also a global record.[44] Corruption is rife, particularly in central government procurement, with highly visible scandals fueling the government's legitimacy deficit.[45] With anemic economic growth rates failing to keep pace even with population growth since 2017 and medium-term projections no better, prospects for the future are not encouraging.[46]

This mixed picture is not new. At many points since South Africa's transition, it has been possible to look back at impressive achievements yet at the same time find present and future challenges daunting.[47] And what we see in South Africa we see across much of the democratic world. Democracy can be a precarious achievement, not the inevitable endpoint of a benign teleological process. It is the best political system yet devised to combat domination, thereby helping people to realize the Enlightenment's promise. But democracies can and do fall apart, and today many of them are in serious disrepair.[48] The answer is not to give up on the enterprise, but instead to rise to the challenges with the tools of reason and science. It's not just that the alternatives are worse, which they assuredly are. Hope has a performative dimension. Cultivating "a passion for the possible," as Hirschman put it, can broaden horizons—inspiring people to take risks to prevent further deterioration and work for a better future.[49]

The book's title doffs a genuflecting cap to Tom Paine, one of the Enlightenment's most steadfast champions. Paine is inspiring not just because he triumphed over daunting odds and bounced back from many personal catastrophes, but also because he personified Hirschman's passion for the possible. He combined an unwavering commitment to reason with the irrepressible conviction that it could move people to reject dogmatism and fight domination, whether by monarchs, colonial powers, or exploiters of the poor. *Common Sense* is widely credited for galvanizing disaffected Americans to demand independence. His *American Crisis* letters won him comparable acclaim for sustaining them through the darkest days of the Revolutionary War. The rousing effects of his *Rights of Man* on Britain's lower orders alarmed the authorities enough that first they tried to discredit him

INTRODUCTION

and, when that failed, they hounded him into exile—convicting him in abstentia of seditious libel.[50] Paine was a democrat to his core, but not out of any conviction that people's preferences can be amalgamated into general wills, that they can govern through deliberative or other participatory processes, or because democracy promises self-government for all. Rather, he thought it obvious that monarchy is an indefensible source of domination and that democracy is the most promising alternative. Paine also stands as an enduring reminder that good arguments can be efficacious in politics and that it is important not to give up, especially in an era like ours when the path forward seems murky at best.

PART ONE
Renovating the Enlightenment

1

Against Impartiality

Iustitia, the goddess of justice, holds a sword in her right hand and a set of scales in her left. The sword represents the power to punish, while the scales, held slightly above it, signal that fair weighing of the merits comes first. But it is the blindfold, common in depictions of her since the sixteenth century, that proclaims her impartiality. Lady Justice is blind.[1] She screens out any risk of favoritism, special pleading, or irrelevant distraction so as to render decisions that embody unbiased reason. It is this image of justice as, above all, impartial that many in our generation of political philosophers have found alluring. In my view, they are misguided. Lady Justice is indeed blind; she cannot help us see what justice is or what it requires.

My goal is to establish that arguments about the justice of political arrangements do not turn in any important way on the idea of impartiality. To the extent that impartiality does play a role, this is either in the application of ideas about justice that have been defended on some other grounds, or impartiality turns out on inspection to be a stalking horse for those other grounds. Put differently, disagreements about the justice of political arrangements cannot be settled by appeals to impartiality. Rather, hostility to domination, or something close to it, usually does the heavy lifting. If I am right, people would do better to recognize that debates about impartiality are confusing red herrings and focus instead on the sources of domination and the means of preventing it.

Why bother? Partly because impartiality is an attractive nuisance. People who become seduced by the prospect of defending accounts of justice that are rooted in impartiality waste their time on quixotic ventures. Worse than wasting time, however, chasing impartiality over the horizon pulls its advocates in unfortunate political directions. A big part of impartiality's allure is the expectation it fosters that we can come up with principles that are beyond the rough and tumble of politics. This, in turn, leads partisans of impartiality to embrace insulated agencies, typically courts, as their institutional instruments of choice. The connection is, to be sure, not necessary, but there is an elective affinity between commitments to impartiality and embracing institutions that are thought to shield its requirements from politics. Courts are not what they are cracked up to be, however. The upshot is that bad philosophy motivates bad politics. Or so I will argue.

Some clarification of terms is in order. Resisting domination does the heavy lifting, I am arguing, but what is domination? To some extent different people mean different things by it. Especially when they invoke it implicitly as they often do, they are unlikely to define it exhaustively or even clearly. Domination is, in any case, what Wittgenstein described as a family resemblance concept.[2] There is plenty of recognizable overlap among its various meanings, but no single definition captures every intelligible use. So we should not expect too much of definitions.

That said, by domination I will mean the illicit use of power to control people or their choices. This control can be direct or indirect, and more or less conscious, though there is usually a presumption that it is alterable: domination can be stopped or mitigated if those responsible for it alter their conduct. Domination can be trivial, but political philosophers who write about justice are usually concerned with serious domination. This might not always rise quite to the level of Locke's admonition that one "can no more justly make use of another's necessity, to force him to become his vassal" than a stronger person "can seize upon a weaker, master him to his obedience, and with a dagger at his throat offer him death or slavery."[3] But people are usually assumed to have basic interests, including the wherewithal to survive and thrive, at stake.[4] Common reasons for regarding the use of power as illicit are that it compromises those basic interests, that it is arbitrary, or that it is unauthorized.

Denying that impartiality will resolve disagreements about justice does not make it irrelevant to those disagreements. Implementing laws and policies requires institutions that depend on impartial administration. People who violate that kind of impartiality by engaging in self-dealing, bribery, and other kinds of corruption, perpetrate injustice. But that is not what political philosophers usually have in mind, and not what I have in mind, when rejecting impartiality as the basis for justice. Exceptions arise when the rules are themselves compromised. This was well illustrated in Robert Cover's exploration of the quandaries faced by nineteenth-century American judges who had to adjudicate litigation over the fugitive slave laws.[5] But at issue were the unjust laws they were charged with enforcing, not the idea that judges should generally be impartial. Their dilemmas would be material to our concerns here only if recognizing that the injustice of the fugitive slave laws depended on embracing impartiality. That is what I mean to deny.

I begin by considering the most formidable case for justice as impartiality I know of, set out in Brian Barry's 1995 book by that name. His argument relies on a distinction between first-order impartiality, which he agrees is hopelessly vulnerable to well-known objections, and second-order impartiality, which he endorses as immune from them. I show that, despite its apparent appeal, Barry's distinction is untenable, so that his attempt to rescue impartiality as the bedrock of justice fails.

The best reconstruction of his argument shows him to be committed to nondomination instead. In section II, I propose an interpretation of impartialist ventures that makes a degree of historical sense of them, but which also makes it easier to see why they are such a tough sell today. The social democratic welfare states that Barry's generation saw as achievements for impartial justice were in fact time-bound products of the postwar era that would erode as the conditions that gave rise to them dissipated. I end by arguing that, rather than pursue the mirage of impartiality, Barry would have done better to recognize that there are no impartial principles of justice and stick with his earlier defense of majority rule democracy. Doing so offers the best available bet to vindicate the view of justice geared to diminishing domination that he has embraced, implicitly or explicitly, all along. By the same token, others who think that giving courts the authority to limit democratic politics in the name of what justice is alleged to require are playing with fire. Courts are unlikely to promote the causes that their proponents seek over time; they are all too easily hijacked by people with agendas other than, and sometimes antithetical to, preventing domination.

I. Barry on First- and Second-Order Impartiality

At least since William Godwin noted that impartiality might mean allowing one's mother to be killed in a fire in order to save a great benefactor of mankind, people have worried about bedrock commitments to impartiality.[6] Godwin was a radical (utilitarian) partisan of impartiality, but most people treat his example as a reductio ad absurdum that illustrates the infirmity of buying into impartiality hook, line, and sinker. Ignoring impartiality is also problematic, however. It opens the door to the dangers of nepotism and related practices that are no less grating to widely shared sensibilities. This means that distinctions have to be drawn to make sense of the expectation that in some contexts people think that justice requires impartiality, while in others, it seems permissible—perhaps even mandatory—to prefer kith and kin over strangers.[7]

Barry distinguished two kinds of impartiality to avoid these and related difficulties. First-order impartiality concerns the decisions people make about what to do: where to eat and live, whom to associate with, and so on. Barry defined this first-order impartiality as "a requirement of impartial behavior incorporated into a precept." Second-order impartiality, by contrast, supplies the justification for basic legal, moral, and political principles. It does not depend on or require first-order impartiality of people in their daily lives. Second-order impartiality "calls for principles and rules that are capable of forming the basis of free agreement among people seeking agreement on reasonable terms."[8] I am skeptical of the "seeking" part of this, which limits the class of acceptable principles to those that people can be motivated to agree upon, but I will not pursue that matter now.[9] Here my focus is on second-order impartiality itself, and in particular Barry's insistence that what sets it apart from unacceptable theories is that it is impartial among particular conceptions of the good life. In this he shares Rawls's impulse to discover principles of justice that are not biased in favor of particular conceptions of the good, though Barry pursues his agenda by reference to T. M. Scanlon's "reasonableness" test, which obliges us to embrace principles if we cannot supply reasonable grounds to reject them.[10]

In making his case, Barry distinguished those who insist that their particular conceptions of the good pass this reasonableness test, whose claims he thought he could refute, from those who resist the test itself.[11] Barry did not deny that there are people who reject his account of reasonableness or that "they have to be taken seriously" as a political matter. But he insisted that "the only response worth making is to try to defeat them politically, and, if necessary, seek to repress them by force."[12] Barry thus portrayed himself as a Leninist on behalf of reasonableness, but not on behalf of a particular conception of the good life. If, however, it turns out that his account of reasonableness conceals a particular conception of the good life on which it depends, then this becomes a distinction without a difference.

Unfortunately for Barry's argument, that is the case. Moreover, it would be true of any version of impartiality that does the kind of work Barry needs it to do. If such an account remains genuinely second-order in his sense, then concrete political principles cannot be derived from it; if concrete principles can be derived from it, then it embodies a particular conception of the good. My view is that in the end, the only political arrangements on whose behalf we should be Leninists are democratic arrangements. The reason is not that they are impartial, but that they hold out a better chance of mitigating domination than do the going alternatives.

Let's start with the view of the good life that lurks in Barry's Scanlonian exercise. As illustrations of why impartiality should be affirmed, Barry maintained that no one could reasonably reject guarantees of full religious liberty and the right to practice any sexual orientation.[13] If you recognize that the importance of freedom of worship "in the way you think right" is integral to "your own ability to live what you regard as the good life," you will be bound to concede that it is important to others as well. Likewise, "if the expression of your sexual nature is important to your living a good life, as you see it, then again you are asked to accept that it is equally important to those with a different sexual orientation from yours." For Barry, this legitimates an absolute constitutional ban on all discrimination based on religious belief or sexual orientation.[14] By contrast, Barry maintained that the right to abortion does not merit constitutional protection because there is enduring disagreement about its permissibility. Accordingly, he concluded, "there is no way round the point that there are different evaluations of the gravity" of allowing a fetus to be aborted "when put in the balance against the ability of women to control their own fertility."[15]

Notice that what is at stake here for Barry does not turn on the harm done to the fetus, but rather on the irresolvable disagreement about the justifiability of abortion.[16] He might well have been right that this disagreement is irresolvable, but that scarcely distinguishes abortion from the cases that he treats differently. There has often been, and in some quarters continues to be, no less enduring or intense disagreement about the gravity of permitting religious disestablishment or homosexual conduct. What is alleged to differentiate them from abortion, for Barry, is their relevance to a person's "ability to live what you regard as the good life." But that is unconvincing. Many women would reasonably insist that not having to bear an unwanted child is no less vital to the ability to live what they regard as the good life than is freedom of religion or unhampered sexual practice. If Barry had a reason to distinguish among these cases, he did not supply it. It is hard to imagine what a compelling reason could be.

Barry's biases about the good life shaped his application of his reasonableness test elsewhere. Consider his contention that courts should not generally make policy in democracies, but that they should require legislatures to implement their policies in equitable ways. "The key to this approach," he argues, is to distinguish "what gets done and how it gets done." Such principles as "non-discrimination, equal educational opportunity, and equal access to healthcare speak to the question of 'how' and are appropriate subjects for judicial review." Questions about "what," on the other hand, "speak to the overall level of expenditure and the general organization of the service," suiting them better "to the government and legislature, even when they too involve questions of justice."[17]

Barry's position sounds appealingly impartial at first blush. Many who would agree, for instance, that courts should not require governments to support the arts might nonetheless think it legitimate for them to intervene if a government decided to do so but then declared blacks or Jews ineligible to apply for grants. Yet while reasoning of this kind led Barry to endorse the U.S. Supreme Court's 1983 decision in *Bob Jones University v. United States,* which denied tax-exempt status to universities that prohibit interracial dating, he rejected my suggestion that the *Bob Jones* logic should be extended to religious institutions that deny women access to the priesthood.[18] Catholic women who aspire to become priests should not be protected from this inequitable treatment, he said, because this would interfere with essential matters of Church doctrine. "If you believe that the sacraments have efficacy only if administered by a man, you can scarcely regard the sex of the person administering them as irrelevant." This must be beyond dispute, according to Barry, because "being a Catholic entails acceptance of papal authority."[19] Notice the mission creep that Barry engaged in to make this seem plausible. The suggestion was not, after all, that the Church be ordered to admit women to the priesthood, but simply to proscribe as inequitable tax subsidies for religions that decline to do so. This is in line with Barry's admonition that government benefits must be given impartially or not at all.

What is really going on here, I think, is that denying the tax-exempt status does not seem worthwhile to Barry because he does not judge the Catholic proscription of women priests important enough to compromise the free exercise of religion. But that reflects Barry's judgment about which things are most important for living a good life. Others will take a different view. Barry did not say what he thought should be done if a church were to exclude blacks from the priesthood, as Mormons did until 1978, though it seems he would have no difficulty with that either. For Barry, the question allegedly turns on whether the belief in question is essential to practicing the religion.[20] But what, then, about *Bob Jones*? It would be child's play for those who promulgated their exclusionary racial policy to reframe their objections as essential to the practice of their religion; indeed for many of them, no reframing would be needed. I suspect that the real reason Barry could not bring himself to say that *Bob Jones* was wrongly decided has nothing to do with impartiality. Rather, it is that proscription of miscegenation has been so closely linked to the domination of American blacks for so long that this distinguishes it from what strikes Barry as the comparatively benign matter of excluding women from the Catholic priesthood.[21] Just as Michael Walzer has pointed out with regard to appeals to equality, once we dig into invocations of impartiality, we find assumptions about resisting domination doing the real work.[22]

Comparable considerations apply to Barry's discussion of rights and economic guarantees. Though he rejected Mill's harm principle (which he dubbed the "negative" harm principle) on the grounds that preventing harm is not the only justification for government action, Barry embraced a "positive" harm principle, which, he claimed, passes the Scanlonian test. "We all have a legitimate complaint based on justice," he says, "if our society fails to provide us with what is needed to avoid harm."[23] The reason: "What is harmful is deleterious to the furtherance of virtually any conception of the good." Accordingly, we do not have to invoke "any particular conception of the good to arrive at the conclusion that rules of justice must prohibit the doing of harm."[24] His list of what the positive harm principle requires includes "security against the deliberate infliction of injury and death by other people, and the provision of sanitation, potable water, shelter, and heat (as required by the climate) and medical care." It also requires "a supply of food adequate to provide for normal growth, work at full capacity, enjoyment of leisure, pregnancy, and childrearing." Satisfying these "vital interests" has "absolute priority," he insisted, "over any other use of society's resources."[25]

Barry's defense of his positive harm principle put him squarely in what, since Rawls, has been known as the resourcist camp in arguments about justice. Rawls's motivation had been to avoid questions about the sources of human welfare, focusing instead on the resources people need regardless of their particular conceptions of the good. He acknowledged that his view rested on a "thin" theory of the good, but he insisted that this depended only on "general facts" about society and "the laws of sociology and economics." It was not biased in favor of particular conceptions of the good life. But just as critics like Roemer and Shapiro pointed out that Rawls's thin theory was thicker than he acknowledged, the same is true of Barry.[26]

Barry's resourcism privileges some conceptions of the good life over others in several ways. One, as Andrew Reeve noted, is that Barry's use of "virtually" excludes conceptions that do not include being protected from harm.[27] Barry heaped scorn on this in a reply to his critics, insisting that he meant only to exclude wildly idiosyncratic conceptions of the good, such as the suffering that Mother Teresa considered a gift from God, the beckoning afterlife that made Hamlet unhappy with the proscription of suicide, or the Munchausen patient for whom being diagnosed with an illness turns out to be an asset.[28]

But we can agree with Barry that avoiding harm is integral to most reasonable conceptions of the good life, yet still balk at his notably heftier contention that insisting on rights to protection from harm by the state does not require contestable assumptions about the good life. Particularly on Barry's capacious view, which, as we have just seen, includes harms due to bad luck as well as the malevolent actions of others—not to mention rights to cradle-to-grave state guarantees of the necessities for commodious living—*harm* is manifestly a placeholder for a contestable set of views of the good life. Most obviously, Barry's account excludes rugged bootstrapping views that assign an important role to triumphing over adversity and providing for one's own security from harm, at least in significant part—to say nothing of providing the wherewithal for leisure. Barry's account also excludes views at the opposite end of the ideological spectrum. His declaration that people are entitled only to enough food to work "at full capacity" loads the dice against views, like Philippe Van Parijs's, that detach people's just claims on social resources (in Van Parijs's case, to an equal share of the highest sustainable social wage) from any expectation that they be required to work.[29]

And this is the tip of the iceberg. Barry's "absolute priority" requirement stands in need of both substance and mechanisms of enforcement. His remarks about equity and institutions understate how demanding these requirements would be—philosophically, legally, and politically. Barry's advertised stance appears strongly conditioned by democratic considerations: that there should be constitutional requirements for his list of social and economic rights, but that it should be left to legislatures to institute them subject to his constraints about equitable allocation already discussed. But this is problematic in ways that reveal the impossibility of hiving off second-order impartiality as a domain that can yield concrete judgments, yet avoid the difficulties of first-order impartiality with which Barry was all too familiar.

The example of medical care establishes the point. Assuming, for now, that a just overall social budget for medical care could be agreed on, there would still be no way to divide it up that would not seem, and indeed be, inequitable from some reasonable point of view. Some ethnic and racial groups are more susceptible to particular diseases than others. Should we invest extra in research on and treatment of diseases that afflict particular groups? If so, which groups should count, and who should bear the opportunity costs? Women live longer than men. Should that entitle them to less lifetime medical care or more? Arguments can be made on both sides. Should we treat illnesses that result from bad genetic luck differently from those that include a behavioral component—and if so, how much should behavior be factored in? Must nonsmokers get lung transplants before smokers, and should addicted smokers be preferred to recreational ones? As I have noted elsewhere with respect to the debates Rawls ignited about moral arbitrariness, there is no impartial way to stipulate the extent to which people should be held accountable for differences in weakness of the will.[30] How, then, are courts meant to decide whether and to what degree any contested allocation of the medical care pie passes Barry's equitableness test?

These difficulties spill over into questions about the size of the medical care budget itself, subverting Barry's attempt to distinguish the amount of provision from how it is divvied up.[31] One need not reflect for long on the opportunity-cost dilemmas opened up by dialysis machines, artificial hearts, or the research on cures to cancer, AIDS, Ebola, and other fatal diseases to see that the possibility of investing in lifesaving medical technologies is elastic, if not limitless. Interpreting Barry's absolute priority requirement literally would therefore mean that medical care has the potential to consume the entire government's budget, raising problems for the other social and economic guarantees that are also accorded absolute priority over "any other use of society's resources."[32] As the South African Constitutional Court discovered when it sought to delineate the limits of a constitutional right to medical treatment for someone dying of renal failure in 1997, there is no theoretically compelling solution to these tradeoffs.[33] Certainly, Barry's theory offers no help. If everyone who needs kidney dialysis is covered but those in need of artificial hearts are not, cardiac patients will reasonably feel aggrieved. And their distress will only intensify if the state is also underwriting the wherewithal for people's leisure. As this example illustrates, drawing the budget line for an inherently scarce good inescapably involves equitable considerations. It is thus self-contradictory to declare that courts should police equity in public provision impartially while keeping out of decisions about what the level of public spending should be.

The difficulties are compounded once we turn to issues about taxation and the distribution of income and wealth. Barry's full analysis of this subject was promised in a volume he never completed.[34] However, he did say that his distinction between the "what" and the "how" of justice did not apply here—at least not in the same way.[35] Instead, he took the obverse (and in some ways more Rawlsian) view that there should be a constitutional requirement of the main contours of a just distributive regime, but that judges should keep out of the technicalities of its implementation.[36]

As we have seen, hiving off the areas that are immune from judicial review is easier said than done once costly resources are included within the ambit of what courts should protect from politics. This arose in the U.S. context when theorists like John Hart Ely and Ronald Dworkin tried to vacuum up much New Deal and Great Society social policy into the ambit of judicial review by imperatives that are comparable to Barry's positive harm principle: in Ely's case footnote 4 of Justice Stone's opinion in *Carolene Products* mandating protection of "discrete and insular minorities," and in Dworkin's case his principle of equal concern and respect.[37] In any case, Barry never filled out his account of the just distributive regime that should be constitutionally protected, much less derive it from second-order impartiality via his Scanlonian test. However, in subsequent writing he made no secret of his view that justice requires much less inequality and notably more steeply progressive taxation than that which prevails in advanced capitalist democracies.

But how much less, and how much steeper? Most of what Barry had to say that bears on these questions was set out in his last book, *Why Social Justice Matters*, published in 2005. His goal there was to help combat the sharp increases in inequality and declines in progressivity that had occurred in Britain and the United States over the preceding decades. Accordingly, most of the book is spent documenting the extent of the changes and exposing specious arguments that had been put forward to justify them. He makes short work, for instance, of the 1994 report on inequality and taxation commissioned by then Labour Party leader John Smith that laid the groundwork for Tony Blair's New Labour.

Barry points out that the report offers no justification for its bald assertion that no one should pay more than half of their income in taxes. He also notes that the New Labour credo was a major departure from the standard views of progressivity embraced by social democratic parties (including the British Labour Party) for decades, and that a 50 percent limit could not have been expected to make a dent in the inequality that had been growing since the 1970s—as, indeed, it did not. All this is true, but it is also true that Barry never offers a defense of the traditional social democratic stance on progressivity embraced by "old-fashioned adherents of social justice" from the standpoint of justice as impartiality. He simply points out that effective tax rates on the wealthy had been 70 percent as recently as the 1970s, and that even with a top marginal rate of 99 percent, "the more pre-tax income people have the more they would have after paying their tax."[38]

II. Impartiality or Democracy?

At this point, it is worth stepping back to ask why Barry, Rawls, Scanlon, and the other Kantian-inspired contractualists have poured so much energy for so long into deriving accounts of justice from ruminations about impartial human reason. There is a pull-the-rabbit-out-of-the-hat quality to the whole enterprise that calls to mind Aesop's quip that after all is said and done, more has been said than done. Obviously, you can't derive something from nothing. It is scarcely surprising that these expeditions from reason to justice become laden, along the way, with contestable assumptions about what is good for people, how they can know and secure it, at what cost, and to whom. No one should be surprised that the contestable assumptions carry more freight than the advocates of these ventures admit, or that people who are skeptical of the assumptions have trouble staying along for the ride.

Barry's work is unusual in this genre in that his writing about justice was embedded in, and addressed to, actual distributive conflicts. Yet his confidence that the moral positions he took reflected the dictates of impartial reason was never shaken. To some extent, he was a creature of his era. Western intellectuals who were born, as he was, in the 1930s, came of age during the heyday of the social democratic welfare states that were built after the war. They saw themselves, as Tony Judt has noted, as defusing old political animosities and, more importantly, as "detached from any doctrinal project." These thinkers had grown up in the aftermath of the Depression and experienced firsthand the horrors of war driven by ideological extremism and the shortages that followed. But they found themselves, in the 1950s, in an era of unprecedented prosperity and peace, "where politics was giving way to government, and government was increasingly confined to administration."[39] It could all too easily seem to them that, after a protracted struggle, the Enlightenment dream of basing collective life on reason's dictates was finally coming true. This helps explain why they embraced the social democratic welfare state as a benchmark for normalcy, with the implication that departures from it would stand in need of justification. As we have seen, this is the basis of Barry's stand in *Why Social Justice Matters*.

But, as Judt also points out, this apparent new normal was in fact a precarious and time-bound achievement. It rested on the unusual confluence of military exhaustion, unprecedented postwar growth helped along by the Marshall Plan, favorable demographic trends, and the protected pocket of geopolitical stability created by the early Cold War.[40] Starting in the mid-1960s, it came under increasing stress as populations aged, growth slowed, and offshore competition forced latent tensions between high wages and full employment to surface. Ronald Reagan, Margaret Thatcher, and the New Right might have seemed like a radical departure from normalcy, but their ascendancy really reflected tradeoffs and conflicts of interest that became manifest once the tide that had lifted all boats began receding in the 1970s. The costs of welfare states were escalating with no obvious respite in view. The "social rights" that T. H. Marshall had famously portrayed as the culmination of three centuries of evolution had worn thin, much to the chagrin of Barry's generation.[41] Many of them reacted with rage to the advent of the New Right and with incandescent fury to the subsequent adoption of its neo-liberal pro-market, anti-welfare agenda by New Labour in Britain and comparable backtracking on traditional social democratic agendas in Western Europe. They saw this as a retrograde selling out of the postpolitical achievements of European social democracy. Thus it was, as Judt says, "that the very generation which came of age in the Social Democratic paradise of its parents' longings was most irritated and resentful of its shortcomings."[42]

These considerations help explain why liberals of Barry's generation thought they could find an impartial rationale for the postwar welfare states, one that brackets disagreements about interests and values yet assumes that there are ways to serve them that all reasonable people must, on reflection, affirm as fair. But we live in a different world today, one in which all vanguardist political solutions are suspect. This is no less true of vanguardist solutions that rest on appeals to armchair speculation about reason than earlier ones that invoked the historic mission of the proletariat. In our world, direct focus on resisting domination makes more sense than defending impartialist ventures. And combating domination is best served by betting on democracy, the worst system—as Churchill said—except for the others that have been tried.[43]

This is true for reasons both theoretical and practical. On the theoretical front, Robert Dahl noted more than half a century ago that the trouble with claiming that certain rights should be protected as anterior to democratic politics is that there is endemic disagreement about which rights these are.[44] Dahl was thinking of natural rights theorists, but the resourcists following Rawls confront the same difficulty. There is a garbage-in, garbage-out quality to their ventures: assumptions are made about what people are and what they need, and those assumptions are then deployed to generate the desired results, as we have seen. It is not surprising, therefore, that there are as many resourcist theories as there are resourcist theorists.[45] This is not to deny the value of resourcist arguments. But their proponents should not pretend that they embody, or are products of, the dictates of impartiality. In my view, for instance, people have an interest in access to the wherewithal to avoid domination, but those who reject this commitment to nondomination will be unpersuaded. I think that when push comes to shove they are few and far between, but they exist and my disagreements with them cannot be resolved by appealing to impartial principles.

On the practical front, some worry that democracy—based as it is on majority rule—does nothing to guarantee protection of people's basic interests. That is true, but there are no guarantees in politics. The real question is: majority rule compared to what? Fondness for judicial review has been a distinctively American preoccupation, but it is worth noting that, like Tony Judt's disappointed European social democrats, the main champions of judicial review in the United States were born between the wars and hit their intellectual strides during the Warren Court era (Dwight Eisenhower appointed Earl Warren Chief Justice in 1953 and he served until 1969).[46] People like Ronald Dworkin, John Hart Ely, and Laurence Tribe championed that Court. Many in their generation expressed mounting distress as much of its work was undone by the Burger (1969–86), Rehnquist (1986–2005), and Roberts (2005–) Courts. This calls to mind Brian Barry's irate response to the assault on the British welfare state that began in the late 1970s. They saw the Warren Court's achievements as vital for protecting individual rights and for the health of American democracy; its eclipse, they thought, seriously jeopardized both. Also reminiscent of Barry, much of their commentary portrayed the situation as a departure from sound practice that would return once sanity was restored, and the Court could once again do its proper job.[47]

Just as Judt's 1960s European intellectuals were blind to the reality that their social democracies were not the new normal, many of their American counterparts missed the degree to which the Warren Court was a massive historical outlier. More attention to the longer sweep of American history, and the Taney (1836–64), Waite (1874–88), Fuller (1888–1910), White (1910–21), and Taft (1921–30) Courts, might have alerted them to this reality. Given decisions like *Dred Scott* or *Plessy v. Ferguson,* the Court's complicity in undermining Reconstruction and limiting the Civil War Amendments in the *Slaughterhouse* and *Civil Rights Cases,* or its evisceration of much New Deal and other reform legislation during the *Lochner* era, there was plenty of evidence at the time that the Warren Court was unusual.[48] Certainly Eisenhower got more than he bargained for in appointing Warren, "the biggest damn fool mistake I ever made." He was a former California attorney general and then its Republican governor, who had been the moving force behind the internment of U.S. citizens of Japanese descent during the war, who was confirmed 96–0 by the U.S. Senate, and whose subsequent trajectory was predicted by no one.[49]

Most judges are not like that. They are conventional establishment figures who, if they do stray, are more likely to do so in the direction of public opinion as expressed through elected branches rather than away from it.[50] Lord Devlin might have overstated things in declaring that judges reflect the views of the man on the Clapham omnibus, but not by much.[51] When the U.S. Supreme Court refused to strike down Georgia's proscription of homosexual conduct in 1986, homosexuality was still illegal in half of the states. By the time the Justices reversed themselves seventeen years later, thirty-six states had repealed the ban.[52] When public opinion is seriously divided, the Court tends to duck. *Roe v. Wade* is sometimes advanced as the exception that proves that rule.[53] The Court rewrote the law of abortion in the face of a divided public, hoping—as Justice Blackmun intimated in his majority opinion—to settle the question.[54] As the next half century of political mobilization and litigation culminating in *Roe*'s reversal underscored, this failed.[55] More usual is the story of school desegregation. Despite the extravagant claims often made for the Court's 1954 decision in *Brown v. Board of Education*, reversing *Plessy v. Ferguson* and declaring "separate but equal" unconstitutional, it seems clear that the advances that have occurred in desegregating schools were achieved through legislative action, not courts.[56]

It is difficult to show that judicial review matters for the prevention of domination. Authoritarian governments routinely flout courts when they are intent on oppression, as anyone who lived through fascism, communism, the era of Latin American "disappearances," or South African apartheid will attest. Democracies do vastly better from the perspective of nondomination, but there is no compelling evidence that judicial review has much—if anything—to do with this. Rather, it seems clear that democracy does the heavy lifting. Countries like Britain, Sweden, Norway, and until recently the Netherlands, which have shown little appetite for judicial review, have not done demonstrably less well at protecting basic rights than has the United States. This is to say nothing of the fact that those with more resources are often better positioned to take advantage of judicial forums to protect their interests than those with fewer resources.

As early as 1956, Dahl registered skepticism that democracies with constitutional courts could be shown to have a positive effect on the degree to which individual freedoms are respected when compared to democracies without them. He developed this view more fully in a seminal article the following year.[57] Subsequent scholarship has shown that Dahl's skepticism was well founded.[58] Indeed, it is plausible to wonder whether the popularity of independent courts in democracies has more in common with the recent trend toward creating independent banks than with the protection of individual freedoms. These "independent" institutions signal to foreign investors and gatekeepers at international economic institutions that the capacity of elected officials to engage in redistributive policies or interfere with property rights will be limited. That is, they might be devices by which governments can signal their willingness to limit domestic political opposition to unpopular policies by taking them off the political table.[59]

It is worth noting here that the growth of inequality since the 1970s that so troubled Barry has been more extreme in the United States, with its Bill of Rights and judicial review, than in any of the other advanced democracies.[60] No doubt there are many reasons for this, but one nonnegligible contributor has been the role of money in politics, which makes both parties disproportionately dependent on large financial contributors. This, in turn, has been aided and abetted by the Supreme Court, which starting in 1976, has struck down repeated attempts by Congress to limit money's role in politics and has recently expanded its prohibition to regulation of corporate political expenditures as well.[61] Instead of arguing that courts should be empowered to protect people's basic interests from the paper tiger of majority tyranny, those who are concerned about domination would be better advised to invest their energy in protecting competitive democratic politics from courts that undermine its integrity and effectiveness.

A full defense of this view would take us too far afield.[62] Instead, I will conclude by noting that in earlier work Barry defended majority rule against theorists like James Buchanan and Gordon Tullock, who had advocated shielding various entrenched constitutional provisions from democratic politics by means of supermajority and even unanimity requirements.[63] This is the best way, they had argued, to limit the likelihood that we will have solutions imposed on us that we do not want. Barry was the first in a long line of theorists to point out, in his 1965 book *Political Argument,* that Buchanan and Tullock were wrong because unanimity rule privileges the status quo.[64] If we assume as much uncertainty about whether our interests are served by the status quo as by possible departures from it, he showed that the best default presumption is to embrace majority rule.[65] Barry's earlier view in *Political Argument* is more appealing than his subsequent excursion down the blind alley of justice as impartiality.

If this overstates the change in Barry's views, it is because, as I showed regarding his different treatment of blacks and women when discussing *Bob Jones,* hostility to domination also turns out on inspection to do much of the subliminal work beneath Barry's subsequent concern with rising inequality. For instance, a good bit of his outrage at what he follows R. H. Tawney in describing as the "repulsive consequences" of inequality is that, beyond some threshold, it "makes even policies aimed at ending poverty harder to enact." Barry also endorsed my argument that the poor become disempowered in highly unequal democracies due to wide empathy gaps (the possibility of upward mobility eludes them and the rich become so insulated that they can ignore them), while middle-class resentment is diverted into stigmatizing them as undeserving.[66] But these are arguments about the vulnerability of the poor to domination, not about inherent evils of inequality.

Barry also had much to say about the changing role of the media in democratic politics.[67] He took particular issue with the 1987 decision by the Federal Communications Commission (FCC) in the United States to abandon the fairness doctrine that had required balanced presentation of controversial public issues, usually by including several points of view. The advent of cable and satellite television meant that the original rationale that had led to its adoption in 1947, the scarcity of channels, no longer obtained. Barry correctly pointed out, however, that the new status quo did not produce a competitive marketplace of ideas because the FCC did nothing to prevent already concentrated media markets from becoming even more so. Again, his compelling objection here is to the way in which a few wealthy individuals and their media conglomerates undermine competitive democratic politics. This is an argument about domination, not the intrinsic desirability of impartiality.

III. Conclusion

This emphasis on power is, in the end, what separates my commitment to nondomination from Barry's justice as impartiality. Like other resourcists following Rawls, Barry thought of his view along the lines of Aristotle's instrumental goods: they consist of the wherewithal to pursue final goods, or things that Aristotle described as "good in themselves."[68] But whereas Aristotle thought of final goods as universal and invariant, Barry tied himself up in philosophical knots to try and show that the instrumental goods that he defended by reference to his positive harm principle do not presuppose a particular conception of the good.

This forlorn endeavor is beside the point. My power-based account is indeed biased in favor of some conceptions of the good: to wit, those that are compatible with mitigating domination when it cannot be escaped. It rests on skepticism of any sharp distinction between means and ends, partly because we are so often unsure of our ends. We recast them as our environments evolve and as the means we deploy to pursue them play out. Means/ends dichotomies warrant skepticism, also, because of their affinities with vanguardist politics to which a commitment to nondomination is constitutionally hostile. This entails tolerating, even welcoming and institutionalizing, a degree of uncertainty into our thinking about what justice requires that is out of kilter with much of the legal and philosophical literature, and betting instead on democratic politics.

Those who fear this course, and want democracy constrained by impartial requirements of justice, have a cure that is likely worse than the disease. Philosophically, we have seen that their ventures are bound to fail. Politically, the institutions they depend on can do more harm than good. Courts have long been touted as the least dangerous branch, essential to checking the unnerving specter of majoritarian politics.[69] But Madison's fear of "majority factions" in Federalist 10, amplified by Alexis de Tocqueville half a century later, has always been longer on hype than on evidence.[70] The greater danger is the minority tyranny that develops when the rich and powerful subvert democratic politics. As we have seen, courts have been aiders and abettors of this subversion more than brakes on it. Expecting them to behave differently in the future would, at best, be a triumph for hope over experience.

2

On Sen versus Rawls on Justice

Amartya Sen's vision of justice is agreeably humane. He sees people as developmental creatures whose well-being depends on achieving their potential in healthy and satisfying ways. This reflects something of an Aristotelian cast of mind, at least with respect to Sen's picture of the structure of human psychology. Whereas utilitarians tend to focus on preference-satisfaction and egalitarians typically traffic in arguments about the distribution of resources, Sen operates with a more fully rounded idea of human well-being. But, as with other neo-Aristotelians like Alasdair MacIntyre, Sen resists Aristotle's view that there is a fixed list of human purposes or virtues. Rather, he thinks that justice is to a considerable extent about enabling people to develop and fulfill their own capabilities. His idea of a better world is one in which more people have the freedom and wherewithal to achieve their best potential, and he sees a large part of the task of promoting justice as identifying—and removing—obstacles to realizing that vision. This means that, although he has strong egalitarian impulses and often recommends anti-elitist policies, Sen is strongly committed to the idea that human freedom lies at the core of justice. Despite his antipathy for preference-satisfaction as a moral yardstick, he resists appeals to externally identified "interests" that might trump an agent's sense of his or her priorities and purposes.[1]

Sen has long—and rightly, in my view—been concerned to get political theorists to focus on important questions of justice in the real world. Part of why he resists what he describes as Rawls's "search for transcendental justice" is that it can divert attention to difficult (perhaps unanswerable) questions that are irrelevant to identifying severe injustices and deciding what to do about them.[2] Sen is skeptical of the path taken by Barry, Scanlon, and the other neo-Kantians who follow Rawls in trying to derive impartial theories by appeal to what members of a political community can, in principle, be brought to affirm or at least not to reject. He doubts that their thought experiments can yield universally valid principles, and, perhaps echoing Rousseau's critique of Hobbes, worries that the principles they affirm fetishize local values.[3] Rawlsians, he thinks, get bogged down in minutiae that do not need to be resolved in order to address the major questions of justice. My own philosophical priors and views about justice are closer to Sen's than they are to Rawls's, but I nonetheless think that Sen's effort fails. His arguments against Rawls are less than telling, and, given what he has said elsewhere, Sen's defense of his own account of justice is surprisingly undeveloped in the long-awaited synthetic statement of his view, *The Idea of Justice*. Moreover, once we dig into Sen's substantive claims about justice, it becomes clear that—as with Barry—the convincing ones trade heavily on antipathy for domination.

My discussion here mirrors the geography of Sen's book. I start with his critique of transcendental political theory (section I) and the comparative approach that he proposes in its stead (sections II and III). I show that he overstates his differences with Rawls on matters of both method and substance, and that his alternative appeal to a comparative outlook cannot do the philosophical work that is needed to sustain his vision of justice. Really, his argument depends heavily on his appeals to a version of Adam Smith's impartial spectator. Sen fails to deal with obvious criticisms of it and he deploys it selectively to legitimate positions that he finds congenial. Most of his claims are not convincingly defended. Where they withstand scrutiny, as with slavery or draconian oppression of women, this is because they obviously involve domination (section IV). Last, I turn to his claim that democracy is an important vehicle for advancing the cause of justice. This is a significant contribution, but Sen's account is marred by lack of attention to the dynamics of democratic politics. As a result, he misses opportunities to advance our understanding of when and how democracy is likely to serve the cause of justice (section V).

I. Against Transcendental Theory

Rawls did not use the term *transcendental* to describe his enterprise, but Sen deploys it to capture its Kantian flavor. Traditional social contract theorists like John Locke had construed political institutions as the result of a foundational agreement made by people in order to protect natural rights that were believed to be rooted in natural law. Individuals were seen as having abandoned the state of nature to avoid the costs of protecting those rights themselves, thereby enhancing their freedom and security. Rawls was writing in a different age, when agreement on the existence of natural law and natural rights could no longer be assumed and in which decades of mordant criticism had dispatched the idea of a pre-political state of nature from serious consideration by theorists of justice.

Rawls's Kant-inspired move was intended to revive the social contract tradition while eliding these well-known difficulties. Conceding that there had never been a social contract, he nonetheless asked what contract people might buy into if they were in a position to do so. And, rather than pre-political people, he asked actual people—his readers—to consider what they thought people would choose behind a veil of ignorance that shielded them from knowledge of their age, sex, race, IQ, physical prowess, aspirations, and other specific facts that would allow them to bias things in their favor. Stripped of such knowledge, people would be constrained to reason in general terms.

In this way, universalizability would replace natural law as the standard for evaluating political institutions.

Sen is skeptical that people could ever be induced to agree on a theory of justice in this way. He also thinks it is unnecessary for them to try to do so in order to tackle some of the most pressing matters of justice in the real world. He captured this vividly in a lecture with the pithy image of a man locked in an unbearably hot sauna who calls urgently to a friend outside to lower the temperature, but elicits the response that he must be told the ideal temperature before acting on the request.[4] A neophyte might wonder whether Sen was making a point about poor judgment in choice of friends, but anyone who has been raised on the steady diet of abstruse meta-debates, thought experiments, and contrived examples that make up so much professional political philosophy will resonate with his frustration.

More specific analogies that Sen invokes to make the same point are that people who disagree on the relative merits of a Picasso and a van Gogh can agree that the *Mona Lisa* is the greatest painting of all time, and that people who might argue about whether Kilimanjaro is higher than Mount McKinley know that Everest is the highest mountain on earth.[5] The *Mona Lisa* stands out over the centuries while debates about lesser works come and go. From a distance Everest obviously towers over the rest. By the same token, Sen's open impartiality of critical distance might get us to focus on the questions that matter most. These are, to be sure, vivid cautions; Sen's impulse to focus our critical energy on serious injustice is deeply congenial—at least to me. It articulates well with my contention in chapter 3 that we can recognize severe kinds of domination without believing that there could be a general theory of what a society without domination would be like, or even being able to come up with a complete ranking of the severity of different types of domination. But how do Sen's observations capture what differentiates his project from Rawls's?

Rawls's commitment to ideal theory, as he called it, had three distinctive features: he thought we should reason about justice under relatively favorable conditions; he thought that we should mostly ignore enforcement problems until we are clear about what justice requires; and he thought that, if we do this, we will be able to determine which of the various theories of justice on offer is best.[6] Specifically, he argued that, behind his veil of ignorance, people would embrace a system guaranteeing three things in declining order of importance: the most expansive basic freedoms that can be given to all, equality of opportunity, and limits on inequalities gearing them to the benefit of the least advantaged. This scheme would be chosen over the going alternatives, providing an Archimedean standard that we can take to our actual "second best" world to see how it measures up and where it needs improvement.

Sen has little to say about Rawls's bracketing of compliance questions, perhaps because Sen himself pays scant attention to them in developing his own views. Thus while he argues for a view of justice in which people have priorities other than "the single-minded pursuit of our own well-being," he has virtually nothing to say about how that might be sustained in the real world.[7] For instance, in the course of defending the notion that having the power to mitigate an injustice brings with it the obligation to do so, Sen cites with approval Gautama Buddha's optimism that people can recognize such claims on the grounds that a mother embraces a responsibility to her child "because she can do things to influence the child's life that the child itself cannot do."[8] Like Buddha, Sen is encouraged by this observation to opine that humans might recognize obligations to weaker people and other species "because of the asymmetry between us," rather than from some expectation of benefit. Yet the mother-child example ignores the relative strength of familial ties which foster expectations of reciprocity on the part of adult children toward elderly parents, not to mention a mother's genetic interest in her offspring and close relatives.[9] These factors render the example a poor basis for the claim that people can be counted on to act voluntarily on obligations when they have nothing to gain.

The only other example Sen discusses is also less than encouraging. This concerns the third-century B.C. Indian emperor Ashoka, who weakened the prevailing system of institutional rules, punishments, and incentives. He disbanded the army, relying instead on Buddhist-inspired exhortations to his people to reflect more and behave better. Ashoka was in many ways an admirable figure who liberated slaves and indentured laborers, but his vast empire collapsed shortly after his death—scarcely an advertisement for his approach to achieving compliance. Indeed, the real puzzle is why his empire did not fall apart sooner. As Sen admits, commentators have concluded that this was at least partly because Ashoka failed fully to dismantle the administrative system of disciplined rule that he inherited.[10] Sen speculates that another likely factor was the "awe in which he [Ashoka] was held by the people at large."[11] One could debate whether there is a way to ensure that great leaders will come to power when they are needed, but it is beside the point here.[12] If Sen is right that Ashoka's awe-inspiring personality held things together during his lifetime, this also militates against Sen's hope that people can be counted on to comply with obligations that are neither in their perceived self-interest nor backed up by coercive institutions—simply out of a sense of moral obligation.

For all its infirmities, Rawls's original position was at least intended to align self-interested calculation with what he saw as the demands of justice by asking people to reason about what rules they would agree on if kept in ignorance about their particular circumstances, values, and ambitions. And while it is true that Rawls says that in a just society people can be expected to behave reasonably—in accordance, that is, with what justice requires—he was careful, as Sen notes, to say that this depends on their developing the expectation that others will behave in a like fashion.[13] One could read this as conceding that, in the real world, behavioral adaptation will be necessary for people to live in accordance with what justice requires, which is Sen's position.

Alternatively, one could read Rawls, as I am inclined to read him, as following the logic of a base-closing commission. Congress binds itself in advance to accept the results of the commission charged to decide which military bases to close and it insulates the commission from constituency lobbying—concededly a fair procedure. But everyone knows that the government will have to enforce the results after the process is complete, when representatives of districts that have not fared well will be looking for ways to defect. In a like fashion, I read Rawls's assumption on this score to be that, once the principles of justice have been accepted as just behind the veil of ignorance, it is legitimate for the government to enforce compliance with them. Otherwise, his requirement that it is a condition for expecting reasonable behavior of people that they, in turn, may legitimately expect others to behave reasonably, cannot be met. After all, there is no analog, for Rawls, of Marx's "withering away of the state"—even in a perfectly just society. This might be an unduly charitable reading of Rawls, but, even without it, nothing Sen says gives him an edge on the compliance front.

This leaves Sen's claim that what differentiates his approach from Rawls's is his use of comparative reasoning rather than a transcendental deduction designed to come up with a perfect account of justice. Sen insists that, if we adopt his comparative approach, we need not settle every question about justice to settle any question about justice. As his examples of paintings and mountains suggest, we can work with incomplete orderings. But there is less at stake here than meets the eye.

Notice, for one thing, that Rawls deployed both comparative reasoning and incomplete orderings in arguing for his principles of justice. His goal was to make the case that, behind the veil of ignorance, rational people would choose his account of justice over such going alternatives as perfectionism and, most importantly, utilitarianism. Rawls sought to do this by showing that, from the standpoint of the most adversely affected person, the principles he advocated would be more appealing than the others. It follows a fortiori that, if someone could show that some hitherto unexamined principle would do even better than his from that point of view, Rawls would endorse the new principle. So it is wrong for Sen to say that Rawls purported to offer an account of "perfectly just institutions in a world where all alternatives are available."[14] When Rawls characterized his principles as procedural expressions of the categorical imperative, he was just describing the standard by reference to which competing principles should be evaluated—to wit, one that requires endorsement even by those most adversely affected by the operation of those principles.[15] He was not claiming to have set forth a transcendental deduction of the principles themselves.

Moreover, Rawls has been condemned in the literature for letting this case depend on partial orderings. Due to his assumptions about grave risks, he famously equated the standpoint of justice with that of the most adversely affected individual. Rawls was enough of a realist to acknowledge that there may be no relationship between the level of economic development in a country and the condition of people at the bottom. This meant that even under the relatively favorable conditions of moderate scarcity about which he was writing in *A Theory of Justice*, for a given individual this condition might be dire.[16] Given that you might turn out to be one of those people once the veil of ignorance is lifted, you had better be concerned about them. Accordingly, Rawls reasoned that behind the veil of ignorance it makes sense to insist that departures from equality operate to the advantage of the people at the bottom.

As Sen is aware, this insistence opened Rawls to the criticism that protecting people at the bottom might come at a considerable cost to others, even others who are quite badly off.[17] Rawls tried to blunt the force of this criticism by suggesting that helping people at the bottom would have positive externalities throughout the system, a kind of multiplier effect that would benefit everyone. But he acknowledged that the ripple effects posited by his account of "chain connection" might not occur in fact, maintaining that in that eventuality he would nonetheless stick to his difference principle.[18] In effect this means that Rawls's argument for the difference principle rests on a partial ordering in just the same way that Sen's does when he maintains that justice requires intervention in the face of famine regardless of the costs of that intervention to others.

In short, when Rawls speaks of a perfectly just society, this is not a world without conflict, scarcity, or (unlike Sen) self-interested people.[19] It is a world that operates to the benefit of the least advantaged whose condition might be so dire that failing to protect them would be irrational for someone who might turn out to be one of them. In making that case Rawls depends heavily on comparative reasoning and incomplete orderings, with the result that there is a good deal less disagreement between him and Sen than Sen seems to realize. Indeed, Rawls goes so far as to declare himself agnostic between capitalism and socialism on the grounds that it is unclear which of these systems, or possibly some hybrid, best meets the requirements of justice.[20] Thus when Sen advocates a comparative evaluation of economic institutions ("preferring a greater—or indeed lesser—role for the free market") as an alternative to Rawls's alleged "transcendental search for the perfect package of social institutions," he is positing a distinction where there is no difference.[21]

II. Sen's Comparative Theory

If Sen's methodological differences with Rawls are overdrawn, what of his more general complaint that political philosophers are too often preoccupied with questions that divert attention from important matters of justice? It is easy to resonate with the complaint, but Sen's various metaphorical illustrations of what he takes to be at stake make it hard to pin down just what he thinks is wrong and, more importantly, how his approach addresses the deficiencies that he identifies.

Notice that Sen objects to two different activities that he thinks are a waste of time. The first, reflected in the examples of the sauna and the mountain altitudes, concern trivial but not unanswerable questions. Presumably there is an answer to the question what temperature the person locked in the sauna would find most comfortable, just as it would be possible to record the exact height of every mountain on the planet. Sen's point is that for many purposes we just don't need to know the answer; it amounts to worrying about things three points to the right of the decimal when the problem at hand is to its left. When billions live in poverty, debating whether an addiction to plovers' eggs and pre-phylloxera claret is a disability that merits compensation gives political philosophy a bad name.[22] But how does Sen's call for a "comparative" approach help?

Aside from a small number of obvious cases such as slavery and victims of famine, Sen has virtually nothing to say about how to make the comparisons that yield the judgments we should care about. Thus while he is convincing that we should not regard it as indicating the infirmity of a theory that it cannot tell us which out of a 39 or 40 percent tax rate is superior, nothing in his account supplies the basis for distinguishing between, say, a 35 percent top marginal tax rate and a 70 percent one.[23] As this example indicates, Sen's scorn for fussing over small distinctions also fails to capture what is at stake between him and Rawls, since Rawls did not fuss over them either. It is true that Rawls never told us how progressive the income-tax code should be (or, indeed, whether we should rely on income taxes at all), but, unlike Sen, he supplied a criterion to decide the matter. The optimal tax rate for Rawls is whatever rate operates to the greatest benefit of the least advantaged, and it is up to the economists and policy wonks to figure out what that is. Adapting Sen's sauna analogy, a person paying a 70 percent tax rate might well be inclined to yell that it is "much too high!" and quickly lose patience with someone who insisted on being told what the optimal tax rate is before agreeing to a cut in their rate. But that impatience would scarcely amount to a compelling reason to reduce their taxes. Sen's real contention is that we should address the most compelling injustices in the world first, yet he has surprisingly little to say about what makes a claim compelling, or how this is illuminated by "comparative" theory.

Sen's example of the *Mona Lisa* and other artworks puts a different set of issues on the table because it might well be that a group of people who agree that the *Mona Lisa* is the greatest painting of all time will never agree on the relative merits of a van Gogh and a Picasso. Their conceptions of what constitutes artistic excellence might just happen to overlap only concerning the *Mona Lisa*. Here the issue is not preoccupation with trivial but answerable questions that is presumed to be wasting people's time, but, rather, preoccupation with questions to which there is no answer even in principle. Again, while preoccupation with such questions is an activity that is easily condemned, it is hard to see how Sen's call for comparative political philosophy resolves, or even mitigates, it.

Sen spends a good deal of time worrying about the problems for justice that are presented by incommensurable values. To illustrate this, he supplies the example of trying to decide which of three children should get a flute: Anne, the only one who knows how to play it;

Bob, the only one who is so poor that he has no other toys; or Carla, who made the flute. Sen reasons that a utilitarian would likely give it to Anne, an egalitarian would give it to Bob, and a libertarian would give it to Carla. He returns to this example repeatedly, which he takes to illustrate the fact that there is no compelling way to choose among appeals to happiness, economic equity, or entitlement to the fruits of one's labor.[24]

Some of the time Sen's worry seems to be that because different theories rest on incommensurable values, their protagonists will be unable to agree on the right course of action in a given situation. But at other times the problem seems to be one of intratheoretical indeterminacy. Thus he notes that a utilitarian case could be made for giving the flute to Bob or Carla if either diminishing marginal utility or incentives is taken into account.[25] The same could be said of the egalitarian and libertarian arguments, though he does not say so. An egalitarian might give it to Anne on the grounds that giving all three the opportunity to enjoy hearing good music matters more than giving Bob an instrument he cannot play, or to Carla on the grounds that "from each according to her ability to each according to her work" is a sound socialist principle when no exploitation is involved. Alternatively, the egalitarian might make them share it. The libertarian might think that Ann or Bob should get the flute if Carla stole the raw materials or the tools she used to make it from either of them, or if she is a bully who they fear will jab them in the eye with the flute—the child's equivalent of a Nozickian "independent."[26]

Turning to Sen's own account, one might hope that he would deploy the flute example to display the attractiveness of the capabilities-based theory of justice that he has been advocating for decades as a neo-Aristotelian alternative to the widespread focus on people's existing preferences and their utility. He never attempts this, however. Perhaps the reason is that the capabilities approach is also compatible with giving the flute to any of the children. Is it more important that the capability for flute playing be realized (give it to Anne), or to reward the person with the capability for flute making (give it to Carla)? Or maybe it would be better to give Bob the flute, since Anne and Carla have already developed their capabilities and giving it to Bob might motivate him to learn how to play it. Sen emphasizes that it is the opportunity to realize capabilities (as distinct from whether they are realized in fact) that is vital, but that helps little here.[27] Does it matter more that people have opportunities to realize existing capabilities or to develop undeveloped ones? Should we equalize the number of capabilities people have the chance to develop, or perhaps the proportion of their capabilities that they can realize? Are some capabilities more important than others? Should the overall goal be to minimize unrealized capabilities? Does it matter if one of the children could be a better flautist than the others? What, if any, interpersonal comparisons are sanctioned in making the relevant judgments?

Sen notes that his plural conception of human capabilities (which would presumably range over the capabilities to play music, enjoy toys, or build musical instruments in the example at hand) runs into questions about incommensurability, but he never comes to grips with the implications. Remarking it is an open question how difficult they will be to resolve, Sen declares that the "main task is to get things right on the comparative judgments that can be reached through personal and public reasoning, rather than feel compelled to opine on every possible comparison that could be considered."[28] But Sen never tells us how to get the comparative judgments right, or even how to think about them. He never tells who should get the flute! The closest he comes is to say that maybe there will be some convergence of prescriptions—if Carla turns out also to be the poorest child or the only one who knows how to play the flute, or if Bob's poverty "is so extreme, and his dependence on something to play so important for a plausible life, that the poverty-based argument might come to dominate the judgment of justice."[29] Changing the relative circumstances of the players is in effect to dissolve the tensions the example was intended to create—solving the problem by definition. In any case, plausible as the notion that extreme poverty trumps other considerations might be, why would anyone think an impoverished child's life critically reliant on having a flute to play—not least when he lacks the capacity to play it? Perhaps the reason there is no commanding resolution to the flute trilemma on any of the theories, including Sen's, is—ironically—that no important question of justice is at stake.

III. Plural Grounds

Another response to incommensurability that Sen explores is to wonder how serious it is in real life. It has long been a commonplace of democratic theory that people with different preferences and values are often able to agree on outcomes.[30] An example Sen gives is the long list of alternative (and not obviously mutually compatible) reasons that Edmund Burke adduced to persuade Parliament to impeach Warren Hastings in 1789. Another is the list of reasons, Sen maintains, that could be given in support of the proposition that the 2003 U.S. invasion of Iraq was a bad idea.[31] These examples of "plural grounds" capture the reality that in collective life people often need not agree on why they support a proposition. *That* they do so may be enough. Cass Sunstein calls it "incompletely theorized agreement."[32] Democracies endorse it implicitly with the secret ballot that shields people from having to explain the reasons for their choices to others.

Notice that appealing to plural grounds scarcely differentiates Sen from the mature Rawls, whose idea of an overlapping consensus rests on the same logic that Sunstein and Sen both invoke to determine what sort of agreement is needed to sustain an account of justice.[33] Rawls's "political, not metaphysical" move involved recognizing that, just as hiring committees, legislators, and judges routinely agree on outcomes when they could never agree on their reasons for endorsing those outcomes, so there is no reason to require citizens to agree on metaphysical fundamentals as conditions for embracing a particular set of political arrangements. It is the fact of overlapping consensus, for the mature Rawls, that supplies the basis for political legitimacy. Sen calls it "plural grounding," or "using a number of different lines" of argument in support of a proposition "without seeking an agreement on their relative merits."[34] It is basically the same idea.

But appealing to plural grounds resolves considerably less about justice than Sen seems to suppose. Consider his discussion of plural grounds in light of his examples of partial orderings. When Sen says that "we do not need to get all steamed up about identifying the most perfect picture in the world" in order to determine the relative merits of the van Gogh over the Picasso, he overlooks the reality discussed earlier in connection with marginal tax rates: it is the difference between the van Gogh and the Picasso that people are liable to get steamed up about—not the merits of the *Mona Lisa,* about which everyone, by assumption in his example, agrees.[35] In a like vein, people who knew that Everest was the world's highest mountain might well have disagreed over which out of Kilimanjaro and Mount McKinley was higher before there were instruments to provide a definitive resolution of their disagreement.[36] Sen's discussion of plural grounds thus lives in considerable tension with his claim that we should focus on concrete comparisons: it will often be about these comparisons that plural grounds will be absent. Nothing Sen says indicates how he believes that people should decide whether the Picasso or the van Gogh is better, or which mountain is higher.

IV. Impartial Spectators

The only additional help that Sen offers is his appeal to the idea of an impartial spectator, which he takes from Adam Smith. This is a different conception of impartiality from Barry's discussed in the last chapter, but it is no more successful. Sen is careful here not to interpret impartiality to mean splitting the difference among competing claims in a society, as an arbitrator might perhaps be inclined to do. Sen also does not intend to invoke the notion of neutrality that became the focus of debates spawned by the early Rawls's assertion that his principles were neutral among rational conceptions of the good. This is a welcome fact, because the upshot of those debates was that the conception of neutrality Rawls sought cannot be found.[37] Sen dismisses that enterprise as a preoccupation with "closed impartiality" to differentiate it from the "open impartiality" he advocates. This is something more like benevolent disinterestedness than neutrality. Sen thinks of it as reflecting Smith's admonition to adopt the perspective of an impartial spectator who enables us to view our sentiments at "a certain distance." The goal is "to avoid local parochialism of values" by taking account of arguments from outside our culture and traditions so that we scrutinize "not only the influence of vested interest, but also the impact of entrenched tradition and custom."[38] As Smith put it in *The Theory of Moral Sentiments*, in order to survey our sentiments and motives we must try to see them "with the eyes of other people, or as other people are likely to view them."[39] Open impartiality for Sen is a kind of critical distance.[40]

Admirable as such a trait might be, it scarcely does the work that Sen's appeal to comparative political theory failed to do on its own. He never tells us what makes an observer impartial, other than that the ingredients include distance and, sometimes, ideas from other cultures. Nor does he tell us how the views of an impartial observer would help us decide on the resolution of any actual contested question about justice. In his discussion of human rights, for instance, Sen asserts that there is a human right to basic medical care.[41] Perhaps there is, but he says nothing about what to say to those who contest it, or, even if it is granted, how to resolve trenchant disagreements about who is entitled to how much health care, or in which circumstances. In a world in which resources spent on AIDS research could be spent on cancer research, artificial hearts, dialysis machines, or something else entirely, one reasonably anticipates some guidance from a theory that champions the focus on concrete comparisons that bear in consequential ways on real-world dilemmas. Yet nothing in Sen's account of impartiality even hints at how to deal with them any better than does Barry's.[42]

This difficulty extends to Sen's treatment of the nondistributive aspects of justice. For instance, in illustrating the alleged advantages of open impartiality, he remarks that "globally sensitive questioning can be more important in a fuller assessment than local discussions on, say, the facts and values surrounding women's unequal position, or the unacceptability of torture or—for that matter—of capital punishment."[43] He returns to the death penalty several times, suggesting that once people come to view it through "the eyes of the rest of mankind" they will be more inclined to reject it, along with such other disagreeable practices as stoning adulterous women.[44] His text is replete with assertions such as that although many people in the United States or China might be unimpressed by the fact that most European countries have abolished capital punishment, open impartiality can show them that "there would be, in general, a strong case for examining the justificatory arguments that are used against capital punishment elsewhere."[45] This calls to mind Thurgood Marshall's confident insistence (without adducing any evidence) that if only Americans were more fully informed about the actual operation of the death penalty, they would agree with his opposition to it.[46] I wonder.

Sen concedes that listening to "distant voices" does not require us to accept them, but he says nothing about which among them should be heeded—or why. His repeated assertions to the effect that considerations from elsewhere will "enrich our thinking" never generate a reasoned case about why this enriched thinking will take us to the destinations that he believes we obviously should reach. After a while, his combination of cherry-picked arguments from elsewhere and his hopeful deployment of the passive voice (as in the poverty-based argument "might come to dominate the judgment of justice") make *The Idea of Justice* read more like a manifesto for sensible chaps who agree with Sen than an argument that might persuade even an open-minded skeptic. The trouble with spectators is that there are many of them, and impartiality tends to reside in the eye of the beholder.

V. Democracy

To this Sen might object that he has explicitly distanced himself from the claim that there are final answers to questions about justice on the grounds that "our best efforts could still leave us locked into some mistake or other, however hidden it might be," and that, as a result, "the nature, robustness and reach" of theories of justice "depend on contributions from discussion and discourse."[47] This appeal to discussion is central to Sen's defense of democracy in the final chapters of the book. Aspects of what he says there are plausible, but his account is disappointingly rudimentary and marred by missed opportunities to explore the ways in which democracy can advance the cause of justice.

Notice, first, that Sen's appeal to democracy lives in tension with his invocation of impartial spectators, since there is no reason to think that democratic publics will take their advice. Sen characterizes democracy as a system of public reason and discussion. The image he seems to have in mind is an academic seminar writ large, where the best argument wins. But in democratic politics outsiders are easily portrayed as stooges to some unacknowledged local interest or as having agendas of their own. Think of the "impartial" development plans handed out by the IMF and World Bank, the Quartet's roadmap for Palestinian/Israeli peace, or the climate control policies recommended by the Intergovernmental Panel on Climate Change. Moreover, appeals to arguments put forward by outsiders lack democratic legitimacy precisely because of where they come from. Former Supreme Court Justice Stephen Breyer and State Department legal adviser Harold Koh have been pilloried for appealing to a version of Sen's open impartiality in interpreting American constitutional law.[48] If one is going to be committed both to impartiality and to democracy as vehicles for advancing justice, some attention is needed to the ways in which they conflict.

The most suggestive part of Sen's discussion of democracy turns on his well-known observation that democracies seem to be immune from famine.[49] This is surely an advantage, but what does it tell us about democracy's desirability from the standpoint of other features of justice that Sen prizes? Democratic responsiveness to famine has not carried over, for example, to alleviating chronic poverty or reducing extreme inequalities—despite the expectations of many nineteenth- and twentieth-century thinkers to the contrary.[50] This difference suggests that, at a minimum, Sen's view of democracy as a system of "public reason" that promotes "government by discussion" that will facilitate advances toward justice stands in need of pruning by reality.[51]

Famines, like other disasters, are vivid. They garner media attention, as Sen notes, making it hard for governments in countries with a free press—which democracies generally have—to ignore them. The public drama and media attention surrounding famines make it possible to mobilize support for extraordinary action. Moreover, famines and other disasters often strike unpredictably out of the blue. This has two further implications: they tend not to involve fraught moral debates about whether and to what extent people are responsible for their dire straits, and they exhibit a "there but for fortune" logic. People know that disasters can befall anyone. Powerful coalitions are not needed to support responses to them because powerful coalitions do not emerge to block those responses. The kind of laws mandating disaster relief that are enacted in the wake of hurricanes, or to compensate victims of catastrophic terrorist attacks, could never make it through the rough and tumble of normal legislative politics. And, because of their exceptional and, therefore, bounded character, disasters provide opportunities for leaders to demonstrate efficacy. The problem can be solved, and it is usually clear what is needed to solve it. Politicians are often held accountable for events over which they have little, if any, control. Catastrophes can empower them.[52]

Most problems of injustice are not like this. They tend to be chronic rather than catastrophic, systemic rather than episodic, and rooted in enduring conflicts of interest and ideology. Responses to them are less spontaneous than is the case with disasters, and inevitably more contentious as they become embroiled in disagreements about causal and moral responsibility and the likely efficacy of alternative courses of action. They divide people along coalitional fault lines. How feasible it is for politicians to respond to them will depend on calculations about the chances of success, the views of powerful members of their constituencies, and related considerations.[53] Sen might with profit have explored the implications of these features of democratic politics to illuminate the conditions under which democracies are likely to be justice-promoting. For instance, if systemic injustices can be reframed in the public imagination to be more like famines and other catastrophes, more progress might be made with them in democratic politics. But this would take more work than Sen's vague appeals to government by discussion.

Consider, for example, the abolition of slavery. Sen rightly points out that it is not hard to conclude that slavery is unjust, even if we are unsure about many other questions of justice and disagree with others about just why we hold this view.[54] He flirts with the notion that this agreement played a significant role in achieving abolition, but how plausible is this?[55] Certainly, it was not remotely sufficient to end slavery in the United States, as he knows. That took a bloody civil war after various institutional compromises, such as the three-fifths rule in Article 1 of the Constitution and the Missouri Compromise of 1820, had failed to generate the necessary political common ground to resolve it democratically. This is scarcely surprising. The slave economy was deeply entrenched in the South and fundamentally incompatible with the free labor system that prevailed in the North. If the Union was to remain together, one would have to displace the other by force, as eventually happened.[56]

The story of abolition in Britain and the British Empire is more illuminating of the conditions under which democracy can help eliminate injustice. Democratic politics indeed played a role, though this had little to do with public reason and discussion. Rather, it turned on forging and sustaining a parliamentary coalition to support abolition. A small group of Dissenting MPs engineered a vote outlawing the North Atlantic slave trade in 1807, but meaningful enforcement had to wait until they came to hold the balance of power in Parliament in the 1830s. This enabled them to auction their support to governments that were willing to advance the abolitionist cause.[57] Slavery was outlawed in most of the empire in 1833, helped along by £20 million in reparations paid out to slave owners.[58] Enforcement was ramped up outside the empire by aggressive diplomacy and unilateral military action, which escalated to an undeclared war against Brazil in 1850 to end the slave trade there. The United States finally agreed to searches of its ships in 1862, and Cuba was pressured into ending slave imports five years later.

Sen is right that democracy can be pressed into the service of reducing injustice. Indeed, this can happen against expectations. Had there been neoclassical economists around in the late eighteenth century, they would have scoffed at the possibility of abolishing the slave trade. In the absence of a system of multilateral enforcement, Britain had to bear the enormous expense unilaterally—over several decades—without any obvious prospect of a return. These costs included the direct costs of the enforcement regime to the Treasury, as well as the indirect but very substantial costs to the economy.[59] Successive administrations, both Whig and Tory, were cajoled into doing this through the democratic process. It was, by any measure, a remarkable democratic achievement.

Discussion and public reason might have played a part, but they scarcely seem to have been at the heart of the matter. This turned on the Dissenters' ability to forge and sustain a political coalition at Westminster to get the job done. Nor did they confront anything like the entrenched and unified proslavery interests that prevailed in the American South.[60] Slave owners in the empire could be bought off. The East India–based slave traders stood to lose, but they lacked political clout at Westminster. The United States had outlawed the Atlantic slave trade as soon as this was constitutionally permissible, in 1808, but for reasons that had little, if anything, to do with democratic public discussion, or, indeed, even abolition. Rather it was motivated by the desire to limit the growth of America's nonwhite populations and to protect the—by then robust—American domestic slave trade.[61] British domestic commercial interests lacked the incentive forcefully to resist because ending the slave trade posed no immediate threat to the flow of cheap materials, notably cotton and sugar, produced by slave labor abroad. The landed gentry were more worried about other threats.[62] Most workers lacked the vote, but to the extent their views mattered, they had every reason to oppose the threat slavery posed to their wages and employment.[63]

Like responding to famines, and unlike, for example, reducing poverty or inequality, abolishing the slave trade and then slavery were well-defined proximate goals. This is vital when trying to advance justice democratically. It creates a focal point around which to organize a majority coalition without regard to its members' other—quite possibly conflicting—interests, and it provides an achievable goal for which people can be mobilized before their energy and momentum dissipate. This helps to explain, I think, why the more proximate goals of the civil rights movement, such as ending de jure segregation, abolishing restrictive covenants, and integrating institutions like the military and professional sports, were more easily achieved than the more nebulous challenges posed by chronic race-based inequality and soft apartheid in American schools and neighborhoods. Fighting these evils involved pursuing goals that were less proximate, and the coalitions to achieve them have been harder to sustain as a result.

British abolition also shared in common with famine-response the fact that it did not face powerful and well-organized interests on the other side. The case of American slavery reminds us how important a limitation this is on democracy as a tool for abolishing injustice. Even without this handicap, British abolition required imaginative leadership to mobilize and sustain an effective political coalition for the better part of half a century, the strategic use of force, and quite a bit of luck. But the distribution of economic forces in the country and the empire, and of political power at Westminster, meant that there were plausible reasons to try.[64] Sen's work on democracy and famine-prevention points the way to an important research agenda: to understand more than presently we do about the conditions under which, and the means through which, democracy can operate to reduce injustice and improve human well-being. These issues are explored further in part II of this book.

3

On Nondomination

When people experience domination, they often complain of injustice, and rightly so. My aim here is to develop an account of nondomination as the bedrock of justice that makes sense of, and builds on, this common complaint. I doubt that any conception of justice could win many adherents or keep them for long even if it snared them for a while, were it not unambiguously hostile to domination. People demand justice to escape domination. I agree with the tradition of political philosophy, stretching at least from Plato to John Rawls, in which justice is regarded as the first virtue of social institutions.[1] If I am right about the relations between justice and nondomination, this makes nondomination in an important sense the primary political value.

I have previously made the case that the best path for pursuing justice, thus conceived, is to democratize human relationships in a particular way. This involves institutionalizing democracy as a conditioning or subordinate good that shapes the ways in which people pursue other goods. My democratic conception of justice is partly defined contextually, linked to the nature of the goods in question and the ways in which people pursue them in particular historical settings. But mine is also partly a general ideal. It implies the need for participation in decision making as well as rights of opposition as constraints on ways in which people pursue their contextually defined goals. How robust these constraints should be depends on how vulnerable to domination people are in particular settings; the more vulnerable they are, the more demanding should be the constraints.

Vulnerability to domination is operationalized, for me, principally by reference to the notion of basic interests. People have basic interests in the security, nutrition, health, and education needed to develop into, and live as, normal adults. This includes developing the capacities needed to function effectively in the prevailing economic, technological, and institutional system, governed as a democracy, over the course of their lives.[2] People are more vulnerable in collective settings when their basic interests, thus conceived, are at stake than when they are not. If I control resources that you need to vindicate your basic interests, that gives me power over you. This fact legitimates more stringent democratic constraints on our collective endeavors when basic interests are at stake than when they are not.[3] This power-based resourcism, as I have called it, is geared toward mitigating the most serious kinds of domination that permeate human social arrangements.[4]

My aim in this chapter is to differentiate this view from two kinds of alternatives: those whose proponents reject the idea that nondomination is the bedrock of justice, and those who agree with me but understand nondomination differently than I do. The first group divides into partisans of equality, on the one hand, and of freedom on the other. The egalitarians generally think of themselves, like me, as writing about justice, mostly in the wake of the "equality of what?" debate spawned by Amartya Sen's contention that debates about justice are always at bottom debates about some kind of equality.[5] Proponents of freedom are sometimes less clear about their ideal's relation to justice, or at least less explicitly so—perhaps because some of them are skeptical of the very idea of justice.[6] Regardless of whether they see freedom as a feature of justice or an alternative to it, they treat it as the coin of the realm in judging the legitimacy of political institutions. For present purposes I will assume that, like Robert Nozick, freedom's partisans regard their understanding of it as the bedrock of justice.[7] The friends of equality occupy my attention in section I, followed by those of freedom in section II. Having explained why nondomination is a preferable bedrock ideal to those put forward in either of these camps, I turn, in section III, to competing conceptions of nondomination put forward by Jürgen Habermas, Michel Foucault, Michael Walzer, Quentin Skinner, and Philip Pettit. There is considerable overlap among these various views, and between theirs and mine, but there are also notable disagreements. I spell out what is at stake in the alternative formulations, indicating why my own conception, rooted in power-based resourcism, is preferable.

I. Justice, Equality, and Nondomination

If nondomination is the bedrock of justice, one might reasonably ask whether its appeal trades on a prior commitment to equality. On this view, nondomination's moral pull is really the moral pull of equality. If that were true, then energy spent justifying nondomination would be better deployed in making the egalitarian case on which it ultimately depends. This approach seems to me ill-considered, however, partly because nondomination is only trivially associated with equality as a political ideal, and partly because endorsing nondomination instead of equality makes it possible to avoid a number of the philosophical and political difficulties associated with egalitarianism.

When I say that egalitarianism is only trivially associated with nondomination as I conceive it, I do not mean to deny that there is an ultimate sense in which proponents of nondomination acknowledge the moral equality of persons—what Sen describes as basal equality.[8] But it is the idea of nondomination, not that of equality, that does the heavy lifting in my argument. Nor do I deny that a commitment to nondomination has distributive implications, some of which—as we shall see—will be congenial to many who count themselves egalitarians. But I do want to deny that nondomination's raison d'être is to promote equality. I agree with John Kane that there is nothing in the meaning of justice that implies an egalitarian presumption.[9] It is when egalitarian distributive arrangements serve the goal of nondomination that they are desirable from the standpoint of justice.

There has been an influential tendency among contemporary political theorists, at least since John Rawls, to deny this: to think that justice begins with a presumption in favor of equality. The nature of this alleged link turns out, on inspection, to be elusive. Sometimes Rawls writes as if it is embedded in the very meaning of justice, as teased out in his examination of our intuitions about justice via the original position in which readers are invited to speculate about justice while denied knowledge of their particular circumstances. A different supposed path to equality is Rawls's trenchant argument that the differences among us, whether rooted in nature or nurture, are morally arbitrary. A third potential basis for a presumption in favor of equality is Rawls's Kantian interpretation of the principles of justice as procedural expressions of the categorical imperative. A final putative path from justice to equality passes through Rawls's admonition that the state should stand neutral among permissible conceptions of the good life. I take each of these up in turn.

The Original Position and the Logic of Justice

Rawls's device of reasoning behind a veil of ignorance does not generate a commitment to equality; rather, it presumes prior acceptance of an egalitarian presumption. His claim is that, under conditions of moderate scarcity, the principle of insufficient reason that operates behind the veil of ignorance would lead any rational person to choose equality unless an unequal distribution could be shown to operate to everyone's advantage.[10] But the original position is an expository device, not an argument for equality—or indeed for any other distributive principle. Rawls himself noted that it was inspired by a conception of fairness according to which the best way to divide a cake is to require the cutter to take the last slice.[11] Assuming rational self-interest, she will divide it equally so as to maximize the size of her slice. Granting the assumptions, arguendo, this does nothing to establish the desirability of an equal division. If we knew, for instance, that one of the recipients had not eaten for three days, another had three cakes in his bag, and a third was a diabetic who would be made sick by eating cake, then any intuitive appeal of "the cutter takes last" rule would quickly evaporate. The cake cutter's rule seems attractive only in light of a prior commitment to equality. What it offers is a way for self-interest to get people there; nothing less, nothing more.

The same is true of the claim that people would endorse an egalitarian presumption behind the veil of ignorance. Rawls explicitly structured the choice situation to produce this result, so it cannot furnish an argument in favor of the desirability of the result. Had he asked them to make other assumptions behind the veil of ignorance, no doubt they could have been induced to pick a different principle. For instance, as Harsanyi noted in an early critique, had people been characterized as more risk-embracing than Rawls characterizes them in the original position, then they would have been more apt to choose utilitarianism over his conception of justice.[12] If there is to be a presumption in favor of equality, it stands in need of a justification that is independent of an expository device which assumes that its desirability has already been established.

Moral Arbitrariness

What is Rawls's independent argument for an egalitarian presumption? One candidate is his moral-arbitrariness thesis, the claim that differences among us—whether products of nature or nurture—are accidental from a moral point of view. Rawls was right to say that distributive outcomes that are shaped by those differences stand in need of justification. His argument about moral arbitrariness is persuasively subversive of any version of the thesis that losses (or gains) should lie where they fall.[13] Indeed, I have argued elsewhere that Rawls was insufficiently thoroughgoing in his defense of this thesis. His attempt to distinguish capacities, which are said to be distributed in morally arbitrary ways, from the choices people make about how to use those capacities, which are not, fails. There is no good reason to suppose that differences in the capacity to decide to use one's capacities more or less effectively are any less arbitrary, from a moral point of view, than are differences in the capacities themselves.[14] This is, to be sure, a disconcerting conclusion; it threatens to obliterate widespread convictions about ownership and personal responsibility. But that does not mean that Rawls supplies us with convincing reasons to avoid it.

The impulse to defend an egalitarian presumption in the literature since Rawls has been animated by fending off what G. A. Cohen identified in 1989 as "the anti-egalitarian right." The motivating worry was that any conception of fair distribution that ignored rewarding effort and ambition would be so implausible that no one would give it the time of day. This is, indeed, a real possibility unless some limits can be put on moral arbitrariness. It was, presumably, considerations of this sort that motivated Rawls's unsuccessful attempt to distinguish capacities from the uses to which they are put that I have just mentioned. Similar considerations led Ronald Dworkin to propose a view of distributive justice that takes account of the Rawlsian insight about moral arbitrariness but is nonetheless "ambition sensitive." Dworkin's argument requires a view of equality by reference to which people "decide what sorts of lives to pursue against a background of information about the actual costs that their choices impose on other people and hence on the total stock of resources that may fairly be used by them." He tried to achieve this by assigning "tastes and ambitions" to the person, and "physical and mental powers" to his "circumstances," arguing that the former, but not the latter, are irrelevant in deciding how resources should be distributed. In this way he hoped to rescue the idea of a responsible agent.[15]

Dworkin's strategy also fails. The ambitions that it occurs to us to develop, no less than the volitions we are able to form, are greatly shaped—perhaps even determined—by our powers and capacities. When we describe someone as ambitious, we may be describing something basic to her psychology and constitution, but do we have any good reason to believe that this is a product neither of her physical and mental powers nor her upbringing and life circumstances? To "think big," to "resolve to go for broke," to steel oneself through self-control to perform demanding acts: do these reflect ambition or capacity? There are certainly circumstances in which we would say that lack of confidence is an incapacity that prevents the formation (not just the attainment) of particular ambitions. Different people have different capacities to form different ambitions, and those different capacities must be as morally tainted from Dworkin's point of view as any other capacities. Donald Trump is able to develop more far-reaching ambitions than, say, Homer Simpson due at least partly to luck in the genetic pool and the circumstances of his upbringing.

The idea that we form our ambitions in some way that is independent of our resources and capacities assumes, implausibly, that we can conceive of goals independently of our understanding of our capacities and life circumstances. This should be evident to anyone who tries to perform a thought experiment in which she is required to choose her future ambitions while kept in ignorance of powers, capacities, and circumstances. The world is riddled with what I have described as "empathy gaps" which limit the aspirations people find conceivable, let alone plausible, as a result of their lived experiences.

You can readily imagine yourself stepping over a puddle, perhaps even swimming a wide river; but will it occur to you to consider possibilities that are on the far side of an ocean?[16]

Similar arguments can be made about the different abilities to form (or refrain from forming) different kinds of tastes, whether expensive, compulsive, or both. Are we to say of an alcoholic, whose affliction is so severe that he cannot even form the desire not to be an alcoholic, that the preference for alcohol results from his *taste* rather than his *incapacity?* I think not.[17] With all acquired tastes (not just the expensive), experiencing the taste is by definition conditional on the exercise of pertinent capacities. A taste for good beer or even just for beer, a taste for a particular kind of music, perhaps even for any music—these can be developed only through the exercise of relevant capacities. We would not attribute a taste for music to someone who was born deaf, although we might intelligibly say that such a person could wish she could have such a taste. Likewise with beer and someone who lacks functioning taste buds or a sense of smell. Dworkin's motivating intuition here is that people should be held responsible only for the choices they make in life, not for things over which they have no control. A variant of this thesis might be defensible, but his treatment of it is no more persuasive than Rawls's. The result is that Dworkin has not, as Cohen claimed, "performed for egalitarianism the considerable service of incorporating within it the most powerful idea in the arsenal of the anti-egalitarian right: the idea of choice and responsibility."[18]

Cohen himself had a go at this problem, but with no more success than Dworkin or Rawls. Cohen tried to diminish the problem by insisting that we should not confuse the valid claim that our capacities for effort are "influenced" by factors beyond our control with the false claim that people like Nozick mistakenly attribute to egalitarians like Rawls, that those capacities are "determined" by factors beyond our control. Pointing to this distinction enabled Cohen to say that although not all effort deserves reward, some effort does deserve reward. That effort is partly praiseworthy and partly not—although he concedes that in practice "we cannot separate the parts."[19]

To the extent that this is a practical problem, it is a devastatingly large one. The topic at hand is whether and to what extent the state should engage in redistribution or other remedial action to compensate for differences in outcomes resulting from these practically inseparable parts. But it is in any case misleading to say that it is only a practical problem. Once we concede that the very decision to choose to expend effort is influenced by morally arbitrary factors, it becomes evident that the difficulty becomes one of principle rather than practicality. Certainly Cohen offers no account of how that component of effort meriting reward might, in principle, be singled out.

Rawls, Dworkin, and Cohen all write as if the moral-arbitrariness argument generates an egalitarian presumption that would be so radical that no one would take it seriously unless some limits could somehow be put on it. They think that this is essential in order to rescue the idea that people should be held responsible for the choices they make, so that they can fairly be said to deserve the resulting benefits or costs. Yet the going attempts to articulate the limits in question fail, as I have just noted, because the moral-arbitrariness noose throttles the notions of choice and responsibility if it kills anything at all.

But Rawls, Dworkin, and Cohen fail to appreciate that rescuing the ideas of choice and responsibility in order to save a suitably chastened egalitarian presumption is unnecessary if that presumption is thought to rest, in turn, on embracing Rawls's moral-arbitrariness argument. This is true for the simple reason that Rawls's moral-arbitrariness argument, while valid, generates no distributive presumption of any kind. To be sure, differences in our ambitions, tastes, and volitions depend vitally on forces beyond our control; as such they are morally arbitrary for the same reason that differences in our capacities and circumstances are morally arbitrary. All such differences stand in need of justification. But the same is true of similarities in our ambitions, tastes, and volitions. They are morally arbitrary for the same reason that similarities in our circumstances and capacities are morally arbitrary. They, too, stand in need of justification. As Susan Hurley puts it, there is "no more a priori reason to regard difference of position as a matter of luck than to regard sameness of position as a matter of luck: people may not be responsible for either."[20] Rawls's moral-arbitrariness argument establishes nothing more than that every distributive arrangement stands in need of a justification. There is no presumptive benchmark.

The Kantian Interpretation

Perhaps Rawls's most plausible candidate for an independent justification of his egalitarian presumption is the so-called Kantian interpretation of his principles as procedural expressions of the categorical imperative.[21] But a commitment to Kantian autonomy does not entail embracing any particular distributive regime any more than the commitment to moral arbitrariness does. The injunction never to use people exclusively as means to your own ends could no doubt be shown to rule out slavery, but no protagonist in the distributive-justice literature of whom I am aware is advocating the establishment of slavery. The example of slavery is, in any case, instructive here inasmuch as the Kantian objection is not to the distributive dimensions of a slave economy but rather to the abnegation of a person's humanity by making them the property of another. The Kantian objection to slavery would stand even in the face of arguments showing that slaves enjoyed distributive benefits that might otherwise be denied to them. "We give our slaves more than you pay your workers" would not pass muster as a defense of slavery, even if it were true.[22] (Similar points could be made about apartheid, "separate but equal," and related dehumanizing statuses. They are often accompanied by distributional inequity, but it is the dehumanization, not the inequity, that makes them objectionable.)

There are two different objections to distinguish in considering Rawls's Kantian interpretation of his principles. The less fundamental one is to observe that if our goal was to do our best to preserve the autonomy of all (and assuming that we could operationalize that aspiration in an intelligible fashion), what would be needed is a matter for political economists and policy wonks. How much, if any, in the way of redistribution toward equality would be effective in achieving that goal depends on complex considerations about the effectiveness and costs of different redistributive instruments, on the incentive-effects of redistribution on growth, and on the relations between the size of the economic pie and the benefits that trickle down to the least well-endowed. Rawls genuflects in this direction when he declares his theory to be agnostic between capitalism and socialism.[23]

But a deeper objection rears its head when we start to wonder whether preserving everyone's autonomy is even intelligible as a distributional idea. The transition from Kantian universalism to an egalitarian presumption must involve some version of the claim that we are bound to respect the autonomy of all equally. But what can this mean when the injunction we are seeking to obey assumes that we should concede (as Kant, realistically, did) that people use one another as means all the time and merely instructs us not to use one another *exclusively* as means to our own ends? It is difficult to see how this can have any distributive dimension at all. Treat everyone with consideration? With the same *amount* of consideration? What could such an injunction actually mean? Kant's dictum seems more likely to generate aphorisms of good conduct and manners ("Don't be rude!";

"Don't be a bully!"; "Don't be gratuitously mean!") than any distributive principle. The Kantian interpretation of Rawls's principles is just not enough to generate an egalitarian presumption because it is not enough to generate *any* distributive presumption.

But why should we *want* to commit to an egalitarian distributive presumption? Michael Walzer pointed out four decades ago that it is not typically inequality as such that people find objectionable so much as the uses people make of unequally distributed assets. In particular, it is when people use the resources in their control to dominate others that we take exception to their having those resources. It is the use of wealth to corrupt a politician, or to "buy" a place in college for an otherwise undeserving child, that generates resentment.[24] Walzer's solution, to build barriers between the spheres in which different goods appropriately hold sway, confronts difficulties, as I note in section III. But they do not detract from the force of his telling underlying intuition that it is domination rather than inequality that is objectionable.

In arguing against an egalitarian presumption, I should not be construed as throwing my lot in with those who maintain that arguments about justice should abjure distributive considerations. Marx famously held that to understand the dynamics of exploitation we must forsake the realm of distribution for that of production.[25] In the 1990s, such theorists as Iris Marion Young and Nancy Fraser suggested that the distributive paradigm should give way to a focus on recognition and domination.[26] It is unclear what role the term "paradigm" plays in such arguments. Proponents of these views are wrongheaded if they maintain that we can reason fruitfully about justice in the absence of distributive considerations, or even that we can reason fruitfully about the dimensions of justice to which the theorists in question point in the absence of distributive considerations, as Fraser subsequently recognized.[27] Marxian exploitation is in significant part about the distribution of work, recognition is about the distribution of status, and domination is about the distribution of power. Moreover, as I spell out in the course of discussing Philip Pettit's view in section III, there are many settings in which resisting domination requires attention to—and sometimes redistribution of—material and other resources. Rather than conceive of nondomination as an alternative to distributive justice, we do better to think of nondomination as the bedrock of justice and acknowledge that it is often intimately linked to distributive considerations. To think otherwise leads down the path of symbolic victories that at best obscure what justice requires, and often work at cross-purposes with it.

Equality as Neutrality?

Yet another Rawlsian contender for equality as the bedrock of justice piggybacks on the idea of neutrality. Rawls's theory of justice as fairness requires the state to be neutral among competing "permissible" conceptions of the good life and the comprehensive doctrines that give rise to them. For Rawls this means guaranteeing the opportunity to pursue any such conception, and prohibiting government from favoring any particular one or giving "greater assistance to those who pursue it." Instead, the state is admonished to adopt what we might think of as a dis-established stance toward permissible conceptions of the good life: it should guarantee the freedom to pursue any of them, but it should not promote one—or some—above the others.[28]

This might seem like an unequivocal bedrock egalitarianism, since the protections and guarantees of disestablishment are equally available to all—but this is not really so. Notice, for one thing, that Rawls was unperturbed by the unequal effects of his institutional neutrality. He acknowledged that his favored regime would have "important effects and influences on which comprehensive doctrines endure and gain adherents over time," which it would be "futile to try to counteract."[29] Furthermore, Rawls's neutrality rule is anti-egalitarian in a more immediate sense than is captured by this admission because different permissible comprehensive doctrines do not fare equally well under its strictures. Most obviously, someone who either has no religion or whose comprehensive doctrine includes the belief that religious practice has no place in the public square gets exactly what she wants from Rawls's scheme, whereas someone who favors an established church (not to mention a fundamentalist one) does not. The defense of Rawls's "neutral" stance toward permissible conceptions of the good, after all, was never that all would fare equally well, but rather that all would enjoy as much freedom as it is possible to have, consistent with guaranteeing a like liberty to all.[30] The partisan of an established church has more religious freedom in the disestablished regime than would the nonconformist in a regime with an established church, but it remains true that the former fares less well than the latter in Rawls's disestablished regime. Concededly, there is a residual sense in which this principle treats adherents to all comprehensive doctrines alike: they are all guaranteed the maximal religious freedom that is compatible with a like liberty for all. But try selling that as equal treatment to someone who favors religious establishment. Equality is not doing the contentious work here.

More importantly, the preceding discussion only deals with the state's appropriate stance toward comprehensive doctrines and permissible conceptions of the good. It does not touch the procedures by which Rawls classified them as permissible or impermissible to begin with. He was unequivocal that the process for doing that is not procedurally neutral. As noted earlier, procedures behind the veil of ignorance were self-consciously gerrymandered to induce the reader to embrace Rawls's conception of justice as fairness—including the thin theory of the good, which sets the limits of permissibility. It follows that judgments about acceptability of comprehensive doctrines and conceptions of the good cannot be said to result from a neutral process. As for later formulations, Rawls remained forthright that justice as fairness cannot guarantee "an equal opportunity to advance any conception of the good." It allows the pursuit only of permissible conceptions, defined as "those that respect the principles of justice."[31] The only sense in which the mature Rawls appealed to procedural neutrality was in claiming that it embodies "a political conception that aims to be the focus of an overlapping consensus." Famously, the overlapping consensus "includes all the opposing philosophical and religious doctrines likely to persist and to gain adherents in a more or less just constitutional democratic society."[32] The overlapping consensus "seeks common ground—or if one prefers, neutral ground—given the fact of pluralism."[33] Whatever this means, it cannot be that the justness of a political order depends on its embodying neutrality as common ground, because the defense of neutrality as common ground is that it is (said to be) compatible with a just political order. The defense of procedural neutrality is not itself procedurally neutral. A fortiori, it cannot be a stalking horse for a bedrock commitment to equality.[34]

II. Domination: A Particular Kind of Unfreedom

If inequalities are objectionable only to the extent that they facilitate domination, questions arise: What is domination? How do we know it when we see it, and why should we care about its presence? Answering them requires attending to the relations between nondomination and freedom. If we think of freedom as the summum bonum, as some theorists propose that we do, then nondomination would stand in the same relation to freedom as I have just been arguing equality stands to nondomination. Nondomination would be an instrumental good, when it is a good, geared to realizing freedom. I want to say something different. Nondomination is more closely related to freedom than it is to equality; indeed it is a kind of freedom. As a result, the literature on freedom is indeed relevant to understanding the sources of domination and its amelioration, as we will see. But nondomination merits independent demarcation, so as to avoid our being caught up in controversies that need not be resolved to make a compelling case for nondomination as the bedrock of justice.

Nondomination is a negative term, defined as the antithesis of domination. I will have more to say about its negative and reactive character later. Here my focus is on the particular constraints on freedom at which it is directed. That is, before focusing on nondomination we should say something about domination. Four features of domination merit particular attention.

Domination is, first, a type of unfreedom that involves a significant human element. A natural chasm or a medical condition can limit our freedom, but we would not identify either as a source of domination. We experience domination when our freedom is curtailed because we are in the power of others—be they slaveholders, torturers, spouses, or employers. This is not to insist that domination always results from intentional action. Domination might not always be intended, and it can be a byproduct of political, social, and economic structures. Such structures are not reducible to human agency, but they could not exist without it. This human element differentiates domination from other kinds of unfreedom, which means that appeals to eliminate sources of domination are always in some sense—however attenuated—directed at changing things that human beings do.

Domination is also a distinctive kind of unfreedom in that it is generally taken to be alterable by those who are responsible for it. A parent's freedom is curtailed by a crying infant, but this is not domination because the infant is powerless to do anything about it. When a person or state of affairs is indicted as responsible for domination, the presumption is triggered that relevant agents can behave differently in ways that would alleviate the domination—at least in principle. People can, of course, be wrong about what will work; they might attribute their powerlessness to the vindictiveness of an angry god who can be appeased only by making a human sacrifice. Or they might correctly identify ethnic hatred as a source of their oppression and be right that in principle it could be eliminated, yet no one in fact may know how to accomplish this. Describing unfreedom as domination alludes to the possibility of its elimination. Realizing that possibility is another matter.

This is not to say that all sources of domination in the world can be curtailed. Limiting the power of investment bankers might involve enhancing that of government regulators, and it is an empirical question whether the regulators are more or less prone than the bankers to engage in domination. Foucault might have been right that throwing off one domineering yoke typically creates new possibilities for domination, but it is an open question whether this is always so. Even if it is, some kinds of domination will be more severe than others, and some kinds will be borne by people who are more vulnerable to its deleterious effects than are others. Any full-blown account of nondomination would have to investigate these differences. My power-based resourcism is intended as a step in that direction.

Domination is, third, a kind of unfreedom that carries the whiff of illicitness. Our freedom is often curtailed when we are in the power of others, but this is not domination unless that power is somehow abused or pressed into the service of an illegitimate purpose. Children are in the power of parents, students of teachers, workers of employers. In all these cases their freedom is limited. But we only think of it as domination if those in positions of authority abuse their power in some way, as when an employer or teacher demands sexual favors as a condition for a promotion or a good grade. When people accuse one another of domination they do it in order to question the legitimacy of a power relationship. Even domination fantasies underscore this; they involve fetishizing dungeons, slavery, or other illicit forms of control. When we say someone is domineering we express disdain; calling them powerful connotes no necessary negative valence. Wars of domination are not regarded as just, whereas wars to escape its yoke are seen as defensible. There are exceptions, to be sure. Sports teams can be said to dominate one another without prejudice to the dominator and economists sometimes talk neutrally of one choice as dominating another, but these really are exceptions. Domination as such is seldom defended as desirable. When it is, as by Nietzsche, this is generally condemned as amoral promotion of an übermensch syndrome—or worse.[35]

This inevitably raises the question: who identifies illicitness, and how? I have adopted a two-pronged approach to this challenge, involving qualified deference to contextual knowledge or "insiders' wisdom." The idea is to agree, but only up to a point, with Alasdair MacIntyre and Michael Walzer that the values guiding human social practices should be defined by the participants via procedures that have evolved over time as appropriate for those choices.[36] Insiders command the relevant street-level knowledge to distinguish licit from illicit uses of authority. But our deference to them should be qualified because external judgments appropriately kick in when basic interests are at stake. So it makes sense to respect parental judgments about the medical treatment of their children, but not when the child of Christian Scientists will die as a result of being denied a blood transfusion. It makes sense to defer to managerial practices that have evolved within firms, churches, and universities, but not when they become smokescreens for perpetrating rape. And it makes sense to require schools to accommodate parents in matters of sexual mores, but not when it comes to denying children vital knowledge about sexually transmitted diseases. If basic interests are compromised or threatened, the state rightly takes an interest. What it should do depends on the seriousness of the threat to basic interests and the availability of remedial instruments that do not create more serious forms of domination than those that they prevent.[37]

Fourth, a distinctive kind of particularism is invoked when people speak of domination and nondomination that need not be present when people refer to freedom or the lack of it more generally. This particularism is linked to domination's rootedness in human collective arrangements. If domination is always, ultimately, because of the actions or practices of others, then any charge about domination naturally leads to pointed questions about those actions or practices. Whose? What? How do they produce control, and why is it illicit? As we will see, this means that arguments about domination involve claims that are invariably rooted in specifics. Perhaps people are unfree in some existential sense if determinism is true, if we are "being towards death" as Heidegger said, or for some other reason unrelated to human social relations.[38] Domination, however, is rooted in the particular.

A different tack, taken by Philip Pettit, is to treat nondomination as the political mechanism to realize the philosophical ideal of freedom. I will have more to say about Pettit's institutional arguments later. Here I will just say that to treat nondomination as the instrument for achieving freedom, as Pettit does, undersells nondomination's importance as a normative ideal in its own right rather than as an instrument to achieve some other benefit. Moreover, I worry about a defense of nondomination that makes it hinge on our first buying a particular contestable view of freedom. Pettit contends that nondomination is the best available instrument to realize his theory of freedom as "discursive control." Some elements of this account of freedom are appealing to me; others I find problematic.[39] I think it is a mistake to hold the case for nondomination hostage to prior resolution of these issues.[40]

Max Weber held that existence of domination requires "the actual presence of one person successfully issuing orders to others."[41] My conception is broader in that I think domination can (and often does) occur without explicit orders emanating from identifiable agents. Domination can result from inadvertent and unconscious actions, as a byproduct of the distribution of resources, and it can be embedded in structural relationships. My conception is narrower than Weber's, however, in that I regard domination as arising only from the illicit exercise of power. Compliance is often compelled in armies, firms, sports teams, families, schools, and countless other institutions, but this is not domination unless it is deployed for an illegitimate purpose. In sum, domination differs from other types of unfreedom in that it focuses attention on particular and alterable human sources of illicit unfreedom, and it avoids the difficulties inherent in generalized commitments to freedom or equality. As a result, I think the ideal of nondomination supplies a superior basis for political analysis and argument. It can appeal to people who think freedom and equality the highest goods because it captures much of what motivates them to prize those ideals in the first place (I take this to be a plus). We might regard it as part of the overlapping consensus or the incompletely theorized agreement among liberals, who value freedom, and egalitarians, who value equality.[42]

III. Conceptions of Nondomination

The preceding discussion suggests that nondomination is to be preferred as a bedrock political commitment either to freedom or to equality, but it does not tell us everything we need to know about nondomination. In recent decades various commentators have countenanced the idea, but they have meant different things by it. In addition to Jürgen Habermas, Michel Foucault, Michael Walzer, Quentin Skinner, and Philip Pettit have also appealed to the ideal of nondomination in their political arguments. Each of their views has something to commend it, but each also exhibits limitations, which combine to suggest the wisdom of embracing my alternative account of nondomination.

Habermas

Habermas is well known for grounding his account of democratic politics, with its guiding normative idea of legitimacy, in what people would agree to in the absence of coercion.[43] Just how he unpacks the notion of uncoerced agreement has evolved over time, from earlier accounts of an "ideal speech situation" to later writings on law and democracy.[44] Running throughout his different formulations is the notion of uncoerced rational agreement. Habermas wants to specify procedures and constraints that would enable people to reach genuine agreement, where this means that they would neither be confused by superstition or ideology nor cowed by imperatives for subservience. People would be persuaded by the best argument because it is the best argument. In one way his account is less ambitious than is Rawls's: Habermas does not specify particular institutions or distributive arrangements that he believes would be selected under his ideal conditions. These are not subjects for armchair philosophy on his account; they would result from people's uncoerced deliberations. This renders Habermas immune from the difficulties that Rawls confronts in trying to establish that the institutions he favors would be chosen in the original position or be supported by his overlapping consensus.[45]

Habermas's position is more demanding than Rawls's, however, in that there is no analogy in his evolving account to Rawls's "political, not metaphysical" move. An Enlightenment Kantian to the core, Habermas expects not only that people can agree on the right answers to normative questions about politics, but, if they deliberate properly and in good faith, they can also agree on why they are the right answers. Indeed, without this second-order agreement, their deliberation cannot be called authentic. And while, unlike Rawls, Habermas does not rule out religious and other sectarian motivations for their arguments, he expects people to agree that only secular reasons will be accepted as telling in formal deliberative settings such as parliamentary debates or in legislative processes.[46] His discourse ethics will not settle for mere tactical coalitions or any kind of modus vivendi. His ideal is deliberative agreement in a public square, modeled on his vision of the kind of engaged public intelligentsia that he believes existed in nineteenth-century Europe. But in his view, it has since been compromised by the subsequent evolution of modern economies, societies, and polities.[47]

Habermas's defenders sometimes emphasize that his accounts of ideal speech and communicative ethics are not meant to describe actual deliberative settings: they embody no more than a regulative ideal that is designed to help us reason about the appropriate constraints on, and preconditions for, democratic politics.[48] Perhaps so, but his regulative ideal nonetheless rests on at least two extravagantly demanding assumptions. One is that people are all Kantians at heart: that everyone can be brought to accept that only views that they can translate into a compelling secular idiom may legitimately hold sway in public political debate. Since there is no good empirical reason to believe this, Habermas's position amounts to unilateral privileging of secular universal views—a kind of rationalist overreaching that assumes what he needs to establish. This might be congenial to people who already agree with Habermas, but it is unlikely to persuade those most in need of persuasion.[49] Imagine trying to convince a religious fundamentalist that requiring their religious views to be defensible in a secular idiom if they are to play a role in politics does not amount to bias. The goal of limiting domination should not be held hostage to the possibility, however speculative, that minds might in principle meet.

A different profligate assumption is that a set of constraints could be established that would banish the threats of power and coercion from political debate. This is needed for his venture to get off the ground, because deliberation in power-laden settings is inherently suspect. Even if, per impossible, procedures could be devised to achieve this result, it is unclear what would have been established. The Habermasian enterprise consists of setting as preconditions for democratic politics the very issues that give rise to the need for them. It is just because power is endemic to human interaction that imperatives arise to manage power relations so as to mitigate the possibility of domination when it cannot be escaped. But for these imperatives to be useful they must be rooted in an understanding of how power actually operates, not in a series of speculations about what the world would be like if it was not there.[50] The Habermasian gambit ignores the reality that motivates this project: that power relations are endemic to human interaction. Without them, democratic politics would be unnecessary.

Foucault

Foucault's view of domination is more appealing than Habermas's because it is rooted in recognition of the ineradicable character of power. In a series of histories of human social relations ranging from family life to sexuality, to insanity, to imprisonment and other forms of social control, he has exposed the dark underbelly of the Enlightenment.[51] Foucault offers riveting illustrations of the ways in which naked coercion was displaced by subtler mechanisms of control—often masquerading as instruments of liberation. Compelling as Foucault's histories frequently are, from my point of view his outlook falls short in three ways.

It is, first, too reductionist. I am enough of a Foucauldian to believe that speculating about what politics would be like in the absence of domination is a fool's errand, but I differ in thinking there is more to human interaction than the power relations that suffuse it. Put this way, Foucault might not have dissented from my claim, but he never said anything to suggest that the power-dimensions of human interaction are importantly distinguishable from its other features. Power surely is exercised in classrooms, firms, families, and churches in the normal course of events, but much else happens in them as well: enlightenment, production, love, and worship. Reducing these activities to the power relations that permeate them misses the basic challenge from the standpoint of nondomination: to enable people, as much as possible, to pursue the activities that give life its meaning and purpose while limiting the potential for domination that accompanies those activities. It was this that led me to develop the notion of democracy as a conditioning or subordinate good, aimed at domesticating the power dimensions of human interaction while leaving the other goods people pursue as unfettered as possible.

Foucault's outlook lacks the tools, second, to distinguish licit from illicit exercises of power. The pursuit of goods inevitably involves exercising power—if only because so much of human social life is hierarchically ordered. But hierarchies are not intrinsically objectionable. As I noted in section II, it is the abuse of hierarchies for illicit purposes that is objectionable. To be sure, whether or not a hierarchy is being thus abused will—and should—often be in contention. This is why I argue for mechanisms to facilitate that contention and for a series of interrogatories about hierarchies that are designed to flush out illicit uses and prevent their atrophy into systems of domination. These concern the extent to which particular hierarchies are inevitable, escapable, chosen, insular, and self-liquidating.[52]

A third, concomitant, failure is that Foucault's work fails to evaluate different uses of power. In his terms, he does nothing to help us distinguish between more and less malevolent forms of domination. On my account, by contrast, domination that involves people's basic interests is worse than that which does not. A billionaire might be in a position to dominate a spouse who knows that she stands to lose millions in the event of a divorce due to a prenuptial agreement, but this warrants less concern than a spouse who faces destitution in the event of divorce if she is not guaranteed the basic necessities for survival. Both are relationships of domination, but one is worse. Just because ubiquitous power relations make the potential for domination ever-present, it matters to be able to decide which are the most important from the standpoint of justice. My power-based resourcism facilitates the relevant comparative judgments.

Walzer

Walzer's view has the merit of focusing on the ways in which people deploy the resources they control to dominate one another. He is right, moreover, that using resources germane to one sphere of human activity to achieve influence in another can be a source of domination because it is often a source of illicitness. Yet while he makes a good case for resisting this kind of domination, he has surprisingly little to say about how such resistance can be made effective—about how the boundaries between spheres should be kept robust. Nor does he have anything to say about how disagreements over what the goods germane to different spheres are should be settled.[53] In contrast, I maintain that every domain of human interaction should be subject to democratic conditioning constraints. These vary with time and circumstance, but they always include mechanisms to participate in decision making about the nature of the goods in question and rights of opposition to try to get them changed.

Walzer was also wrong to think that transgressing the boundaries he describes is the only, or even the principal, source of domination in the world. As recently as the 1950s, in most American states there was no such thing as marital rape by conclusive legal presumption, and the doctrine of interspousal tort immunity shielded husbands from liability for assault and other forms of harm perpetrated on their wives. After decades of opposition from the women's movement, both the marital rape exception and interspousal tort immunity have been abolished—but this had nothing to do with insulating the sphere of domestic life from the norms outside it. On the contrary, it required a frontal assault on the accepted values governing the definition of marriage and actively transgressing the boundaries that protected the "integrity" of the family from egalitarian values that prevailed outside.[54] My notion of democracy as a conditioning good involves deference to prevailing values, but only to the extent that this does not render people vulnerable to domination by compromising their basic interests. Being vulnerable to someone who can rape or assault you with impunity compromises your basic interests.

Skinner

Quentin Skinner approaches nondomination through the lens of what he calls the neo-Roman or republican conception of freedom. In his view, the neo-Roman account captures the best understanding of the negative libertarian tradition which he hopes to rescue from Hobbes and his successors. Although the Hobbesians might have "won the battle," Skinner is not ready to throw in the towel and admit defeat in the longer war. His project is to make a compelling case that the republican tradition offers a version of negative liberty that is superior to the Hobbesian one, a version that appeals to the idea of an independent status that is marked by the absence of domination.[55]

As Skinner notes in *Hobbes and Republican Liberty*, while there is some variation in how Hobbes defined liberty in various writings, in *Leviathan* he seems clearly to be operating with a prototype of the negative liberty view. By talking of liberty by reference to the absence of external impediments, describing the liberty of the subject by reference to "the Silence of the Law" and what "the Sovereign hath praetermitted: such as is the Liberty to buy, and sell, and otherwise contract with one another; to choose their own aboad, their own diet, their own trade of life, and institute their children as they themselves think fit; & the like," Hobbes seems clearly to be thinking of individual freedom as connoting a zone of action in which the individual is left alone by the state to do as she or he pleases.[56] Despite his soon-to-be-anachronistic absolutism, then, Hobbes won the historical battle on this reading by advancing the negative libertarian view of freedom.

I have noted elsewhere that there is some plausibility to this account, but, by failing to appreciate what is problematic in the distinction between negative and positive freedom, Skinner draws the wrong moral and political conclusions.[57] The difference between negative and positive freedom is usually seen as residing in the fact that, whereas negative libertarians focus primarily on impediments to action, positive libertarians are centrally concerned with what the agent is able to do. Writers like Rousseau and Hegel are seen as positive libertarians because they conceive freedom as what Charles Taylor has described as an "exercise" concept rather than an "opportunity" concept. For positive libertarians, freedom consists in exercising human capacities to achieve our characteristic potential, and we are unfree to the extent that this possibility is attenuated or blocked by deleterious social arrangements.[58] Positive libertarians generally link individual freedom to participation in social and political institutions—participation in ways that will lead people to realize their potential.

It has been conventional since Berlin wrote to criticize positive libertarians on the grounds that their doctrine wrongly assumes that we can know what people's potential is, so that we can then design collective arrangements to facilitate their attaining it.[59] The limiting case of this difficulty is embodied in Rousseau's slogan that, by being required to obey the general will, people can be "forced to be free."[60] If people are coerced into certain types of collective participation in order to achieve a particular goal or conception of the good life, then it is hard to see in what meaningful sense they can be said to be free. As a result, Berlin and his followers are often taken to be right in maintaining that the positive conception of freedom is incoherent.

Skinner wants to go part of the way with Berlin, agreeing that the positive conception is problematic. Yet Skinner believes that the Machiavellian, or neo-Roman, conception of freedom that he champions has been misclassified as a positive one on the grounds that it requires active participation of citizens—in the military as well as in the civic life of the republic. But, for Skinner, Machiavelli's requirement of civic service is an instrumental requirement of freedom for republican citizens. It is necessary so that they can protect themselves from the external domination of aggressive neighbors and the internal domination of power-hungry domestic elites. As a result, Skinner resists the suggestion that a negative conception of freedom cannot include requirements of civic service, holding that it is, indeed, superior to the Hobbesian negative conception.[61] Freedom is the antithesis of slavery on this account; we are free when we are independent beings and virtuous acts of public service are necessary to secure that status. As Skinner puts it, "the paramount distinction in civil association is between those who enjoy the status of *liberi homines* or 'freemen' and those who live in servitude."[62]

Skinner's focus on domination as the relevant source of unfreedom for politics is appealing. But by buying into the negative/positive liberty dichotomy in order to rescue the negative view from Hobbes and his successors, Skinner misses what is at issue in the debate and what is most objectionable about the Hobbesian account of freedom. In my view we should agree with Gerald MacCallum that the debate between negative and positive libertarians diverts attention from what matters most in arguments about freedom and domination. It perpetuates arguments that cannot be resolved because protagonists on both sides are right about the demerits of each other's arguments.[63]

MacCallum pointed out that any assertion about freedom minimally involves reference to agents, restraining (or enabling) conditions, and action. My suggestion is that we endorse MacCallum's account but modify it by noting that when we talk about *political* freedom, a fourth term enters, having to do with legitimacy; it may be thought of by reference to the question *why*, in virtue of what authority, is the agent free?[64] This reference to authorizing conditions is vital to my account of nondomination, as it provides both the invitation and the basis to distinguish licit from illicit constraints on, or exercises of, freedom.

Skinner contends that, claims to the contrary notwithstanding, MacCallum's account is really a version of the doctrine of negative liberty. "Insofar as MacCallum's analysis suggests a negative understanding of freedom as the absence of constraints upon an agent's options (which it does), this ['that the only coherent account that can possibly be given of the concept of liberty is the negative one'] is also the implication of his account and of those that depend on it."[65] But this claim misses MacCallum's point. His argument was that all accounts of liberty contain both negative and positive elements, some of which are usually implicit—that negative libertarians focus mainly on constraints while positive libertarians concern themselves with enabling conditions.

To be sure, MacCallum acknowledged that all intelligible concepts of freedom or liberty involve some notion of constraints or their absence, but just because this element could never amount to an account of freedom, talk of freedom from constraint or restraint did not make an account "negative." The opposition itself should be eschewed, on his account, because constraints and enabling conditions can easily be redescribed as one another. In effect, arguments between negative and positive libertarians are analogous to arguments over whether a prisoner is unfree because of the presence of a locked door or the absence of a key. It is thus misleading to think of negative or positive language as indicative of any significant conceptual difference.[66]

Skinner's discussion in *Hobbes and Republican Liberty* builds on his earlier discussion of MacCallum, and what he says there about republican liberty makes it clear that he has not appreciated the force of MacCallum's thesis. In terms of my modified version of MacCallum's schema, by focusing centrally on the independent status of the agent, Skinner wants to reduce liberty to the first and fourth terms in the quadratic relation—inasmuch as the status of the agent as a freeman or slave depends on the prevailing legitimating authority. That this is a partial account of freedom becomes evident when we reflect on the fact that it is silent about the second and third terms in the relation—the actions to be performed and the restraints (or enabling conditions) that hamper (or facilitate) their performance.

Why does it matter? The answer that motivated MacCallum, and motivates me, is that what is consequential in discussions about freedom is not which vocabulary is used but rather what different people are actually able to do, or are prevented from doing, in the world. Skinner would be correct to say that a slave is unfree even if a comparatively benign slave owner allowed him or her some discretionary resources and range of choice, because of the slave's compromised status as a person.[67] But as I noted earlier, virtually every political theory on offer today condemns slavery so that establishing Skinner's case does not settle much that is at stake among the various contending views. To this Skinner might respond that his neo-Roman ideal rules out other subservient statuses as well, such as serfdom, apartheid, patriarchy, and caste systems. I am happy to concede that too, but continue to wonder who the serious protagonist is on the other side.

Anatole France famously mocked "la majestueuse égalité des lois, qui interdit au riche comme au pauvre de coucher sous les ponts, de mendier dans les rues et de voler du pain."[68] The elimination of formal subservience is surely consequential from the standpoint of nondomination. When status hierarchies are present, they invariably become a focus of contention, but eliminating them is seldom sufficient to undermine domination. Someone with the *status* of a free citizen might confront such enormous obstacles to performing a range of actions routinely enjoyed by others that we would be disinclined to regard him as immune from domination. In recent decades many corporations have fired employees and then rehired them as independent contractors at reduced salaries, and without employment benefits, to do the same jobs that they were doing before. Their *status* as independent persons has been enhanced, but it would be hard to make a convincing case that they are less vulnerable to domination than they were previously.

This was MacCallum's point: instead of trying to reduce freedom to one or another of its relational components, we should embrace his antireductionist account. The schema itself is formal and empty, reflecting what we might describe as the analytical grammar of freedom. MacCallum's hope was that, rather than continue to engage in endless debates about "kinds" of freedom, by embracing his account we could change the subject: focus instead on the conditions in the world that shape not only the status of agents, but also the actions they might aspire to perform, and the resources and constraints affecting those aspirations. Hobbes's nascent negative libertarian view is surely impeachable from this perspective, but the deficiency is not remedied by counterposing to it a neo-Roman view that reduces claims about freedom to claims about the status of agents.

Pettit

Considered from the standpoint of actual institutional arrangements, Skinner's account is conducted at a pretty high altitude. Pettit's discussion in his book *Republicanism: A Theory of Freedom and Government* and subsequent writings has the advantage of engaging with institutional arrangements more directly. And there is much in what he has to say that is congenial from the perspective of my institutional arguments. I agree with his contention that democratizing power relations is generally the best path to mitigating domination. More particularly, I agree with his claim that this implies not only a presumption in favor of inclusive participation in decisions by which one is affected, but also a presumption that people should always be free to oppose decisions ("contestation" is his term) with which they disagree—even when these decisions have been arrived at by legitimate democratic means.[69] I also agree that it is the capacity to interfere with someone, rather than actual interference, that is often key to having power over them and that needs institutional managing with an eye to preventing domination.[70]

Despite these points of agreement, Pettit and I have substantial disagreements. These derive from the fact that Pettit's discussion pays surprisingly little attention to the relative seriousness of different kinds of domination; that his definition of domination blinds him to the ways in which power can be used to undermine domination as well as to cause it; (conversely) that his account of social movements and civic associations underestimates the ways in which they can operate to foster domination rather than undermine it; and the reality that his account of the democratic state as the principal instrument for resisting domination is hamstrung to the point of impotence by his republican theory of institutions.

The first set of disagreements is rooted in Pettit's decision to define domination exclusively by reference to the capacity for arbitrary interference in the choices of another without attending to the nature or importance of those choices. At the outset of his discussion he genuflects to the proposition that "domination in some areas is likely to be considered more damaging than it is in others; better be dominated in less central activities, for example, rather than in more central ones."[71] But he never defines centrality, and considerations having to do with it play no role in his institutional recommendations, as we shall see. He talks briefly about how "extensive" domination is, by which he means the number of issues over which people are free to choose, and at greater length about the "intensity" of domination. It is less than entirely clear just what this means, but it has to do with the degree to which those with power can act with impunity. Absolute tyrants exercise domination with greater intensity than opportunistic spouse batterers who figure they can count on lax enforcement of the laws against spouse beating.[72] But neither the number of choices nor the intensity of domination go to the importance of the choice in question, about which Pettit has virtually nothing to say.

The implications of this omission become clear in his discussion of egalitarianism. He distinguishes "material" from "structural" egalitarianism. By "structural" Pettit means the "powers" which "include all those factors that are liable to affect political, legal, financial, and social clout." He thinks both relative and absolute equality with respect to these things are important because whether or not someone is a potential victim of domination depends not only on his or her own powers, but also on the powers of others. "In the land of the blind," as he says, "the one-eyed man is king."[73] Because a person's "absolute score in relation to the intensity of nondomination is a function of their relative score in regard to powers," attending to the "power-ratio in the society as a whole" is essential to Pettit's nondomination project.

With respect to these power ratios, Pettit argues, accordingly, that increasing inequality is presumptively a bad idea because there is what he calls "diminishing marginal productivity" to increasing your relative power, whereas moves toward equality are desirable.[74]

Leaving the plausibility of these claims to one side, Pettit distinguishes them from what he has to say about "material" inequities, where there is no egalitarian presumption.[75] The reason is that attempts to impose egalitarian redistribution may themselves involve domination on the part of the state. This is not offset by the same kind of diminishing marginal productivity that holds with respect to powers. "The money that will enable me to do something, poor as I am, will enable you to do exactly the same things."[76] Pettit concedes that the utility derived from money might be of diminishing marginal value, "but the capacity to buy things, and its capacity therefore to extend undominated choice, does not." As a result, while his nondomination project is committed to "structural egalitarianism," it is "not essentially committed to any sort of material egalitarianism."[77]

Pettit's myopic focus on the number of choices ignores how important the choices are from the point of view of avoiding domination. It is also innocent of the ways in which material resources are often integral to resisting domination. Funding health insurance through the tax system reduces the exit costs for those who must otherwise obtain it from employers and spouses, limiting the latter's capacity for domination of those who depend on them for it. This is why I argued in *Democratic Justice* that when the social wage is low, stringent democratic controls of domestic and work life are warranted from the standpoint of nondomination, though I also argued that the unappealing intrusiveness of stringent controls suggests that a high social wage regime with fewer intrusive controls is preferable.[78] The less my ability to vindicate my basic interests depends on my relations with you, the less power you have over me—and hence the less capacity to dominate me.[79] Pettit does at one point describe nondomination as a primary good.[80] This makes it odd that he ignores its evident connections to material resources. Locke said that "a man can no more justly make use of another's necessity, to force him to become his vassal," than can he "with a dagger at his throat offer him death or slavery."[81] If we agree with Pettit, as I think that we should, that the capacity to exert power (rather than its actually being asserted) is often key to domination, then we should resist his attempt to banish the material resources needed to vindicate people's basic interests from the theory of nondomination.

A second disagreement between us concerns Pettit's insistence that having the capacity for arbitrary interference in the lives of others constitutes domination of them. On my account having that capacity does not itself constitute domination; rather it creates the potential for domination. This distinction might sound like hair-splitting, but it has significant consequences. The playground bully might have the capacity to beat up any of the smaller children, but might be widely known only to beat up black children. Does he dominate the children who are not black?[82] Senator Joseph McCarthy had the capacity to interfere arbitrarily in the lives of many Americans, but those on the political left plausibly lived in fear of him in a way that others did not. To say that McCarthy dominated all Americans who could have been interfered with by him misses this, trivializing the plight of those who had good reasons to live in fear of him. Today, the United States has the capacity for arbitrary interference in Cuba, Mexico, Canada, and Fiji, but it stands in very different relations to them from the standpoint of domination. Cuba has endured explicit coercive interference for decades; Mexico periodically feels the pressure of American "soft power"; Canada is subject to the influence of a stronger but largely like-minded ally; and Fiji is unaffected by American power in any of the ways that are relevant to the other three.

Moreover, Pettit's position diverts attention from the ways in which interference can mitigate domination. The strongest child in the playground can be a bully, but he might instead be the person who protects weaker children from bullies. If this is common knowledge, then the mere fact that the strongest child has that inclination might deter the bully or embolden the weaker children to resist or report him. When Saddam Hussein's forces invaded Kuwait in 1990, U.S. President George H. W. Bush led a coalition of forces to eject him. Bush saw this as an opportunity to institutionalize a new post–Cold War world order geared to facing down international aggression and fostering expectations and incentives to minimize it in the future. He deployed American might in the service of that goal. This involved creating norms of international authorization and regional participation in the containment effort, and going no further than was necessary to block Saddam Hussein's aggression. In effect Bush stopped the bully without himself becoming a bully.[83] Unfortunately, his son undermined those norms twelve years later by his unilateral invasion of Iraq to topple the regime—a rogue action of the sort that his father's policy had sought to forestall. Pettit's formulation is insensible to these distinctions, and therefore also to the significance of the Obama administration's decision to engineer the collapse of Muammar Gaddafi's regime in Libya in 2011.[84]

A third set of worries about Pettit's institutional arguments concerns the degree to which he believes that empowering social movements and other forms of civic association to resist majoritarian politics is advantageous from the standpoint of nondomination. In Pettit's vision of democracy, it is essential that people be "able to contest decisions at will and, if the contest establishes a mismatch with their relevant interests or opinions, [be] able to force an amendment."[85] His vision is one in which civic associations and social movements serve as oppositional buffers against majority tyranny, fielding complaints and organizing them into effective contestatory politics in support of progressive change. The image that "suggests itself," he tells us, "is that of popular movement, widespread controversy and debate, and progressive, legislative adjustment." As examples he cites the women's movement, the green movement, the gay rights movement, and the movements in support of ethnic minorities and indigenous peoples. "Any democracy that is going to serve republican purposes has to be able to give a hearing to evolving allegiances and commitments," Pettit insists. It must be open to "deep and wide-ranging transformations."[86]

One difficulty with this is Pettit's manifest assumption that social movements and civic associations will in fact be organized in support of change that Pettit regards as progressive. Opposition movements have indeed organized to advance the goals he enumerates, but they also organized to enact Proposition 13 in California, to force repeal of the federal estate tax on multimillionaires, and to outlaw gay marriage and affirmative action. Perhaps the most effective such movement in the United States since 2009 has been the Tea Party movement that emerged to resist Barack Obama's agenda on health care reform, environmental legislation, and financial regulation. As these examples suggest, there is no particular reason to suppose that empowering social movements to resist democratic government will, on balance, lead to progressive change as Pettit supposes. He implicitly acknowledges as much in his endorsement of gag rules designed to depoliticize debates about criminal penalties when he notes that "challenges to criminal-justice practice are generally heard in a public, politicized forum, with a variety of bad effects." By this he means harsh sentences that experts know to be ineffective deterrents.[87] But perhaps people care more about retribution than they do about deterrence.[88] Who is Pettit to decide which issues should be subject to empowered civic contestation and which taken off the political table by gag rules? His

Republicanism might be an appealing manifesto for those who share Pettit's values. Whether it supplies a sound political basis for limiting domination is dubious.

Pettit underestimates the difficulties of his position, I think, partly because of his faith in deliberation to push politics in what he takes to be felicitous directions. He supposes that, following an appropriate round of deliberation or appeal, people will accept outcomes that go against them if they are in the general interest. "All that is necessary is that they be assured that the judgment is made according to their ideas about proper procedures and that it is dictated, ultimately, by an interest that they share with others."[89] Pettit's contestatory vision of the democratic process is one that "is designed to let the requirements of reason materialize and impose themselves."[90] This confident deployment of the passive voice can be encouraging only to the extent that we share Pettit's faith that losers in the contestatory process will accept the legitimacy of their defeat. One did not have to spend much time listening to Rush Limbaugh, Sean Hannity, Glenn Beck, and the leaders of the Tea Party movement to realize that they never had any intention of conceding the legitimacy of any aspect of the Obama administration's agenda and that they deployed every resource they could muster to derail as much of it as they could. To the extent that they were successful they saw themselves as effective resisters of domination, and on Pettit's account they would be right.[91] On my account, by contrast, we should have preferred them to fail because they did not have basic interests at stake, whereas those who stood to lose (or not to get) health insurance or unemployment insurance did.

Pettit defends deliberative contestatory forums partly because he thinks them superior to an account of political contestation based on bargaining. He is inspired by the vision of the eighteenth-century American founders according to which "citizens have equal claims and powers" and "public matters are decided by deliberation on the basis of considerations that have common appeal—they are not biased in favor of any group, or even in favor of the status quo—and agreement serves as a regulative ideal as to how things should be decided."[92] Like Joshua Cohen and Habermas (whom he cites approvingly in this regard), he thinks that engaging in deliberation will cause people to discover, and perhaps even manufacture, the requisite common ground. "The trouble with bargaining contestations," by contrast, is that "they are only available to those who have sufficient negotiating power to be able to threaten other parties effectively; if you want to force a change of bargain, then you had better represent an interest group which pulls some weight."[93]

This is a non sequitur as a defense of deliberation in the real world. Deliberation can sometimes lead people to discern and then move toward areas of agreement, though, for reasons discussed in chapter 5, I wouldn't count on it.[94] But in arguing for deliberation's superiority to bargaining, Pettit never confronts the reality that people cannot be forced to deliberate, and that those who are disinclined to do so can and do press deliberative mechanisms into the service of stonewalling change—in effect to bargain. For this reason, I have argued that if we want to press deliberation into the service of reducing the kinds of domination that should concern us, then rights to insist on it should be limited to people with basic interests at stake. To be sure, they might deploy those rights to bargain instead of to deliberate, but at least in that instance it is those who are vulnerable in ways that we should care about whose interests are being protected.[95]

For a stark illustration of what can be at stake here, consider Pettit's closely related contention that losers in the legislative process should enjoy access to forums in which they can limit what they take to be the deleterious effects of a policy enacted by the majority by "editing" it in the application.[96] During 2009 and 2010, the investment banking lobby in the United States engaged in a huge lobbying effort, which almost succeeded, designed to scuttle the Obama administration's plans for investment banking regulation in the wake of the 2008 worldwide banking crisis. They failed to derail it entirely, though they weakened it considerably, ensuring, among other things, that many of the most contentious matters having to do with systemically risky behavior by banks deemed too big to fail would be determined later by regulators.[97] It does not require giant leaps of imaginative foresight to predict that these regulators would become objects of relentless campaigns to defang the legislation further by "editing" it in the application. After the 2010 banking regulation bill passed in Congress, I asked a partner at one of the largest investment banks whether they would now be out of the proprietary trading business. His answer was "it will be five years before it will be clear whether we can kill that part." He thought it a pretty good bet that they would, and he turned out to be right.[98] This is editing in the application in the real world.

A final disquieting feature of Pettit's institutional stance is the assumption running through his writing that the power wielded by governments is more malevolent than the power wielded by other actors—whether powerful individuals or other corporate agents. Because the government establishes itself as a collective agent with the capacity to interfere arbitrarily in the affairs of any individual, it is potentially a threat to everyone. This means that although proponents of nondomination should look to the state as an instrument to limit the malevolent effects of private *dominium,* "they will remain alert to the danger of giving the state the sort of license that would introduce a dominating form of public *imperium.*" If its capacity for action "is insufficiently fettered or its range of responsibilities too large, the government is liable to become a domineering presence in its own right."[99]

This worry leads Pettit to embrace an exceedingly long list of constraints on majoritarian politics. In addition to the deliberative and other contestatory rights already discussed, he is a fan of multiplying checks on collective action through bicameralism, supermajority requirements, separation of powers, judicial review, federalism, appeals processes against administrative decisions, ex-ante measures to limit their effects, independence for national banks, exemptions and special treatment for minority cultures, turning politically charged matters over to "professionally informed bodies," and using gag rules otherwise to limit the writ of electoral politics. Despite his acknowledgment that vetoes can block legitimate change, Pettit's discussion of these matters seems to be entirely innocent of the literature on veto players from Brian Barry to George Tsebelis, which has made it clear that, as veto players become stronger and veto points multiply, so does protection of the status quo and those who have the resources to wait out opponents.[100]

There is a curious paradox to Pettit's view here. On the one hand he expresses considerable skepticism that nonstate actors are powerful enough effectively to reduce domination in modern societies. This he describes as the strategy of "reciprocal power"—in effect relying on private and other decentralized resources as means for combating domination. Pettit notes that the trade union movement "almost certainly advanced the nondomination of workers in the industrial world of the nineteenth century," yet he insists that there is "very little reason" to be attracted to their strategy of direct action which confronts "too many problems to be taken seriously." Instead, he argues that "the strategy of having recourse to a state looks by far the more attractive option."[101] On the other hand, we have seen that his list of preferred institutional devices to separate, disperse, check, and veto state action is so extensive that it is unlikely to have a meaningful impact on private domination.

Trade unions are a case in point. Organized and widely supported as they were in Britain and the United States in the middle part of the last century, they could not possibly have enjoyed the success that they did without strongly supportive legislation from successive Labour governments in Britain and the passage of the Wagner Act in the United States in 1935. Yet it was the whittling away at those protections at the behest of business-oriented interest groups and their supporters, through exactly the kinds of "contestatory politics" Pettit champions, that led to the evisceration of private-sector unions that began in the United States in the 1950s and took off in both countries in the 1980s.

Pettit seems to be at cross-purposes with himself. On the one hand he agrees that efficacious action by democratic governments is likely essential to any project of rooting out entrenched systems of domination. On the other he seems to be so fearful of democratic politics and government that he wants to hem them in at every turn, insisting that "every interest and every idea that guides the action of a state must be open to challenge from every corner of the society; and where there is dissent, then appropriate remedies must be taken."[102] Given the many opportunities for special pleading, forum shopping, and delay that are disproportionately afforded to those with time and resources on their side by Pettit's model of dispersed power and institutional checks, it is hard to imagine governments in the world as he envisages it doing much of anything at all—let alone tackling entrenched systems of domination. This tension is puzzling. It is as if for all his attention to the centrality of domination in his theory, Pettit fails to notice much domination in the world around him. He also seems, generously, to attribute his own sunny disposition to all mankind. His is a world in which progressive contestatory pressure combined with faltering prodding from a semi-incapacitated state can be expected to get people to give up domineering positions as they are persuaded that this is in the general interest.

I am inclined to a darker view of the human social condition. It assumes that people in positions of advantage seldom give them up unless the status quo becomes costly to them, and that among the things a government committed to nondomination must do is increase the costs of maintaining the status quo to the powerful when the basic interests of those who are vulnerable to domination by them are at stake. Most people in poor and middle-income countries and poor and middle-income people in rich countries are vulnerable to serious domination in many situations because their basic interests are either compromised or so precariously met that their dealings with others are inevitably laden with the possibility of domination. Tackling that reality seems to me the starting point for any plausible theory of the distributional and institutional arrangements needed by a principled commitment to nondomination. Pettit's focus on the numbers of choices people have without reference to their importance misses this, and, as with Sen, his faith in civic-minded deliberation to encourage progressive social action reads like a manifesto for the sensible chaps party. His account of public institutions is a recipe for protecting the status quo, which could only be appealing from the point of view we share if one did not perceive it as heavily laden with domination. In this respect our disagreement has less to do with the meaning of domination than it does with our perceptions of how power is distributed in the world and how politics works.

Pettit's fulsome embrace of institutional sclerosis has been conventional among republican thinkers since the American founders wrote *The Federalist*. Fear of majority tyranny prompted them to build many of the institutional features Pettit finds so appealing into the American constitutional model partly because there was no other way to get the constitution ratified and partly out of what turned out to be the mistaken conviction that it would prevent civil war. It has become clear, since then, that consociational institutions contribute little, if anything, to democratic stability, and nor do they limit the propensity for majority tyranny. The evidence strongly suggests that inclusive economic development is the best predictor of democracy's survival, while different kinds of institutional arrangements appear to have a negligible impact—though presidential systems are somewhat less stable than parliamentary ones.[103] That is scarcely an advertisement for the beneficent effects of separation of powers. As far as majority tyranny is concerned, there is no evidence that adding bills of rights and constitutional courts to democratic systems makes any difference as far as the protection of minorities is concerned.[104] Imperfect as competitive parliamentary systems might be, they turn out to be the stablest democracies and at least as good as any other from the standpoint of protecting vulnerable minorities. Given the propensity of republican arrangements to protect entrenched systems of domination and powerful minorities, the reasons to reject them in favor of parliamentary systems seem to me to be decisive.

IV. Nondomination Revisited

Nondomination is the bedrock of justice. Though it is often connected to egalitarian considerations and appeals to a kind of freedom, I made the case that it should be differentiated from both. Egalitarians might still resist this case, arguing, in the spirit of the "equality of what?" literature, that my argument commits me to a principle of equality of nondomination. But that is not my view because domination ranges from the trivial to the momentous, and I have argued that only the most serious forms of domination merit government's attention. This might provoke the retort that I really favor equality of nondomination where basic interests are at stake. But I resist that characterization too, because even within the realm of basic interests some violations are worse than others and I agree with Judith Shklar and Casiano Hacker-Cordón that preventing the most extreme forms of cruelty and deprivation should trump remediation of other kinds of domination involving basic interests.[105]

This might provoke the further retort that my implicit principle is to equalize elimination of the most egregious sorts of domination, but this seems to me to be trivially egalitarian at best. It strains ordinary usage, and most people who count themselves egalitarians would not recognize it as such. Moreover, it belies the extent to which comparing extreme cases of domination often involves judgments that verge on the incommensurable—if they are not in fact impossible to make. During the 1970s, defenders of the National Party government in South Africa would sometimes deflect criticism by asking: why are you attacking apartheid when worse things are going on in Uganda? It was not clear to me then, nor is it now, that it was possible to evaluate the assertion embedded in this question and intended to supply its rhetorical force. A dispositive comparison of the two cases would surely involve many complex judgments, some of them counterfactual, that made it difficult to know where to begin.

Allowing oneself to be drawn into the comparative debate seemed to me in any case to be worse than a waste of time. Unlike the trolley-bus examples that sometimes give moral philosophy a bad name, these cases were unconnected—at least from the perspective of the perpetrators.[106] The evils of apartheid bore no relation to the domination then being committed, to the north, by Idi Amin. Opponents of both regimes might face choices about where best to deploy their efforts, but they would likely have at least as much to do with judgments about the chances of success in either place as with a determination of which was ultimately worse. Arguments about those choices could never, in any case, furnish a justification for the evils being perpetrated in either place. Rather than allow oneself to be manipulated by disingenuous demands for an egalitarian metric of moral equivalency, the better course was to confront those evils on their own terms—showing why and how they could be stamped out.

Nor are my prescriptions egalitarian—at least not conventionally so. Rather, I view the power-dimensions of human interaction through a Hirschmanesque lens in which there is a tradeoff between the importance of enhancing democratic voices and reducing the costs of exit for the vulnerable.[107] In employment relations, for instance, I argue that where exit costs for the vulnerable are high due to the lack of a robust social wage, then government should insist on more voice within the firm: stronger safeguards for unions and other protections for workers. Likewise in the domestic context I argue that a divorce law regime that protects the vulnerable at dissolution of marriage legitimates greater laissez-faire with respect to what goes on within marriage than would otherwise be the case.[108] True, I argue that a low exit-cost/low-regulation regime is better than a high exit-cost/high-regulation one, which leads to my defense of a comparatively robust social wage. But this flows from two considerations, neither of which is egalitarian: my power-based resourcism and my general presumption that, while it is important to vindicate people's basic interests, it is always best to do this in ways that interfere as little as possible with what goes on within civil institutions and practices.[109]

To appeal to nondomination is to appeal to a certain kind of political freedom that human beings have the power to diminish or enhance. Though not constitutionally hostile to all hierarchies in human affairs, nondomination as I understand it is sensitive to the reality that legitimate hierarchies often atrophy into illicit systems of domination. The institutional challenge is to police the potential for domination via democratic constraints, but to do this as unobtrusively as possible. This view of nondomination is political all the way down, and it takes no position on larger metaphysical debates about the possibility and meaning of human freedom. Nor does it treat freedom as the summum bonum for which people can strive. My account takes a minimalist tack on identifying common human interests as basic, and on the possibility that those interests can meaningfully be tracked by political institutions. It is a reactive ideal that appeals to human ingenuity to design and implement practices that can ameliorate sources of domination as and when they arise. As a result, it always operates at the margin—eschewing the project of designing a basic structure for society as a whole.

Nondomination as I have defended it is Foucauldian in recognizing that power relations are ubiquitous to human interaction, but I demur from Foucault's refusal to discriminate among kinds of domination or to address questions about what to do about it. Doing that seems to me to be the main constructive project suggested by Foucault's central insight. Nondomination as I defend it involves threading the needle of institutional design without depending on large assumptions about human communication and deliberation that infect the arguments set forth by Habermas and Pettit. It depends on a view of freedom which, like Skinner's, involves abjuring the negative libertarian account we have inherited from Hobbes. But rather than try to replace it with the status-based negative liberty view that Skinner finds congenial, I reject the negative/positive dichotomy in favor of a relational view that involves thinking about unfreedom as it relates to agents, restraining and enabling conditions, actions, and systems of authorization. This buttresses the reactive character of my account because, rather than push us in the direction of general theories of freedom, it directs us to focus on specific people, circumstances, possibilities, and authorizing institutions to get at the contours of domination and what to do about it.

To the extent that general presumptions are warranted, I agree with Pettit that democratizing the power dimensions of human interaction is the best way to go and that this means creating mechanisms for inclusive participation and opposition. But I differ from him in holding that their form and intrusiveness should depend on the nature of the interests at stake, with basic interests operating as the trigger for enfranchisement. And because I agree with Pettit's claim that rooting out systems of entrenched domination will typically require efficacious action by governments, I dissent from his embrace of republican institutions that are replete with veto points and other consociational elements. These can make it all too easy for those controlling entrenched systems of domination to stonewall change, and they do not—in any case—deliver the benefits of protecting vulnerable minorities from majority tyranny that are often claimed for republican institutions.

It is well known that James Madison offered a trenchant defense of republican institutions in *The Federalist*. At the time he was thirty-six years old, and the bulk of his political experience lay ahead of him. Perhaps this is why much of what he wrote about political parties and competition in *The Federalist* reads like someone who is trying to learn to swim by walking up and down next to a lake while discussing the theory of swimming. What is less well known is that the mature Madison rejected the republican thinking that is famously attributed to him and to which Pettit and other contemporary republicans appeal. His years in the rough and tumble of politics in Congress, as secretary of state, and as the fourth president of the United States convinced Madison that democratic competition is the best available guarantor of the values that republicans seek to protect. In 1833, three years before his death, he was unequivocal that "if majority governments . . . be the worst of Governments those who think and say so cannot be within the pale of republican faith. They must either join the avowed disciples of aristocracy, oligarchy or monarchy, or look for a Utopia exhibiting a perfect homogeneousness of interests, opinions and feelings nowhere yet found in civilized communities."[110] Subsequent evidence suggests that the mature Madison was right that democratic competition offers the best hope for mitigating domination. As a result, working to protect and refine it is the best path forward for those who regard nondomination as the bedrock of justice.

PART TWO
Fortifying Democracy

4
The New Authoritarianism in Public Choice

(with David Froomkin)

The ideas of economists and political philosophers, both when they are right and when they are wrong, are more powerful than is commonly understood. Indeed the world is ruled by little else. Practical men, who believe themselves to be quite exempt from any intellectual influences, are usually the slaves of some defunct economist. Madmen in authority, who hear voices in the air, are distilling their frenzy from some academic scribbler of a few years back.

John Maynard Keynes

These are alarming times for democrats. Recent years have seen falling public confidence in democracy across the developed world. Many democracies have at least flirted with authoritarian presidentialism, including Hungary, India, Turkey, Poland, the Philippines, Brazil, and the United States. Authoritarian nationalism, under the aegis of charismatic leadership, is on the rise in countries like Austria and the Netherlands. Many of us used to think that this kind of politics was a relic of the 1930s, at least in the advanced democracies. Now we are not so sure. Book titles like *How Democracies Die, How Democracy Ends,* and *The Road to Unfreedom* capture the new sense of gloom.[1]

These political developments coincide with a new strand of academic argument advocating the transfer of power within democracies from legislatures to chief executives on the grounds that this will produce more rational—and more efficient—governance. This impetus toward executive concentration garners ideological ballast from an unexpected source: a public choice critique of legislative politics whose progenitors made quite different institutional prescriptions. Defenders of executive concentration such as Eric Posner and Adrian Vermeule, William Howell and Terry Moe, and Francis Fukuyama are not themselves public choice theorists, but they invoke arguments about the sources of legislative dysfunction that are rooted in public choice theory.[2] And like the classical public choice theorists, they associate the rationalization of government with promarket policies. The institutional recommendations have changed but not the analysis of the legislative process that underpins them. That this analysis is largely erroneous has not stopped it from contributing to growing skepticism of democracy. This chapter is an effort to push back.

We begin by revisiting the earlier public choice critiques of legislative politics. In section II we turn to the new arguments, exhibiting their affinities with the classical arguments. Whereas the public choice theorists of the 1960s and 1970s typically prescribed checks and balances, and particularly judicial review, as the best remedy for the irrationalities that allegedly plague democratic legislatures, the new authoritarians maintain that presidential leadership is better. We refute their arguments in sections III and IV. We show that, like the classical public choice theorists, the new authoritarians mischaracterize the pathologies of legislatures while ignoring defects of the constraining institutions they advocate.

In their skepticism of democratic legislatures the new authoritarians are wrong for the same reasons that the classical public choice theorists were, but their credulous embrace of executive power is misguided for different reasons. Strong chief executives are more easily captured and manipulated than are legislatures, as the corruption that runs rife from Russia to Venezuela underscores. Executive aggrandizement facilitates clientelism by streamlining patronage, personalizing politics, and weakening parties—aggravating the legislative dysfunction to which the new authoritarians claim to be responding. However lacking in accountability legislatures might be, strong independent presidents are not the solution. Moreover, the proponents of presidential control of the executive branch dramatically overstate the extent to which executives can be unitary and the extent to which presidential elections can function as robust mechanisms of political accountability.

I. The First Wave

The early social choice literature provided conceptual resources for libertarian attacks on big government. This is not to say that the likes of Kenneth Arrow, Charles Plott, and Allan Gibbard had ideological agendas; they did not.[3] But by showing that majority rule can produce arbitrary and sometimes manipulated outcomes, they provided ammunition for others who were determined to limit the power of democratic legislatures as much as possible.[4] Public choice theory emerged out of social choice theory in the 1950s and 1960s, championed by scholars who were suspicious of government in general and democracy in particular. Public choice theorists like James Buchanan, Gordon Tullock, William Riker, and Barry Weingast deployed the social choice critiques of majority rule to defend extensive constitutional restrictions on democracy.[5] In the United States, this meant robust support for courts to limit legislative interference with markets and property rights. If not ideological in motivation, there was a certain myopia to the early social choice literature, rooted in its—sometimes tacit—acceptance of Jean-Jacques Rousseau's construction of the challenge of democratic government: to discover a general will that embodies the "common interest." Rousseau had famously, if vaguely, characterized this as "what remains" when we start with individual wills and then deduct the "pluses and minuses that cancel each other out."[6] Arrow and his progeny unpacked this by reference to the concept of a social welfare function. This they conceived of as the collective analog of an individual welfare function in economics, exhibiting standard features of economic rationality: that it should express transitive orderings of social preferences. Majority rule's infirmity derived from its alleged inability to converge, or remain, on a social welfare function thus defined.[7]

The early literature took this neo-Rousseauist construction of the problem for granted. As a result, it ignored defenses of majority rule in the tradition stretching from John Locke to the mature James Madison, Joseph Schumpeter, and modern pluralists following Robert Dahl and Adam Przeworski, for whom the value of majority rule has nothing to do with that definition of collective rationality.[8] Indeed, writers in this tradition often see the possibility of Arrovian cycling as an advantage of majority rule. Some argue that democracy functions best when parties replace one another in government over time, institutionalizing contestation over policy.[9] Some defend it as more likely than the going alternatives to get the truth to influence decision-making in politics.[10] Some note that cycling provides present losers with incentives to remain committed to the system in hopes of prevailing later rather than reach for their guns.[11] Sean Ingham argues that popular control is consistent with the findings of social choice theory because governments can be accountable to multiple groups simultaneously.[12] Nicholas Miller made the logic underlying many of these arguments explicit by pointing out that the Arrovian and pluralist conceptions of stability contradict one another.[13] Those who deployed the early social choice findings to attack majority rule's irrationality really meant that it failed to meet their narrow, not to say stilted, test of collective rationality. For them, majority rule imposes arbitrary or manipulated outcomes on society and should be kept to a minimum.

Some public choice theorists extended their criticisms of democracy well beyond the alleged irrationalities of majority rule that social choice theorists had identified. They viewed the democratic process as a net drain on social welfare. Majority rule was identified as giving rise to rent seeking, as majority coalitions seek private benefits at the expense of public good provision—not least the public good of a well-functioning market system.[14] But the democratic process could not be relied upon even to yield effective majority rule, since officials often had stronger incentives to provide benefits to special interests at the expense of the majority.

Some significant work in public choice was addressed to the perceived problem of rampant bureaucracy, but this problem was secondary to legislative irresponsibility. Stigler's seminal analysis of regulatory capture focused not on bureaucracy but on the tradeoff that elected officials make between responsiveness to votes and to money.[15] Others argued that electorally unaccountable bureaucrats might be even likelier than legislators to engage in rent-seeking behavior at the public expense by lobbying for bloated budgets.[16] But these problems were subsidiary to the fundamental problem: the incentive for legislators to abdicate responsible stewardship of the public fisc. Bureaucracy posed additional problems due to agency slack, but they were rooted, ultimately, in the dearth of legislators' incentives to engage in adequate monitoring.

The libertarian case eventually drew flak for leaning on misleading features of the social contract metaphor, in particular the idea that the alternative to collective political action is no collective political action. In fact, even a night-watchman state geared exclusively to ensuring peace, protecting private property, and enforcing contracts is itself a collective-action regime, financed by and imposed on those who would prefer some alternative.[17] This characteristic libertarian blindness was dramatized in Nozick's assertion that the fundamental question of political theory is "whether there should be any state at all."[18] In the modern world this is a bit like saying that the fundamental question of dental theory is whether people should have any teeth at all. The question is not whether there should be collective action but rather what sort.

During the 1980s and 1990s, the analytical collective-choice literature moved on to other topics and became less explicitly political. This was partly because it attracted a new generation of scholars who were more interested in technical questions than political outcomes, partly because renewed attention to game theory and institutional analyses ushered in different research agendas, and partly because the advent of rational choice Marxism made the field less the preserve of the ideological right.[19] Instead of inhabiting a few outposts like Washington University in St. Louis, George Mason, and Rochester, rational choice theory swept the mainstream of political science, but in a more domesticated—if not scholastic—form.[20]

But in the real world the assault on legislatures continued. On January 20, 1981, President Ronald Reagan declared in his Inaugural: "In this present crisis, government is not the solution to our problem, government is the problem."[21] This became the bumper sticker for the ascendant New Right on both sides of the Atlantic, fueled by the oil shocks and stagflation of the 1970s, fiscally strapped welfare states, and the prospect of growing dependent populations as the baby boom generation eyed retirement. In the United States, the Republican revival fed on and bolstered the idea that out-of-control public spending had to be reined in no matter what—with Congress ritualistically lambasted as unequal to the task.

Reagan was a harbinger of things to come. In his 1986 State of the Union he demanded: "Give me a line-item veto this year. Give me the authority to veto waste, and I'll take the responsibility, I'll make the cuts, I'll take the heat."[22] Congress demurred, but a decade later Bill Clinton persuaded Congress to adopt the Line Item Veto Act. The Supreme Court struck it down two years later, however, as violating the Constitution's Presentment Clause by letting presidents make unilateral changes to parts of spending statutes.[23] George W. Bush and Donald Trump would both call for line-item vetoes that could pass constitutional muster by sending statutes to the legislature for up-or-down votes once items had been struck out by the president. Ironically, Bush would get behind trillions in unfunded federal spending mandates by borrowing to fight wars in the Middle East and adding free prescription drugs to Medicare, while Trump's combination of tax cuts and defense spending hikes would add more than $1.9 trillion to the deficit—scarcely evidence of fiscal rectitude in the executive branch.

If Congress has had second thoughts about handing this much budgetary power to the president, the same is not true of the new authoritarians in public choice. There has always been an authoritarian undercurrent to the public choice literature, rooted in its portrayal of a minimal Weberian state as somehow prior to politics. The view that any more robust state would involve illicit legislative behavior loads the dice in favor of a government that does nothing more than monopolize the use of violence, protect private property, and enforce contracts—irrespective of whether a majority of the population, even a substantial one, would favor more expansive social policy. But this latent authoritarianism was obscured by social contract metaphors that take for granted the conceit of organized collective life without government and technocratic arguments that ignore the distributive dimensions of every regime of collective action or inaction.

The differences between democracy and dictatorship did not make it onto many early public choice research agendas, perhaps because of the libertarian suspicion that all governments are potential sources of expropriation.[24] It is possible, however, to defend autocracy by appealing to classical public choice premises. For instance, Hoppe maintains that autocracies (which he calls "monarchies") will expropriate less than democracies on the grounds that democratic governments typically have shorter time horizons than autocrats.[25] This is reminiscent of Olson's claim that stationary bandits will engage in less expropriation than roving ones, with the twist that a democracy is portrayed as more like a roving bandit.[26] Public choice theorists have also worried that democracy is distinctive in exacerbating the growth of bureaucracy. Gordon Tullock, Arthur Seldon, and Gordon Brady opine that "the bureaucratic problems of democracies would be much worse than those of a despotism" on the grounds that democracy exacerbates rent seeking.[27] There have been other libertarian attacks on democracy, but the distinctive public choice critique focused on its alleged tendency to produce deviations from efficiency. Restrictions on democracy were seen as appropriate, not to protect individual rights, but rather to prevent inefficiency.[28] Yet the "rent seeking" that they deplored was in effect, as Dowding and Hindmoor observe, "another name for democratic politics."[29]

II. The New Authoritarianism

Like their classical predecessors, the new authoritarians indict Congress, attributing poor legislative performance to legislators' incentives to favor special interests at the collective expense. But they differ in contending that transferring power to the executive—and especially the chief executive—is the answer. Posner and Vermeule, Howell and Moe, and Fukuyama all argue for executive concentration by appealing to efficiency—if in different ways. Posner and Vermeule appeal to expediency, arguing that legislative processes take too long to respond to pressing issues—if they do at all. Howell and Moe invoke coherence, arguing that legislative outcomes are marred by inevitable compromises among various interests. Fukuyama makes both arguments, claiming that U.S. executive weakness is "making the operation of the government as a whole both incoherent and inefficient."[30]

The central thrust of this new scholarship is to view executives as able to avoid the collective-action problems that plague legislators. Because legislatures are composed of many actors, none of whom internalizes the benefits of optimal policymaking, they face efficiency-undermining collective-action problems. Chief executives, by contrast, are unitary actors, from which it is alleged to follow that the prerogatives of the office are better aligned with the incentives of the officeholder. The primary focus of these scholars is not on relations within the executive (a subject we take up below), but their approach resembles recent arguments that have been developed by unitary executive theorists in the conservative legal movement. These scholars share the classical public choice concern with rent seeking, but they view empowering chief executives as a way of disciplining both Congress and bureaucrats in the interest of efficiency. Federalist Society founder Steven Calabresi provides an elegant summary of this perspective, arguing that Congress faces a "redistributive collective action problem" to which presidential leadership provides a solution.[31] The usual pork barrel incentives lead legislators to promote excessive public spending, but a single chief executive, representing a national constituency and motivated to govern effectively, will likely prioritize fiscal responsibility. In its essentials this is the same as Posner and Vermeule's claim that legislatures face distinctive collective-action problems that are best obviated by a powerful chief executive.[32] As a result, we should be neither surprised nor troubled to see increasing concentration of executive power at the expense of both legislative chambers and the courts. The founders might have intended ambition to counteract ambition, but the executive turns out to be a better counteractor than the other branches. And that, we are told, is good. The executive has consistently "proved capable of acting with dispatch and power, while Congress fretted, fumed, and delayed."[33]

This claim is pressed into the service of a larger critique of Madisonian separation of powers in the age of the administrative state. Posner and Vermeule present themselves as sympathetic in principle to Madisonian checks and balances, and they consider, in formal terms, which distribution of power across branches will produce the socially optimal level of checking. One conjecture is that multiplying checks can reduce overall checking of the most powerful branch, which they take to be the executive, because weaker branches will free-ride on one another as checks against executive aggrandizement.[34] They also conclude that the legislature, as a diffuse institution, is poorly structured to resist executive encroachment. The interest of the president is more closely aligned with the institutional prerogatives of the presidency than the interest of an individual legislator is aligned with that of Congress. Legislators will therefore find it hard to coordinate so as to check the expansion of executive power.[35]

Posner and Vermeule make two predictive arguments for executive concentration on the basis of expediency, one based on energy and the other on capacity. The executive will amass power over time first because it can respond rapidly to crises. The legislature will defer to executive action in times of crisis, ratifying constitutional excesses after the fact.[36] What begins as the response to a crisis tends to become quickly enshrined in law, and the purview of the administrative state grows. Second, in the era of the administrative state, they note, 98 percent of U.S. federal government employees work in the executive branch.[37] Congress simply lacks sufficient capacity to resist executive encroachment.[38]

Posner and Vermeule's normative stance is often left implicit, embedded in their contentions that more authority should shift from the legislature to the executive and that the president should control the activities inside the executive branch without legislative oversight. They endorse a "plebiscitary presidency," in which the president is subject to regular elections but governs unencumbered by checks and balances between elections, as optimal. Congressional oversight, to the extent it still exists, only hinders administrative efficacy. If the natural course is for Congress's power to wane, Posner and Vermeule want to speed it up. Against Madison's dire warning in Federalist 47, they argue that their plebiscitarian brand of presidentialism will not produce tyranny because of the check imposed by the president's responsiveness to popular opinion. As a result, "the plebiscitary presidency is constrained, not tyrannical."[39] Regular elections mean that presidents must remain responsive to public demands, even if they are no longer subject to effective legal constraints.

Posner and Vermeule maintain that presidents can be effective only when they have "credibility." Because the president, unlike Congress, has strong incentives to govern effectively, this "forces the executive to adopt institutions and informal mechanisms of self-constraint that help enhance its credibility."[40] Their argument recalls North and Weingast's argument that autocrats have incentives to create institutional constraints on their power in order to achieve their governance objectives, although Posner and Vermeule shift focus from constitutional constraints to the de facto constraints of political coalitions and public opinion.[41]

Posner and Vermeule do offer telling criticisms of checks and balances, long a staple of public choice prescriptions. These constraints are sometimes defended as needed to protect minorities, but in reality they privilege the status quo and those who benefit from it.[42] They can also produce "utility drift" or "policy drift" when changing circumstances erode the efficacy of once-effective policies.[43] In short, Posner and Vermeule are right that the proliferation of veto points hinders effective government action to address pressing social problems.

But as reviewers like Graham Dodds were quick to point out, Posner and Vermeule's positive case for increased executive power is notably more robust than their normative case.[44] They frequently rely on the principle that "ought implies can": if the executive is bound to encroach on legislative supremacy, then we might as well abandon the latter as a normative ideal.[45] But if they literally believed executive concentration to be inevitable, then it is not clear why they would be so concerned to advance normative defenses of it. So presumably they believe there are choices to be made and, where there are, they put their normative thumbs on the executive side of the scale.

Howell and Moe present a more thoroughgoing normative argument for executive empowerment, but their case also exposes more fully the defects of this stance. If Posner and Vermeule focus on the impotence of legislatures, Howell and Moe stress their maleficence. In contrast with the unitary executive, supposed to represent the whole of the public, the loyalty of the legislature is divided among multiple principals, with the consequence that legislation is the piecemeal product of negotiations among them. It is therefore unsurprising, they argue, that Congress produces hulking legislative packages too complex for voters to understand and packed with special interest giveaways. The problem is not that Congress "cannot set the agenda" but that it does.[46] Howell and Moe's proposed solution is a procedural reform "giving presidents broad and permanent agenda-setting power, and thereby moving Congress to the back seat of policymaking and presidents to the front."[47]

According to Howell and Moe legislators have incentives to be "parochial" and "myopic."[48] They expect presidents to be more attuned than legislators to the long-term implications of policy decisions, because presidents are more motivated by legacy concerns—indeed, they assert (citing only anecdotal evidence) that this is the "motivator that most forcefully drives presidential behavior."[49] Presidents, accountable to national constituencies, also have better incentives to consider the national interest rather than the interest of particular constituencies. Howell and Moe's argument that legislators are focused on parochial concerns recalls a recurring public choice trope: the choice that legislators face between allocating funding to public goods or targeted spending. Howell and Moe are concerned that legislators represent the interests of their constituents rather than those of the whole—whereas a president can allocate externalities in ways that produce coherent and holistic solutions to policy problems. They thus see empowering the president as a means to bring about superior economic efficiency in policymaking.

Howell and Moe share the classical public choice preoccupation with rent-seeking benefits that are extracted from the pie without generating productive activity. In this intellectual universe, any deviation from the smooth operation of markets, except when needed to correct market failures, is suspect. Part of their market-oriented bias results from the fact that public choice theorists often focus myopically on the ways in which government action might detract from efficiency, but as Carpenter and Moss point out, regulatory capture can occur by preventing prudential regulation as well as by securing regulatory policies that cater to industry interests.[50] Howell and Moe speak the language of coherence and effectiveness, but their conclusions consistently lean toward less government—as they explicitly note.[51]

It is telling that Howell and Moe cite the Affordable Care Act as illustrating legislative action run amok, a "cobbled-together patchwork that denies the country genuine reform" and contains "one special-interest victory after another, in a bill that is more than a thousand pages long."[52] One consequence of adding institutional constraints on majority rule is increasing the number of pivotal players who are capable of extracting rents in exchange for approving legislation, a dilemma worse in the case of the ACA where every Democratic vote was pivotal. Congress abandoned the public option, which would have kept private insurers honest in the short run and offered a path to a single-payer system in the longer run, because Senator Joseph Lieberman, heavily funded by Connecticut insurance interests, threatened to pull his support for the bill unless it was dropped.[53] For reasons discussed below, any suggestion that the executive branch would have been less susceptible than Congress to industry lobbying on this legislation is implausible.

Fukuyama attacks checks and balances in a like vein. He is especially critical of legislative oversight of administrative agency decisions. Fukuyama argues, plausibly, that "Madisonian democracy" has given rise to "vetocracy" that benefits special interests at the expense of the public and, less plausibly, that legislation is particularly subject to these pathologies.[54] The decision to abandon the ACA provision—that candidate Barack Obama had run on in 2008 along with the public option—to empower the federal government to control costs by negotiating drug prices with pharmaceutical companies was made in the White House in response to industry pressure in 2009, replicating the giveaway that the George W. Bush administration had created with Medicare Part D six years earlier.[55] Donald Trump ran on a similar promise to negotiate drug prices in 2016, but he began backtracking during his first month in office and included big pharma benefits in his bill to replace NAFTA the following year. As for empowering administrative agencies, one only has to mention the almost complete industry capture of financial and mortgage regulators in the run-up to the 2008 financial crisis to make it obvious that, whatever the problems created by lobbying Congress, immunizing administrative agencies from legislative oversight is not the solution.[56]

From the 1950s to the 1980s, the favored strategy of public choice proponents was empowering courts to "constitutionalize" provisions that would protect property and contracts from legislative interference. But as the scholarship surveyed here demonstrates, public choice premises can also be deployed to defend enhanced executive power. Fukuyama provides a motivation for this shift, claiming that, in the United States today, "the courts, instead of being constraints on government, have become alternative instruments for the expansion of government."[57] He endorses the "ossification" thesis, also advanced by Posner and Vermeule, according to which excessive judicial review frustrates administrative efficacy. This might seem curious, since Fukuyama's goal is "to cut the state back," but judicial review can just as well frustrate a deregulatory agenda as advance it. Whether ossification exists is an empirical claim about which the jury remains out.[58]

As Elena Kagan observes, most legislative delegation to the executive until the 1980s had been from Congress to administrative agencies, not to the president.[59] The real transformation has not been increasing delegation by Congress but increasing administrative control by the president. Ostensibly, Congress is the principal to which federal agencies should be accountable. But beginning with the Reagan administration, presidents have moved aggressively to solidify control over the federal bureaucracy. This new presidential assertiveness coincided with Congress's increased willingness to transfer oversight functions to the executive office of the president.

Perhaps it is not coincidental that a congressional deregulatory agenda abetted the rise of "presidential administration." Congress found it easier to pursue deregulation through expanded presidential control than through the legislative process. Empowerment of the Office of Information and Regulatory Affairs (OIRA), established by Congress as part of the Paperwork Reduction Act of 1980, mandated pre-publication review of any new executive agency rule. This process, controlled by the White House, has been one of the most effective routes (perhaps second only to appointments) for presidents to stymie the regulatory process. Kagan argues that presidential administration can be used for proregulatory as well as antiregulatory purposes, but there are structural limits to the efficacy of presidential control as a force for proregulatory ends. Congress has the sole authority to appropriate money, and the OIRA review process can only delay or obstruct agency rulemaking, not initiate it.[60]

Kagan suggests that the rise of presidential administration is primarily due to presidents' ability to serve as more efficient and accountable intermediaries between agencies and the public. She argues that "the President has natural and growing advantages over any institution in competition with him to control the bureaucracy. The Presidency's unitary power structure, its visibility, and its 'personality' all render the office peculiarly apt to exercise power in ways that the public can identify and evaluate."[61] Presidential control, on this view, ought to increase the accountability of the regulatory process by making agency decisions more transparent and clarifying relationships of responsibility. Kagan's analysis dovetails with Posner and Vermeule's suggestion that there is a natural tendency for power to gravitate over time from the legislative to the executive branch.

Alarmed at the celebration of these developments by the likes of Posner and Vermeule, John Ferejohn and Roderick Hills have proposed institutional reforms to resist the encroachment of executive power on legislative prerogative.[62] They are right to be concerned, even if the accumulation of executive power is not as unidirectional or relentless as the literature we have reviewed here suggests. It is true that Congress has often ceded its own capacity voluntarily. During the Truman administration, Congress gave up substantial budgetary and oversight capacity on national security to the executive without so much as a whimper.[63] More recently, Congress has dismantled sources of expert counsel like the Office of Technology Assessment, along with cuts to the Government Accountability Office and the

Congressional Research Service on top of the pitiful funding allocated to congressional staffing.[64]

But it is not all a one-way street. In battles over Russian sanctions after 2016, Congress forced the Trump administration to adopt measures it opposed and that the President decried as unconstitutional.[65] Moreover, when Congress has surrendered legislative capacity, this is not always due to institutional incentives. Sometimes it is a consequence of political ideology, as conservative activists have found it easier to reshape the legislative branch than administrative agencies. And even though Congress is typically more willing to defer when the presidency is occupied by a copartisan, the 116th Congress recognized the importance of strengthening congressional capacity, including by increasing funding allocated to staffing and expert counsel.[66] While the institutional incentives are powerful, there is more room for agency and choice than the new authoritarians suggest. For those of us who are unpersuaded by their normative claims, that is good news.

III. Against Executive Concentration

The normative case that the new authoritarians make for enhanced executive power is even weaker than their mechanical analyses of institutional incentives. They argue that executive concentration can restore accountability to a profligate, sclerotic, and captured government, but the opposite is more likely true. Just as parliamentary systems facilitate better accountability than presidential systems, so executive aggrandizement within presidential systems is likely to increase corruption and clientelism while offering less democratic accountability.

Personalized Politics

Instead of a "constitutionalist fallacy" in public choice in favor of delegation to courts, the new authoritarians embrace a presidentialist one.[67] They imagine that the unitary executive can somehow pursue the public interest impartially, that presidents are more likely than legislatures to prioritize spending on public goods over targeted transfers to favored interests. In fact, presidents can and do give away rents too—as we noted with respect to healthcare legislation. The main difference is that the rents will be less widely distributed, going to the president's cronies rather than allies of more diffuse groups of legislators. Indeed, executive aggrandizement should be expected to exacerbate clientelism due to the more streamlined distribution of pork. We might call this the pluralist case for preferring legislative supremacy as a lesser evil. If politics is going to be concerned with the allocation of private goods to constituencies, then it is better to allocate them more widely, rather than to fewer beneficiaries. Presidentialism reduces turnover in coalition membership.[68] This will likely result in less rotation in the interests patronized under presidentialist politics and fewer cross-cutting cleavages. This might be one contributor to the greater instability of presidential systems than parliamentary ones, identified long ago by Juan Linz.[69]

One consequence of making a single office the focal point of political competition is to magnify the importance of personality in political competition. But personalized politics frustrates accountability. Political competition under presidentialism tends to be less partisan and hence less programmatic, with a corresponding increase in clientelism.[70] Personalization thrives on charismatic leadership, potentially exacerbating instability and facilitating authoritarianism. Dismayed by the election of President Trump (and by its grim implications for their theory), Howell and Moe have suggested that strengthening the presidency would help to combat the rise of populist politics.[71] Recent political dynamics in Eastern Europe, Turkey, and Latin America suggest that this is wishful thinking.

Weak Political Parties

The drawbacks of presidentialism are compounded by weak parties, but presidentialism weakens them still more. One mechanism is through personalization, which detracts from party branding and discipline. Another is that strengthening presidents shifts the center of political gravity away from the legislature, diminishing connections between voters and parties. Powerful presidents' usurping of legislative agendas also exacerbates the diffusion of responsibility, permitting legislators to dodge accountability. When their political fortunes depend less on party loyalty, they have correspondingly diminished incentives to conform to party discipline. Party leaders in the legislature will also evade accountability, as when Nancy Pelosi's leadership position remained secure despite leading Democrats to four successive defeats from 2010 to 2016. That would be much less likely in a parliamentary system. In short, weakening parties erodes their political accountability without fostering a concomitant increase in presidential accountability.

Legislatures also perform better on the dimension of accountability because they institutionalize a role for the opposition, something conspicuously lacking in the executive branch. Legislatures provide forums for minority parties, offering them both institutional resources and public platforms. Archibald Foord characterizes the "loyal opposition" as valuable for accountability because it has a strong incentive to scrutinize the government: "The immediate purpose of Opposition criticism is to check, prevent, and rectify any abuses of which government may be guilty."[72] Voters benefit from this scrutiny. The opposition's hope to become a future government aligns with the voters' desire to gain information about government malfeasance. Legislatures have opposition leaders and ranking or shadow members, but there is no shadow president. Once the campaign is over, the loser loses her public platform—another reason that enhancing presidential power diminishes accountability to voters.

Limits to Presidential Control

The new authoritarians' defense of executive power relies on criticizing legislatures, but it neglects the serious principal-agent problems that undermine effective presidential governance. For one thing, principal-agent dynamics within the executive erect obstacles to the development of good policy. In a complex bureaucratic system like the federal government, it is hard for a leader to gather necessary information and monitor subordinates effectively. Legislative power offers resources that can enhance accountability and the quality of policymaking.

The new authoritarians largely ignore the glaring challenge that executives cannot in fact be unitary. They are complex organizations composed of many actors with differing motives and visibility. Ironically, this is a standard insight from public choice, which has seen much ink spilled over the problems of principal-agent relationships. Agents tend to be imperfectly responsive to the demands of their principals. Ron Suskind gives several examples from the Obama administration. Tim Geithner repeatedly deferred action on President Obama's order to research how to break up the big banks until Obama finally gave up asking.[73] Larry Summers, based on his own political calculations, presented Obama with a stimulus plan that his economic advisers knew to be inadequate.[74] Suskind concludes that "when a staff of thousands is designated to express the will of a single man, bad process can spell disaster, no matter the clarity of best intentions."[75] The Obama administration was far from unique in this respect. Oliver North's overzealous interpretation of Reagan's instructions resulted in his Iran-Contra debacle. It will likely be decades, if ever, before we learn what rogue exploits occurred in the Trump White House. Weberian bureaucracies are supposed to operate efficiently due to smooth transition of commands downward and information upward, but as these examples suggest, principal-agent dynamics within the executive thrive on serious information asymmetries. So much for the efficiency of "unitary executives."

There are also more basic problems with information gathering in bureaucratic systems, analogous to the failures of command economies to pool information efficiently. Even the best-intentioned agents face daunting challenges in gathering accurate information. Moreover, bureaucratic processes may be vulnerable to cooptation by special interests, as the example of the Dodd-Frank rule-making process attests.[76] Agencies rely on consultation in order to gather information, and well-heeled groups are well placed to influence this process. By contrast, legislators have at least intermittent incentives to be responsive to the majority of their constituents in the face of interest group pressure.[77] The obvious solution is better legislative oversight, for which presidential leadership is no substitute.

Posner and Vermeule might respond that the problem is that currently the executive is not as unitary as it ought to be. But it is hard to see why a more unified executive would avoid the principal-agent challenges we have identified; it might well make them worse. In any case, our discussion of the infirmities of presidential supervision of agencies mirrors their ought-implies-can challenge to legislative oversight. If an argument from feasibility does not suffice in the one case, neither can it in the other. Moreover, their prescription may be contraindicated. Presidents are often less effective coordinators of agencies than they imagine, and there is some evidence that Congress is well equipped to perform this function by passing interagency coordination legislation.[78]

Limits of Presidential Responsiveness

Relations between voters and the president are also beset by information problems. Presidential elections are practically useless as accountability mechanisms, partly because of formidable information asymmetries and partly because voters face massive coordination problems. Posner and Vermeule rely on responsiveness to public opinion as the main check on the executive, but they overlook the capacity of leaders to manipulate the public to advance their own agendas. Druckman and Jacobs reveal that presidents have great latitude to mold public opinion through strategic agenda setting and issue framing.[79] Presidents use polling to frame issues such that they can claim the mantle of public support, while at the same time they focus on policy concessions to their favored policy-demanders. In this respect, executive power is surely more concerning than legislative power, since legislators have less capacity to control political narratives and to set agendas. Moreover, legislators have greater proximity to their constituents and consequently greater capacity for responsiveness.

Voters also face daunting coordination challenges in attempting to defeat presidential incumbents. Even if they can obtain accurate information about poor performance, they must coordinate not only to remove the incumbent but also to select a successor. The sheer size of the presidential electorate makes this a daunting undertaking. We should certainly expect this problem to be more severe for a population of 328 million than for 435 members of Congress (or for 650 members of Parliament, perhaps a more apt comparison). Posner and Vermeule do acknowledge the electorate's agency challenge, but they fail to see that the answer is to look for reforms that would make the American system function more like a parliamentary one—not less.

Posner and Vermeule argue that the main check on executive power is public opinion. They claim that, in contrast to the moribund state of constitutional law, "electoral democracy is alive and well."[80] But five years after the publication of *The Executive Unbound,* Posner seemed to have lost his nerve.[81] As the prospect of a Trump presidency loomed, Posner began waxing nostalgic for the separation of powers (even as he warned that it would provide little respite). He focused on the possibility of administrative resistance to presidential power, considering the ability of civil servants to resist Trump's orders.[82] But Posner warned that Trump would, over time, have the ability to reshape the civil service (like the courts) in more congenial directions. Ultimately, Posner and Vermeule offer nothing but hope that public opinion will rein in rogue presidents, however fanciful that might be.

Empowering chief executives is not likely to foster responsiveness to the preferences of the median voter. That desideratum would be better satisfied under legislative primacy and majority rule. Of the new authoritarians, Fukuyama is the most perceptive (or the most frank) about presidential power's dearth of democratic credentials. He associates legislative power with democracy and executive power with state capacity, arguing that the United States suffers from "too much 'democracy' relative to American state capacity."[83] But it is not majority rule that is to blame for congressional dysfunction. Rather, it is republican checks and balances and weak congressional parties.[84]

Presidential Decision Processes

It is fortunate that executives cannot be unitary, because they would be pretty terrifying if they could. Hierarchical decision processes are ill-suited to yield well-reasoned results, because deliberation in hierarchical settings tends to consist of kissing up and kicking down. There is always a trade-off in decision making between the costs and benefits of acquiring information. Expediting decision making comes at an informational cost. There can therefore be value in slowing down the pace of policymaking. The legislative process takes time, but if time devoted to information gathering helps to ensure a fuller airing of the testimony of affected interests, then it might be time well spent. The supposed virtue of executive "energy" is often a vice. The most disastrous military misadventures—think of Vietnam and Iraq—tend to be pitched with urgency.

Narrowing the range of interests consulted in the policymaking process is also often a disadvantage. Irving Janis's discussion of groupthink suggests that executive decision making is more vulnerable to this pathology than what goes on in legislatures.[85] Sunstein and Hastie identify another mechanism: deliberating groups that are overly homogeneous—as when all of the members are selected by one leader—tend to make poor decisions.[86] Congress should be expected to have better information than the president partly because it solicits testimony from more diverse arrays of stakeholders.

IV. Misdiagnosis and Prescription

Unlike Posner and Vermeule and Fukuyama, Howell and Moe would not displace the action from legislative politics to bureaucratic processes. They regard increasing the role of presidential leadership in the legislative process as the only feasible solution to congressional pathologies. They are right that legislative fragmentation in the American system undermines accountability. Checks and balances worsen these problems, as we have seen. Presidents and Congress claim credit for legislative successes and blame one another for failures. Against endemic finger-pointing and sclerosis, the impulse to bet on a strong president is understandable. But the solution is not further to undermine Congress; it would be better to strengthen it.

The new authoritarians' argument for executive concentration rests on an indictment of legislatures, but critiquing only the American system as presently configured stacks the deck by focusing on one of the world's most poorly designed legislatures. The new authoritarians are right to draw attention to its pathologies, but their account misses the main sources of congressional dysfunction. Congress today functions poorly, but it does so for reasons having little to do with old or new public choice narratives. They would do better to focus on the causes and consequences of weak parties: the profusion of veto players within and between branches, partisan and misguided gerrymandering, malapportionment of Senate seats, and the role of money in the political system.

To their credit, these authors recognize that checks and balances pose serious obstacles to legislative performance. But, it is worth emphasizing that the American system institutionalizes veto players to a greater degree than any other democracy—save only the "unit veto" that prevailed in the Polish-Lithuanian Commonwealth from the mid-sixteenth century to the late eighteenth century, where any member of the Sejm could nullify all legislation passed in the current session by yelling *Nie pozwalam!* (literally: "I do not allow!").[87] The addition of each veto player produces an additional departure from majority rule, thereby increasing the likelihood of gridlock. The American system today includes three formal veto points—the Senate, the presidential veto, and judicial review—as well as additional veto points embodied in Congress's own rules: most notably the Senate filibuster and intermittently the Hastert Rule in the House.[88]

American parties lack the cohesion of their parliamentary counterparts. Party discipline, always weak, has been exacerbated by the increase in safe seats that empowers unrepresentative voters in low-turnout primaries. The mere possibility of primary challenges often prompts leaders to prevent votes on popular legislation and to hold them on bills that most voters oppose.[89] Despite these defects, historically in the United States parties have been the most important mechanism for making Congress function effectively.[90] Strengthening congressional parties would be a better response than the presidential leadership that Howell and Moe advocate, which, we have seen, is a remedy akin to bloodletting. Strengthening parties also helps lengthen legislative time horizons, mitigating concerns about short-termism.[91]

Howell and Moe, like Posner and Vermeule, register admiration for the Westminster model, but their insinuation that their proposals would harness its benefits within the institutional constraints of the American system is stillborn. The central problem with Howell and Moe's proposal—giving the president the power to require an up-or-down vote on any legislation—is that they want to give the president all the legislative power of a prime minister without any of the checks on executive power that accompany it in a parliamentary system. As we have noted, in parliamentary systems, back benchers can and do remove leaders whose performance falls short, and electoral incentives correspond well to legislative performance. Better reforms to the U.S. system would be to get rid of the presidential veto, the opposite of what Howell and Moe propose, and to give congressional parties more say in the selection of their presidential candidates. They had this before Andrew Jackson led the first populist assault on America's fledgling party system following his loss to John Quincy Adams in the House in the presidential election of 1824 despite beating him in the popular and Electoral College votes.[92] Other plausible measures would be to curtail or eliminate the Senate filibuster and the Hastert Rule in the House, support the moves in a number of states to relocate congressional redistricting from state legislatures to independent commissions, introduce minimum turnout requirements for primary results to be binding on parties, break up some of the largest states, and admit Puerto Rico and the District of Columbia to statehood. Such steps, none of which require constitutional amendment, would combat vetocracy and enhance congressional standing.

The Trump era in the United States saw a few tentative signs that Congress might be willing to start rolling back the imperial presidency. The 116th Congress defied President Trump on foreign policy repeatedly, albeit in largely symbolic ways, such as the House voice vote to repeal the AUMF and the Senate's 98–2 vote in favor of Russia sanctions. In 2019 both chambers invoked the War Powers Resolution to end U.S. involvement in Yemen's civil war. But presidential administration continued unabated in many areas, sometimes taking new and disturbing forms.[93] The Trump administration contemplated and indulged other questionable methods to circumvent Congress, from cutting the capital gains tax through the administrative process (encroaching on one of the few powers still generally regarded as exclusive to Congress) to ordering the construction of a wall on the southern border by declaring a national emergency.[94] Congressional backlash to overreach by the Trump administration might turn out to have been the beginning of real constraints on the imperial presidency, but achieving that would take more defiance than Congress historically has demonstrated.

Posner and Vermeule are mistaken, however, to claim that congressional acquiescence must be a one-way ratchet. The post-Vietnam reforms of the 1970s, which included the War Powers Resolution, are not even the most dramatic example. After Republican victories in the 1866 elections, Congress set out to reclaim a great deal of power from Andrew Johnson. It did so not just with bills facilitating military Reconstruction, passed over his veto, but also by insulating the military command in the South from presidential control, and by passing the Tenure of Office Act to prevent the president from firing executive officers without congressional approval.[95] Despite subsequent constitutional doctrine restricting congressional power over appointments and removals, including the Court's judgment in 1926 that the Tenure of Office Act was unconstitutional, Congress still has the power to structure agencies with some independence from presidential control.[96] Equally important, Congress has powers of oversight and impeachment with which it can make life difficult for an errant president. Strengthening them would do more to make the United States operate like a parliamentary system than continuing to underwrite the growth and concentration of executive power.

The impetus for change is unlikely to come from the judiciary. Were the Supreme Court so inclined, it could do a lot to restrain the imperial presidency, but separation of powers jurisprudence has moved decisively in the direction of increasing presidential control over administration.[97] Recent decisions, even during the Trump era, expressed great reluctance to check presidential discretion.[98] And in the wake of President Trump's judicial appointments, the Court's support for presidential unilateralism will likely increase.

It is particularly important in this situation to press the case for strengthening Congress as an institution and the parties within it. Like the classical public choice theorists, the authors discussed here have done considerable damage to democracy—however inadvertently. The delegitimation of legislative politics—indeed of democracy—wrought by that earlier generation of public choice theorists helped to foster conditions in which the new authoritarians could seem to pose as neutral advocates for efficient public policy and the popular will against a sclerotic and captured legislature. Yet as we have shown here, emancipating chief executives undermines democratic accountability. For democracy to operate as well as possible in the United States, Congress must have the capacity and prestige to constrain the president—even if the American system prohibits its outright control.

5

Collusion in Restraint of Democracy: Against Political Deliberation

Advocates of political deliberation usually defend it as a collaborative activity motivated by the possibility of agreement. Even when agreement proves elusive, deliberation helps people come to grips with one another's views, draw on their different experiences and expertise, and better understand the contours of their enduring disagreements. People's views will be better informed, and the decisions they make will be of higher quality than if they had not deliberated. When study after study reveals most people to be appallingly ill-informed about much public policy, deliberation's appeal seems obvious. Two minds are better than one, three better than two, and so on. Democracy will be improved if its decision making can incorporate, and build on, the benefits of deliberation. Or so it is frequently claimed.[1]

Deliberation should not be confused with argument. When people argue, there is an expectation that one of them will, or at least should, win. Even when we speak of one person making an argument, we see this as something that stands until it is contradicted or challenged and beaten by a better argument. Like the deliberationists, proponents of argument believe it will enhance understanding and improve the quality of decisions. This was the essence of John Stuart Mill's defense in *On Liberty* of the robust clash of opinions: it would lead people to hold better-informed and more accurate views. Mill even went so far as to worry—needlessly, it turned out—that as advancing science expanded the realm of settled knowledge, people would be deprived of argument's benefits. No longer forced to sharpen their wits by defending their views in the marketplace of ideas, they would become mediocre dullards: less able to think for themselves and more easily manipulated by others.[2]

My claim here is that the argumentative and deliberative ideals should be more clearly distinguished than they usually are. They support different and incompatible institutional arrangements. I also maintain that the argumentative ideal is superior because, when appropriately institutionalized, it helps hold governments accountable for their actions. By contrast, the deliberative ideal cannot easily be institutionalized—and perhaps cannot be institutionalized at all—because people who prefer to bargain can easily abuse rules designed to promote deliberation. But deliberation's difficulties run deeper. Its defenders fail to appreciate that, in politics, deliberation and the search for agreement are—to borrow an antitrust analogy—unhealthy forms of collusion in restraint of democracy. They should worry less about voter ignorance, which, as Anthony Downs noted long ago, might well reflect sensible budgeting of scarce time, and worry more when office seekers fail to engage in robust public debates over the policies that, if elected, they will enact.[3]

I. Competitive versus Deliberative Institutions

Joseph Schumpeter's competitive model of democracy, in which governments acquire power by prevailing in a "competitive struggle for the people's vote," gives institutional expression to the argumentative ideal.[4] This was perhaps best exemplified in the Westminster system as it existed from 1911, when the Parliament Act stripped the House of Lords of its real powers, until the late 1990s, when the Lords was reformed to enhance its legitimacy as a second chamber and the

Commons began ceding authority to European and other courts, the Bank of England, and independent agencies. The twentieth century's middle eight decades were the heyday of Parliament's supremacy within the British political system and of the Commons' supremacy within Parliament. Epitomized at Prime Minister's Questions, the sometimes-overwrought weekly gladiatorial clashes over the famous wooden despatch boxes. Parliamentary supremacy thrives on the ongoing contest between opposing policies and ideologies.

Schumpeterian democracy depends on alternation between two strong parties in government. The party that wins the election exercises a temporary power monopoly, but the loyal opposition—a government-in-waiting whose leaders hope to take power at the next election—continually challenges its policies. This system depends on combining first-past-the-post single member plurality (SMP) electoral systems with parliamentary democracy. The SMP electoral system produces two large parties, so long as the political makeup of the constituencies more or less reflects the political makeup of the national population.[5] Parliamentary systems ensure that the parties will be strong because the leader of the majority party is also the chief executive. Government and opposition clash across the aisle continually and compete during elections by offering voters the different programs they plan to implement.

The deliberative model, by contrast, calls for institutions that create incentives to seek agreement rather than victory—or at least agreement as a condition for victory. Rules that require concurrent majorities in bicameral chambers force representatives to find common ground when they can, and compromise when they cannot. Executive vetoes and supermajority provisions to override them create similar incentives. Proponents of deliberation often find proportional representation (PR) congenial for comparable reasons. Instead of two catchall parties that must submerge their disagreements in order to win elections, PR leads to party proliferation, bringing a more diverse array of voices to the political table. In addition to the left-of-center and right-of-center parties characteristic of SMP systems, in PR systems liberals, religious groups, Greens, separatists, and nationalists, among others, can all elect representatives to the legislature to be part of the conversation. Because one party seldom wins an absolute majority, coalition government, which forces parties to seek and perhaps even manufacture common ground, is the norm.

The U.S. system is a hybrid. The SMP electoral system produces two large parties, but the independently elected president weakens them, and the system of checks and balances forces consensus-seeking and compromise to the extent possible. The American founders intended the Senate, in particular, to be a constraining body made up of what Jefferson would later refer to as an "aristocracy of virtue and talent." It has been heralded as such by commentators dating back at least to Alexis de Tocqueville.[6] The idea that the Senate is the world's greatest deliberative body, which first gained currency with Daniel Webster's three-hour soliloquy in defense of the Union in 1850, has been repeated to the point of banality, no matter how scant its connection with reality.[7] I will have more to say about the kind of competition the U.S. system fosters shortly. As a prelude to this, notice that, unlike the Westminster model, which gives temporary control of the government's power monopoly to the majority party and relies on alternation over time as its main mechanism of accountability, the U.S. model divides up the control of power on an ongoing basis. Madison's slogan was that ambition "must be made to counteract ambition."[8] The checks and balances force the players in the different branches to accommodate themselves to one another—hence its affinities with the deliberative ideal.

Up to a point. A major limitation of institutions that encourage deliberation is that they can produce bargaining instead. Juries, for example, are traditionally subject to unanimity requirements that put pressure on their members to talk out their differences until they reach agreement. When this works well, it produces thorough exploration of all the arguments and evidence provided by the contending parties: a poster child for the benefits of deliberation. But a jury can also be held hostage by a recalcitrant crank who has nothing better to do when everyone else wants to go home. His superior bargaining power and stubbornness might enable him to extract agreement from the others, but this will not be deliberative consensus on the merits of the case. What holds for juries also holds for other institutions that we might hope will induce deliberation. When they produce bargaining instead, those with the most leverage will prevail. So it is that small parties often exert disproportionate influence over coalition governments, U.S. senators can use holds and filibuster rules to thwart the will of the majority, and various other supermajority and concurrent majority rules can be deployed to similar effect.

In short, deliberation requires people to act in good faith, but it is not possible to design institutions to induce good faith. "If men were angels," Madison wrote, "no government would be necessary."[9] Indeed, when power is at stake and representatives must answer to constituents, the impulse to bargain will likely overpower even genuine desires to reason collaboratively. In 2009, a number of centrist Republican Senators showed an interest in working with the Obama White House for "cap-and-trade" legislation on toxic emissions control. They soon bolted, however, when confronted with Tea Party–orchestrated threats of primary challenges in their constituencies, should they choose to persist.[10] Since power is endemically at stake in politics, it seems unlikely that there will be much genuine deliberation or that politicians will resist the impulse to exploit rules that might maximize their leverage instead.

An exception that proves the rule is the British House of Lords. Like the U.S. Senate, the Lords is sometimes praised as a deliberative body—though Bagehot famously said that the best cure for admiring the Lords is to go and look at it.[11] Interestingly, the Lords became less partisan and more deliberative after they lost the power to do anything except delay most legislation in 1911. Because there was no longer any partisan advantage to be had, peers who showed up were more likely to be those interested in improving the quality of legislation. The Lords became more of a repository of expertise. And, because they could no longer force the Commons to listen to them, they had incentives to give cogent reasons for their views—to try to persuade.[12] But they have become more partisan and assertive since reforms adopted in 1999 restored a measure of their democratic legitimacy, albeit one at a considerable distance from the ballot box, by radically reducing the membership and phasing out hereditary peers.[13] Meg Russell notes that the remaining peers believe that the Lords has gained legitimacy from these reforms that have "increased their confidence to challenge government policy."[14] The ironic conclusion is that the odds that a second chamber will be home to a dispassionate natural aristocracy moved by lofty thoughts and generous instincts might vary inversely with its power and democratic authority. Its members can be expected to show most interest in reasoned persuasion when there is no other way for them to prevail—the one way for Jürgen Habermas's ideal in which the best argument prevails to triumph in real politics. The British public seems to want some version of this. Polls reveal substantial support for the experts and non-party-aligned members in the Lords and little appetite for their replacement by party representatives.[15]

The various deliberative institutions that have been tried out or proposed in recent years are exclusively consultative. Deliberative polls and citizens' juries have no authority to decide anything. They might affect how people vote, but it is the voting that will be decisive. Objects of theoretical conjecture like ideal speech situations are even more radically divorced from politics, since they depend on armchair speculation about what people would decide in settings that are devoid of power relationships. Questions can and have been raised about whether such speculations add up to anything we should believe, or whether the changes in people's views produced by deliberative polls and other consultative mechanisms tried thus far are really improvements on their pre-deliberative views or simply changes.[16] These issues need not detain us here, however, since my present point is that—whatever its merits—institutionalizing deliberation turns out to be an elusive endeavor. If it is purely consultative, it is not clear why anyone will or should pay attention to it. Yet if rules are created to institutionalize deliberation and give it real decision-making teeth, they can all too easily undermine political competition, empowering people with leverage to appropriate them for their own purposes.

II. Deliberation and Direct Democracy

Some will contest my contention that deliberation can't be institutionalized by invoking another favorite of participatory democrats: referendums. Like deliberative polls and citizen juries, referendums appeal because they hold out the promise of bringing democracy closer to the people. By wresting decisions away from horse-trading politicians and political parties and enabling citizens to consider the pros and cons issue by issue, they invite in-depth reflection of issues on their own merits. And by getting them out of party platforms, they don't have their decisions held hostage to decisions on other matters. A referendum on abortion would give prochoice fiscal conservatives the chance to vote for their preference on abortion without having to support a party that spends more than they want on social programs.

If their decisions can be informed by deliberative mechanisms on the issue in question, this combines two participatory devices that empower citizens at the expense of party elites. In this spirit, some deliberative democrats point to Ireland's 2018 referendum on abortion and its earlier referendum on equal marriage—both of which had their origins in Ireland's deliberative assemblies in which random samples of the population discussed these issues in intensive sessions over a series of weekends—as demonstrating that it is possible to institutionalize deliberation.[17]

Appealing as this might sound, it misses the vital service that parties provide by bundling issues into platforms: it forces them to discount everything they propose by everything else that they propose. To see why bundling matters, consider this: if Americans are asked whether they support abolishing the estate tax—paid only by the wealthiest 2 percent of taxpayers and more than half of it paid by the wealthiest half of 1 percent with estates in excess of $20 million—substantial majorities say yes. However, when asked if they favor getting rid of the tax if this also means getting rid of prescription drug benefits for senior citizens, then majorities say no.[18] In the latter case, they are discounting their preference for the tax cut by their preference for retaining the prescription drug benefits.

That is what political parties do on a larger scale. They bundle issues into platforms, discounting everything they propose by everything else they propose in ways that they believe—or at least hope—will appeal to the broadest possible cross-section of voters. Deciding on issues one at a time sounds like it enhances in-depth exploration and democratic participation. Actually, it involves framing policy choices to obscure tradeoffs just as ballot initiatives and referendums do.[19] Former British Foreign Secretary David Miliband put the point succinctly when commenting on defenders of Jeremy Corbyn's far left manifesto, who insisted that the policies were popular despite Labour's catastrophic defeat in December 2019: "We were sold the category error of confusing opinion poll support for individual policies with support for the programme as a whole."[20]

Brexit was a dramatic illustration. When British voters chose to leave the European Union in June 2016 by a vote of 52 to 48 percent, substantial majorities of both the parliamentary Tory and Labour parties were pro-Remain.[21] This outcome might suggest that both parliamentary parties were out of step with the electorate, as anti-European activists insisted. But the evidence suggests otherwise. A year after the referendum, voters once again elected predominantly pro-Remain Labour and Tory delegations to Parliament. Vernon Bogdanor notes that 16 out of the 23 members that Theresa May's 2017 cabinet had, like her, been Remain advocates a year earlier, and he estimates that overall the Parliament elected in 2017 was more strongly pro-Remain than the Parliament elected in 2015.[22] Even in December 2019, when Labour imploded and many Tories were traumatized by Boris Johnson's Brexiteers, 373 of the 608 or 61 percent of MPs for whom data was available had been pro-Remain in 2016.[23]

The reason is not that British voters were schizophrenic or muddled. More likely, it reflected the reality that when the MPs bundled their constituents' preference for autonomy from Europe with other things they knew are important to those constituents—employment security, access to European goods and services at reasonable prices, and economic growth—they calculated that on balance remaining in the EU is better for their constituents. Considering Brexit in isolation from these other issues is as artificial as offering California voters a tax cut—as was done with Proposition 13 that limited property taxes to 1 percent of assessed value and was adopted by an almost two-thirds majority in 1978—without reference to the downstream effects on the quality of schools, the viability of local government services, and other undiscussed costs.

Some will object that it is not literally the same electorate that votes on ballot propositions and referendums as those who turn out in elections to legislatures. This is often true. Antitax activists were more heavily represented in the yes vote for Proposition 13 and pro-Brexit voters turned out at disproportionately high levels in the 2016 referendum. So it is not surprising that at the same time as the Brexit referendum passed, polling indicated that the median British voter favored the UK's remaining in the European Union.[24] In effect, referendum voters are like members of a single-issue party who are empowered to impose externalities on the rest of the population. By unbundling issues, they create the illusion of greater voter control, but the effect of allowing serial single-issue votes undermines the possibility of programmatic policy.[25] It's like letting a child eat as much candy as he wants without thinking about the stomachache that is coming later or the complaining about it that others will have to put up with.

Single-issue activists invariably turn out in higher numbers for pet causes. As the Proposition 13 example underscores, they might also be better-resourced than their opponents. Proposition 13 was, after all, the start of the antitax crusade whose members were determined to "starve the beast"—cut the size of government by every possible means until it was small enough to be drowned in the bathtub, as Grover Norquist would subsequently put it. Norquist founded Americans for Tax Reform, the group that extracted pledges from Republican candidates for national office never to vote to raise taxes lest they face a primary challenge or the sorts of attacks that Newt Gingrich unleashed on George H. W. Bush for violating his 1988 "read my lips: no new taxes" pledge three years after he made it.[26] And of course, starve the beast does not work anyway: faced with the political costs of cutting programs like Social Security and Medicare that their constituents want and need, Republicans, like Democrats, balk—borrowing the money instead.

Brexit also illustrated the leverage of activists in party governance. Tory MPs, most of whom had opposed leaving Europe, were ill-positioned to stop Brexit after the referendum because the activists on the fringe of the party, who were overwhelmingly pro-Brexit, were disproportionately represented among party members who participate in candidate selection. They could and did threaten to "deselect" MPs who tried to stop Brexit.[27] No doubt this partly explains why, of the 129 Tories who had been pro-Remain in 2016 and were reelected in December 2019, all but 5 had reversed themselves.[28] A comparable dynamic played out in the Tory leadership election following Theresa May's resignation in June 2019. The party's 160,000 members who make the final selection were well to the right of the median Tory voter and strongly pro-Brexit, making it all but inevitable that only a staunch Brexiteer could win.[29]

Brexit also underscores a different kind of incoherence that single-issue unbundling can produce. A large part of the reason that in 2019 no majority in Parliament would vote either for the leave proposal that Theresa May renegotiated with the Europeans or for any of the proposed alternatives to it was that there was no agreement on what those who wanted to leave Europe favored.[30] Hard-core Tory Brexiteers imagined a future in which, unshackled from stifling bureaucratic tentacles emanating from Brussels, Britain would reinvent itself as a hard-charging bastion of capitalism, a kind of Singapore on the Thames. On the left of the Labour Party, by contrast, the aspiration was for more robust state planning and social spending than can be achieved within the EU; a latter-day version of Socialism in One Country. It is scarcely surprising that MPs accountable to such divergent interests—not to mention the plethora of conflicting positions on the customs union, free movement of peoples, and the Irish backstop—could agree neither on Brexit nor on any alternative leave arrangement, and that there was also a blocking coalition against calling a second referendum.

The Brexit referendum obscured these realities because voters did not have to confront what the alternative to remaining in Europe would be. Had they done so—had they in effect been forced to bundle their preference of staying or leaving with their other policy preferences—voters would likely have wound up closer to their MPs and elected to remain in the EU. Their dissatisfactions over Europe would have been handled like they had been in the past—as part and parcel of electoral competition. When Margaret Thatcher, who had campaigned in 1983 on a manifesto that had recognized the EU as "by far our most important export market" from which withdrawal "would be a catastrophe for this country," she nonetheless called for a renegotiation that would reduce Britain's contribution to the EU budget and "shift the Community's spending priorities away from agriculture and towards industrial, regional and other policies which help Britain more."[31] She did this the following year, negotiating an annual UK rebate as compensation for the common agricultural and fisheries policies that worked to Britain's disadvantage.[32] This did not give Eurosceptics everything they wanted, but it dealt with enough of their grievances to be compatible with Conservative victories in the next two general elections. In a like spirit, in 1986 Thatcher secured qualified majority voting instead of unanimity rule on tariffs and other barriers to trade in negotiations over the Single European Act. This curtailed the veto power of countries like France, Germany, and Italy that had locked in advantages for themselves before the UK joined.[33]

The one exception to this approach before 2016 had been the referendum called by Harold Wilson in 1975, the first national referendum in British history, following Edward Heath's taking the UK into the EU two years earlier. At that time, the Tories were predominantly pro-European whereas Labour was conflicted because the unions expected membership to diminish their power and limit the statist agenda favored by Labour left-wingers like Michael Foot and

Tony Benn. Seeking to avoid conflict between them and Labour moderates like Roy Jenkins, Denis Healey, and Shirley Williams, Wilson opted for a referendum to take the issue off the table. The result, a two-to-one victory for Britain to remain in the EU, led Wilson to crow that "it was a matter of some satisfaction that an issue which threatened several times over thirteen years to tear the Labour movement apart had been resolved fairly and finally . . . all that had divided us in that great controversy was put behind us."[34]

But Wilson was wrong. Five years later, left-wingers like Benn disavowed their earlier acceptance of the referendum result and began pushing for Labour to commit to taking Britain out of the EU without another referendum—one of the main issues that triggered the departure of leading Labour moderates to start a new social democratic party that would subsequently ally and then merge with the Liberals to form the Liberal Democrats.[35] The better medium-term course for Labour would have been to hammer out a compromise position on Europe, perhaps by pressing for the EU to accede to the Council of Europe's Social Charter.[36] This would have taken the battle to the Tories in what was then the mainstream of British political opinion. Instead, Foot led Labour to a catastrophic defeat in the 1983 general election (the Tories won a 188-seat majority) on a hard-left manifesto subsequently immortalized by Labour MP Gerald Kaufman as "the longest suicide note in history," a record that would stand for thirty-six years—until Jeremy Corbyn's even longer and more radical program produced an even more devasting Labour wipeout.[37]

Bogdanor defends Britain's 1975 referendum on the grounds that at the time all three major parties favored remaining in the EU, leaving voters who wanted to leave with no way to advance their cause through the electoral process.[38] Yet Bogdanor never asks the obvious question: why did all three parliamentary parties favor remaining in the EU? The reason should by now be plain. When bundling continued EU membership with the other issues that mattered to their constituents, most MPs and party leaders concluded that leaving would not be part of a viable electoral strategy to retain voter support over time. Referendums empower intense single-issue activists to impose their preferences on the rest of society without confronting the costs. People who say that referendums can hold legislative bodies accountable forget to ask the question: accountable to whom?

Representation should be geared to maximizing the chances that public debate will center on the policies that parties, if elected, will implement as governments. As I argue in chapter 6, this is why SMP beats PR, and why strong, centralized parties are better than weak, decentralized ones. Supporting a party in a multiparty system can help voters feel better represented because their representatives' views are likely closer to their ideals than would be the case in a two-party system. But this is an illusion. What really matters is the policies that governments will implement. That cannot be known until after the coalition is formed, postelection. Coalition governments decrease accountability, since different coalition members can blame one another for unpopular policies.[39] Americans got a taste of this when unusual conditions produced a cross-party coalition to enact the Budget Sequestration Act in August 2011, putting in place $1.1 trillion of automatic spending cuts over eight years split evenly between defense and domestic programs, unless Congress passed an alternative by January 2013. The sword-of-Damocles proposal was widely said to be sufficiently draconian that the representatives would be forced to find a compromise. In the event, they did not and the sword fell, with each side blaming the other for intransigence. Perhaps it was a cynical way for both parties to achieve cuts without being savaged by their electoral bases. Whether due to blundering or collusive cynicism, the result was that everyone had an alibi and no one was undeniably responsible for the outcome. Coalition governments live perpetually on such ambiguous terrain, undermining accountability for what governments actually do.

Competition enhances political accountability, but some kinds of competition are better than others. Competition between representatives of two parties, one of which will become the government, enhances accountability, as we have seen, because they run on the platform they will be judged on as governments. Moreover, the need to sustain broad bases of voter support gives them strong incentives to advocate policies that will be good for the country as a whole, or at least for large swaths of the population. Smaller parties represent more narrowly drawn interests: business, organized labor, and ethnic and religious groups. This loads the dice in favor of clientelism, because politicians know that they will be held accountable for how effectively they advocate or bargain for their group's interest in a governing coalition. It is better for parties to compete over what is best for the country as a whole than to bargain over the rents they can extract for their clients. This contrast can be overdrawn, to be sure, because large catchall parties consist of different interests among whom implicit bargains must be struck to keep them in the party. But that bargaining is constrained by the need to propound and defend platforms that can win support from other groups as well; otherwise they cannot hope to become the government.

The sequester episode underscores the fact that the weakness of U.S. political parties is only partly due to republican institutional arrangements. Another source of party weakness is decentralized competition, an artifact of the wrongheaded idea that local selection of candidates somehow makes the process more democratic. In reality, because of their comparatively high rates of participation, activists, whose beliefs and preferences tend to be both more extreme and more intensely held than the median voter in their constituencies, dominate primaries and caucuses. This enables them to force representatives to pursue agendas that the median voter in their district abjures, or to serve the median voter only with the kind of subterfuge that might have been at work behind the Budget Sequestration Act.

Some will say that making the system responsive to voters with intense preferences is a good thing. There is, indeed, a strand of democratic theory dating back to James Buchanan and Gordon Tullock's *Calculus of Consent* in 1962 whose proponents defend vote trading and vote buying on the utilitarian ground that it improves the overall social utility.[40] But democracy's purpose is to manage power relations, not to maximize social utility. The contrary view would suggest that it was right for the U.S. government to abandon Reconstruction when Southern whites opposed it with greater intensity than most voters favored it, and that it was right for the intense preferences of neoconservatives who wanted the United States to invade Iraq in 2003 to override those of more numerous but less fervent skeptics.[41] This is to say nothing of the fact that in politics, preferences are always expressed subject to budget constraints. The intense antiregulation preferences of the multibillionaires Charles and David Koch are massively amplified because their budget constraints differ vastly from those of the typical voter.[42] In short, there are good reasons for the rules of democratic decision making to reflect how many people want something, rather than how intensely they want it.

III. Conclusion

People have theorized about democracy for millennia, yet it is only in the past few decades that the idea has gained currency that democracy depends on, or at any rate can be substantially enhanced by, deliberation. I have sought to show here that this is a dubious proposition. It is hard, if not impossible, to create institutions that will foster deliberation in politics, and institutions designed to do so are all too easily hijacked for other purposes. But deliberation is in any case the wrong goal. Competition is the lifeblood of democratic politics, and not just because it is the mechanism by which governments that lose elections give up power. Institutions that foster competition also structure politics around argument, which Mill was right to identify as vital to the advancement of knowledge and good public policy.

But not any competition. The contestation over governing ideas that Mill prized is best served when two large parties are constrained to compete over potential governing programs. It is compromised by multiparty competition which encourages clientelism as we have seen. And it is damaged even more by competition within parties, which empowers people with local agendas and intense preferences who participate disproportionately in primaries and caucuses. This can render parties vulnerable to the ideological capture of candidates by well-funded groups, as has happened with the Tea Party in Southern and Midwestern Republican primaries since 2009. But it is a more general problem associated with local control of selection processes, in which candidates find themselves compelled to compete by promising to secure local goods. Once elected, they face powerful incentives to engage in pork barrel politics with other similarly situated politicians, protecting public funding for sinecures and bridges to nowhere in their districts. This problem is worse in districts—the vast majority in the United States—that have been gerrymandered to be safe seats, so that the primary is the only meaningful election. It is better for party leaders to seek candidates who can both win in their districts and support a program that can win nationally. The leaders, in turn, are held accountable by the back benchers who remove them when they fail to deliver winning platforms. In sum, two large, centrally controlled parties are most likely to foster the programmatic competition that is best for democratic politics. By contrast, multiparty competition encourages wholesale clientelism and intraparty competition encourages retail clientelism.

Deliberation can be rendered harmless and perhaps, occasionally, beneficial for democratic politics by relegating it to a purely consultative role; but in that case, it is hard to see what the hype surrounding deliberation amounts to. Regardless, the most pressing political challenges in the United States do not result from lack of deliberation. Rather, they stem from the increasing subversion of democracy by powerful private interests since the Supreme Court's disastrous equation of money with speech in *Buckley v. Valeo* almost five decades ago, and the subsequent playing out of that logic in *Citizens United* and subsequent decisions.[43] As politicians have become increasingly dependent on countless millions of dollars to gain and retain political office, those with the resources they need undermine the process by manufacturing—and then manning—huge barriers to entry, by contributing to both political parties in ways that stifle competition, by capturing regulators and whole regulatory agencies, by giving multi-millionaires and billionaires the preposterous advantage of running self-funded campaigns, and by doing other end-runs around democratic politics. Unless and until that challenge can be addressed, debating what deliberation can add to politics is little more than a waste of time.

6

On Political Parties

Political parties are unpopular across the democratic world. Denounced as out of touch with voters, polarized sources of gridlock, gripped by money and special interests, or helpless in the face of populist demagogues, parties are often declared incapable of governing in the public interest. The widespread ennui is reflected in low turnout in many elections, fragmenting parties, and growing support for antisystem causes and candidates. Calls for change are endemic and sometimes acted on, as when legislative paralysis prompts efforts to strengthen executive power. But strengthening presidential authority also means weakening parties in the legislature. Is that a good thing? Such questions prompt more basic ones: what are political parties, and what role should they play in democratic politics? These are my subjects here.

Calling for accounts of what parties are and should be is easier than delivering them. Even the briefest survey reveals great variety. Some parties are highly centralized and tightly controlled from above. Others are decentralized, with vital decisions reserved for annual conventions and mass memberships. Unions, business groups, funders, and other entities play different roles—sometimes formal, sometimes informal. If there is any sustainable generalization, it is that party governance is endemically contested with leaders, officials, back benchers, would-be candidates, and members perpetually second-guessing one another and vying for influence. No status quo is long immune from challenge.

Debates about what parties should be are often shaped by concerns about the gulf between voters and the politicians. Direct participation might have been viable in small city-states and principalities, but it is not scalable to populations in the tens and hundreds of millions, where coordination problems and other challenges limit widespread participation in public decision making. In the modern democratic world this makes representative government all but inevitable. People authorize politicians to act in their stead, and the challenges involve preventing politicians from abusing the power voters give them. Much writing about electoral politics, what is said to be wrong with it, and what would address the inadequacies is viewed—explicitly or implicitly—through this principal-agent lens.[1]

Perhaps voters must cede authority to representatives, but why must they be organized into parties? The imperative to assemble sustainable coalitions when majorities, and sometimes supermajorities, are needed to enact or block legislation makes parties indispensable. Just as voters need representatives in order to be efficacious, representatives need parties for the same reason. But parties are both a help and a hindrance to voters. They help by providing them with information about politicians and by increasing the likelihood that the politicians they elect will be effective in the legislature. But parties hinder by creating additional principal-agent relationships inside legislative parties and between voters and parties. Legislators might collude with one another to the detriment of voters. When back benchers delegate authority to party leaders to enhance their effectiveness, this can also work to the detriment of voters when the leaders develop agendas that voters—and sometimes even their representatives—oppose. These challenges are as old as the American republic. In 1824, when none of four contending candidates won an Electoral College majority, Congress picked John Quincy Adams over Andrew Jackson despite the latter having the most popular and Electoral College votes.

Jackson mobilized the resulting voter anger to create the new Democratic Party that he led to victory four years later, spawning America's two-party system.[2]

Dysjunctions between voters and party leaders are seldom that dramatic, but voters often denounce parties as run by unaccountable elites motivated by their own agendas. Frequent calls for greater grassroots control of decisions, platforms, leadership, and candidate selection all reflect this concern. Likewise with efforts to enhance direct citizen participation via referendums, ballot initiatives, deliberative polls, and new forms of internet democracy. The goal is either to enhance voters' control over politicians or to liberate voters from the principal-agent relationship, entirely enabling them to reclaim the capacity act for themselves. In short, parties might help voters monitor representatives, but who monitors the monitors? Much recent dissatisfaction with parties emanates from the difficulties of doing that effectively.

Here I argue for a different view of the relations among voters, representatives, and parties, one that rejects principal-agent thinking entirely. Rather than start by asking how much authority, and under what conditions, voters should delegate, my point of departure is to attend first to the nature of power relations and then ask how best to manage them both democratically and in the public interest. Taking power relations rather than delegation as the point of departure offers two advantages. It is, first, more accurate historically in that no democracy was ever created through acts of delegation envisaged in the principal-agent story. Rather, power was first centralized in embryonic national states.[3] Demands for democracy came later, as those subjected to that newly centralized power pushed back. Some might invoke the United States as an exception, but that ignores the imposition of a new order on propertyless white men, women, slaves, and African and Native Americans—all of whom would later demand democratic rights. Political parties were vital to the vindication of those demands.

My alternative point of departure is also more appealing analytically because it conditions arguments about governance on the nature of power relations, and in particular on recognizing that power is a natural monopoly. This matters not only by shaping the possibilities for managing power relations in the public interest, but also for the justification of majority rule that lies at the heart of democracy's appeal. This connection to democracy is ironic because it was the seventeenth-century social contract theorists who first discerned the link between the natural monopoly character of power and majority rule, yet they are frequently seen as classic proponents of principal-agent views of politics with little, if anything, to say that is relevant to democratic theory. But we will see that this view misses their insights. Hobbes held that majority does and should prevail when a new state is founded by representatives, as it does when the government is a representative assembly. Locke went further, grounding all political legitimacy in majority rule. Yet neither posited principal-agent relations between the people and their rulers.

Many who agree that parties should govern democratically in the public interest nonetheless disagree about how to structure politics to produce that result. On one predominant view good government results when contending parties are forced to compromise, either by negotiating coalitions in multiparty systems or by legislating across the aisle in two-party systems which, like the American one, have been designed to make unilateral government by one party difficult. Here, too, I defend a minority view: that good democratic government is fostered by competition between large parties with strong incentives to run on programs that will best serve most voters, implement those programs as governments, and then be held to account at the next election. Rather than act as voters' delegates or respond to their preferences, governments try to govern in their interests—hoping to be rewarded accordingly.

I begin by detaching the idea of majority rule that is essential to democratic politics from all principal-agent thinking. But unlike critics of principal-agent views who invoke deliberation and judgment, compromise, or theories of public reason and public justification to constrain parties to govern in the public interest, my focus is on the dynamics of power relations and electoral competition.[4] Drawing on undernoticed logic first explored by Hobbes and Locke, I argue that collective action is ubiquitous to human interaction and that power is a natural monopoly whose exercise is best understood as authorized by majority rule. In section II, I contend that interest-based models of retrospective voting capture the relations between politicians and voters better than preference-based models that trade on principal-agent thinking, however implicitly. I also take up the role of parties in this process, arguing that the American founders were right to treat them as repositories of partisan interests, but wrong to see them merely as such—or at least not necessarily so. The challenge, I contend, is to structure political competition so that partisan parties will govern in the public interest as much as possible.

How best to do this is taken up in the rest of the chapter. In section III I make the case that two-party competition will more likely achieve this than multiparty competition and in section IV that the partisan character of parties limits the Tweedledee-Tweedledum problem—whereby two parties aiming at the median voter will offer the same policies—in healthy ways. I buttress this case in section V by reference to strengths and limitations of Joseph Schumpeter's model of political competition. His great contribution was to portray voters as consumers of policies rather than principals who delegate authority to politicians. But his analogy between parties and firms is problematic because parties cannot be constrained to govern in the public interest if they are as answerable to their members in the way that firms are answerable to their shareholders.

If parties should not be governed by their members, the question arises: Who should govern them? This question is taken up in section VI. There I argue that parties are most likely to engage in programmatic competition geared to the public interest if leaders have great authority in the short term, but over time back benchers choose front benchers who choose back benchers who choose front benchers—sustaining party identities into the future. The system rests on a Ulysses-and-the-sirens logic by which representatives allow leaders to discipline them so as to forgo temptations that undermine programmatic competition. This dynamic model of governance is the best bet for getting parties to govern in voters' interests, fulfilling democracy's promise.

I. Reject Principal-Agent Thinking Root and Branch

Democracy is often portrayed, as Lincoln famously did at Gettysburg, as government not only of and for the people, but also by them. Principal-agent views seem normatively appealing because they embody this idea that democracy is at bottom about the people ruling themselves. The people are the principals, and they delegate authority to politicians as their agents. But how can this work for millions of people who hold different values, interests, and agendas?

The early social contract theorists can help here. Even though they had little to say about democracy, they thought about representative institutions and majority rule by reference to a very different logic than that of delegation. They rejected principal-agent thinking because "the people" cannot literally rule themselves, but they nonetheless saw majority rule as foundational to representative government. Hobbes and Locke both regarded the people as authors of the commonwealth, but neither conceived of the sovereign as an agent whose job was somehow to track, represent, or embody the people's preferences. Consent of the people was the font of political legitimacy, but the relevant agreement was not between them and the government. Rather, it was among the people—"every one with every one" as Hobbes said—to obey the government so long as it governs in their interests.[5] Locke was unequivocal in declaring compliance to be universally binding unless one is willing to risk outright revolution, hoping that others agree. Without endorsing a right to resist, Hobbes also conditioned compliance on the government's doing what he took to be its job: protecting them. That is why he counseled Charles II's Royalist supporters to swear allegiance to Parliament during the Engagement Controversy once Charles—who had fled to Europe—could no longer safeguard them or their property.[6]

Both theorists saw that majority rule offers a way of reconciling the tension between the monopoly character of power and the irreducible diversity of interests and opinions. Having lived through a civil war, they understood that unless power is exercised as a monopoly, destabilizing conflict is a permanent possibility. But if people's desires and interests differ, then any decision will frustrate some of them. The majority will likely prevail as an empirical matter because they will be more powerful, but it also makes normative sense. As Locke put it, "by barely agreeing to unite into one political society," each person "puts himself under an obligation, to every one of that society, to submit to the determination of the majority."[7] The reason? In diverse societies, someone must prevail. Even if everyone could be consulted, "the contrariety of interests which unavoidably happen in all collections of men" would render "the mighty Leviathan of a shorter duration, than the feeblest creatures, and not let it outlast the day it was born in." That is why actual assemblies typically deploy majority rule. "The act of the majority passes for the act of the whole, and of course determines, as having, by the law of nature and reason, the power of the whole." Hobbes also insisted that if people inaugurate a commonwealth by selecting representatives, they are bound by "the major part." He elaborates: "Because the major part hath by consenting voices declared a Sovereign, he that dissented must now consent with the rest . . . or else justly be destroyed by the rest." Like Locke, he rejected unanimity rule as impractical because it turns everyone into a veto player. "If the Representative consist of many men, the voice of the greater number, must be considered the voice of them all."[8]

Contemporary writers in this tradition sometimes pay lip service to power's monopoly character, but they often misconstrue its implications for political accountability. Rather than reason from the nature of power to arguments about how best to render its exercise legitimate, their point of departure is the—sometimes tacit—assumption that unauthorized collective decisions are illegitimate. Among its other defects, this cedes the conceptual high ground to democracy's libertarian critics who—writing in Arrow's wake—are often quick to assert that collective decisions should be kept to a minimum because "the people" cannot authorize them.[9] For Nozick this limits legitimate collective action to what is needed to maintain the power monopoly: "the night watchman state of classical liberal theory."[10] For everything else, anyone may veto collective action. Buchanan and Tullock are less draconian, permitting departures from unanimity rule only when the costs to each person of authorizing those departures exceed those of living with adverse outcomes.[11] Here we see the principal-agent model doing its work: unauthorized collective actions are not legitimate. Because there is no coherent way for "the people" to consent to them, the authorizing authority reverts to each individual—turning her into a veto player. Whereas for Hobbes and Locke the monopoly character of power implies that the people authorize the majority, proponents of principal-agent views struggle to authorize anything because "the people" are not—and never can be—univocal about what they want.

It is better to think about accountability without going down the principal-agent path. After all, the system of rights that libertarians prefer—to private property and state enforcement of contracts—is itself a collective-action regime that imposes costs on those who prefer an alternative.[12] Holding changes to the status quo hostage to unanimity rule entrenches it.[13] The earlier theorists would have been untroubled by the libertarian critique, because their allegiance to majority rule had nothing to do with amalgamating preferences into general wills or social welfare functions. It was rooted instead in managing the power monopoly in ways that prevent people from hamstringing governments. "It is the unity of the Representer, not the Unity of the Represented," as Hobbes said, that transforms a multitude into a governable people. "Because the Multitude naturally is not One, but Many; they cannot be understood for one; but many Authors, of every thing their Representative faith, or doth in their name."[14] Hobbes was an absolutist only in holding that the state's monopoly on power must be supreme; otherwise, we get civil war. But a majority can be sufficient to authorize that monopoly and, if the government is a representative assembly, then it will operate by majority rule as an "absolute democracy."[15] Locke withholds absolute power from all governments, natural rights and the right to resist being indefeasible. But he is unequivocal that legislative majorities can enact laws, including laws imposing taxes, because everyone who enjoys the state's protection "should pay out of his estate his proportion for the maintenance of it."[16]

II. Retrospective Voting and Partisan Parties

Theories of retrospective voting can help incorporate these early modern insights into democratic theory. As Mansbridge notes, these theories abjure principal agent thinking entirely. Rather than seeing governments as trustees or bearers of mandates to implement voters' preferences, they portray them as implementing policies that they believe will serve the interests of most voters, so that majorities will supply ex post ratification by reelecting them.[17] As Page puts it, the retrospective view "orients government responsiveness toward fundamental needs and values of the people rather than ephemeral or weakly held policy preferences."[18] Parties in government do not ignore voter preferences; they govern in anticipation of those preferences. If they govern well and there are good outcomes for most people, they can anticipate satisfied voters.[19] If not, not. They are "Schumpeterian entrepreneurs, motivated to try to attract the votes of future customers" and even mobilize them.[20]

The Schumpeterian view that Mansbridge invokes is often called minimalist and in some ways it is, but it also rests on a useful view of parties as constrained to govern in the public interest.[21] This differentiates it from the American founders' conception of parties as nothing more than institutionalized factions, calling to mind instead the account sketched by Edmund Burke. Like Washington and Madison, Burke held that parties embody specific points of view, but he did not embrace their clientelist contention that they invariably pursue sectional interests to the detriment of others. For Burke a party is "a body of men united, for promoting by their joint endeavors the national interest, upon some particular principle in which they are all agreed."[22] This "particular principle" embodies a partisan point of view, but adherents argue that it will promote the public interest better than the alternatives. The challenge is to structure political competition in ways that increase the likelihood that this will be true.

But what is the public interest? At least since Schumpeter's attack on Rousseau's discussion of the general will and the common good, it has been standard to shift the burden of persuasion to proponents.[23] Theorists sometimes start from the economist's conception of public goods, and some, such as Nozick and Riker, eschew more expansive conceptions.[24] But candidates and parties routinely promise many rivalrous and excludable goods: utilities, education, unemployment insurance, medical and retirement benefits, funds for research and the performing arts, and more. And even when strictly defined public goods are at stake, parties compete over how to allocate the externalities and other costs—as recent debates about infrastructure and environmental protection underscore. When a policy would manifestly deliver benefits or harms to particular groups, as with adopting or abolishing environmental regulations, proponents invariably claim to be doing this in the public interest. They sense that voters discern a difference between shelling out clientelist payouts and governing for the country as a whole, and that they expect politicians to do the latter.

III. Partisan Competition and the Public Interest

I argued in chapter 5 that a major defect of referendums and other decentralized decision-making devices is that they undermine the vital issue-bundling function that parties perform. But parties are by definition partisan, which raises the question: what makes it more rather than less likely that they will govern in the public interest? Several commentators have recently taken up this question, arguing for various constraints on partisanship as a regulative ideal.[25] I agree with these authors that parties should be induced to govern as much as possible in the public interest, but my focus is on the electoral incentives that will most likely have that effect. Here America's founders stumbled onto part of the answer by opting for single-member districts with plurality rule that, under the conditions that prevail in the United States, usually produces two large parties.[26] Two-party systems are distinctive in generating winner-take-all, and therefore loser-lose-all, contests. This incentivizes parties to embrace platforms that will appeal to as many voters as possible, because that last vote your party fails to win might be the difference between winning and losing everything.[27] This need not be true in multiparty systems, where no party expects to form a government on its own. If a party's prospects for expanding its electoral appeal are limited to a particular interest or identity group, satisfying an intensely motivated base will often trump other considerations. This can be an effective strategy if a small party is needed to form a government, as is often the case with Israel's religious parties.

Some will wonder whether there is less to this distinction than meets the eye. The large catchall parties in two-party systems are themselves coalitions that would constitute distinct parties in multiparty systems.[28] In one case the coalition forms before the election and in the other after the election, but perhaps it doesn't much matter. After all, the alternation between left-of-center social democratic policies and right-of-center promarket policies since World War II has not obviously been that different in a multiparty system like Germany's when compared with the United Kingdom's two-party system. They have comparable welfare states, universal health insurance, and environmental regulation. Indeed, if there is a difference, some scholarship suggests that multiparty systems are more responsive to median voters, and therefore more redistributive, than two-party systems.[29]

There are good reasons to suspect, however, that the greater relative responsiveness of PR (proportional representation) systems to median voters was an artifact of features of their economies that no longer hold: large industrial workforces, comprising the bulk of the working population, whose interests were well represented by large left-of-center social democratic parties. The decline in industrial jobs and unionized workforces, accompanied by the splintering of traditional left parties, has led to a new reality in which diminished social democratic parties are protecting a shrinking industrial workforce less effectively, and other workers even less well—if at all. At the same time, splintering among right-of-center parties has produced ethnic and anti-immigrant parties with strong incentives to cater to narrow interests at the expense of most voters.[30]

The winner-take-all dynamic in two-party competition creates stronger incentives for governments to pursue programmatic policies that will appeal to as broad as possible a swath of voters, more so than do the postelection dynamics in multiparty systems. One reason is that those who create the big-tent parties in two-party systems have an interest in internalizing the costs of the deals that they make to sustain the party, whereas in multiparty systems the incentive is to externalize those costs when forming a coalition. If a probusiness party that values industrial peace joins with a prolabor party that values protecting workers' wages, the incentive might be to externalize the costs on the general public in the form of higher prices or on the long-term unemployed in the form of fewer jobs.[31] Likewise, if an agrarian party joins a coalition, the deal will likely include agricultural subsidies for which taxpayers must pay, and higher food prices for consumers.

In two-party systems, by contrast, angering taxpayers, workers, or consumers might be the difference between victory and defeat. Both parties therefore face incentives to avoid alienating voters any more than necessary. That concern must be at the backs of their minds when party strategists negotiate compromises among traditional supporters and interest groups, lest the alienated voters turn out to be decisive in the election. Parties in two-party systems will seek to internalize the costs of the deals they must do as much as possible to minimize that risk, reducing incentives to dole out clientelist benefits to those in the coalition at the cost of those who are not.

Some will claim that this exaggerates the difference, because parties in multiparty systems must worry about alienating potential future supporters. But factoring in future considerations accentuates rather than mitigates the difference. In two-party systems, both parties expect to be campaigning as the same parties into the indefinite future. They build and expect to preserve their identities as parties, anticipating that activists and voters will identify with and support them going forward.[32] Parties in two-party systems do sometimes disintegrate, as happened with the American Whigs during the 1850s and Britain's Liberals early in the twentieth century. This is neither typical nor expected, however. Marriages sometimes end in divorce, but people do not generally marry expecting to divorce. Likewise, parties in two-party systems expect to stay together and try to plan for it. They are composed of what Bawn and Rosenbluth describe as "long coalitions," committed to sustaining their policy brands over time, as distinct from the "short coalitions" that we see in multiparty systems—where uncertainty about future partners makes this harder.[33] After being part of four consecutive grand coalitions, in 2021 Germany's SPD formed a government with the Greens and the libertarian Free Democrats. Multiparty governments are more like hookups than marriages. Gratifying as they might be in the present, all bets are off for the future.

This difference becomes more pronounced as the number of parties grows, as has been happening in recent decades.[34] The greater the number of parties, the less predictable future alliances will be. They might be among ideologically adjacent parties, as is often true in Israel. But they might be among parties from multiple parts of the ideological spectrum, as happened there and in Germany in 2021, or coalitions of even stranger bedfellows—as in Greece in 2015 when the radical left-wing SYRIZA allied to form a government with the far-right ANEL.[35] Parties in such coalitions will not likely identify with others, in what Nancy Rosenblum describes as a common project of "regulated rivalry" geared to governing in the public interest.[36]

An analogy from industrial arbitration can illuminate the different incentives at stake here. When management and unions cannot agree, sometimes they turn decisions over to arbitrators who listen to both sides, do independent fact-finding, and then determine a binding outcome. Expecting the eventual outcome to be a compromise, both sides have incentives to exaggerate their demands. But a different kind of "last-best-offer" arbitration changes the incentives: instead of designing a compromise, the arbitrator must pick one final offer. This dispels incentives to take extreme positions, lest they drive the arbitrator to opt for the other side. Unsurprisingly, last-best-offer arbitration produces less tactical posturing and more realistic offers.[37]

Two-party competition is analogous to last-best-offer arbitration. Everyone knows that the party most voters pick will likely be the government. Accordingly, their incentive is to run on platforms that aim at the political middle. In multiparty systems, by contrast, where everyone knows that the election will be followed by negotiations, the ex-ante incentive is to create a surplus that can be bargained away.[38] This incentive becomes more powerful with identity-based or other single-issue parties that have few, if any, prospects for expanding their electoral support, so that the election is mainly about turning out core supporters. For them, every election is like a base election in the United States, or, put differently, most supporters are more like primary voters in the diverse catchall parties in two-party systems.[39]

A final difference between two-party and multiparty systems concerns accountability. Accountability depends on parties that take clear positions in campaigns and then "muster the cohesion to enact those plans" as governments, giving voters "a clear and easy way to express or withhold their approval at the next election."[40] In two-party systems, the "loyal" opposition is a government-in-waiting; it criticizes the government and defends its alternative. In multiparty systems, by contrast, there is less accountability and no coherent alternative.

There is less accountability because parties can deflect blame for failures to others in the coalition, or to compromises forced on them during coalition negotiations. There is no coherent alternative because no one knows who they will be negotiating with after the next election.[41] Multiparty systems are more representative at the electoral stage, but this comes at the price of accountable government.

IV. Tweedledee and Tweedledum

Some worry that parties with strong incentives to aim at the electoral middle will offer the same policies, giving voters little meaningful choice.[42] That might be true in theory, but in fact partisan conceptions of the public interest operate differently in two-party systems. On some issues, both parties do offer substantially similar policies. The National Health Service in the UK, enacted by Clement Attlee's postwar Labour government in 1946 and put into operation two years later, remains exceedingly popular with UK voters—topping the popularity of all British institutions seven decades later.[43] There are partisan disagreements over funding and coverage at the margins, but the institution is bulletproof politically. Even during the heyday of privatization under Thatcher, there was no question of abolishing the NHS.

But not everything is like that. British railways were nationalized in 1948, reprivatized in 1982, and might be renationalized by a future Labour government. Likewise, in the United States, Social Security, enacted as part of the New Deal in 1935, and Medicare, part of the Great Society in 1965, are so popular that neither party can scrap them, but the parties diverge sharply on other matters. Democrats created strong protections for trade unions in the Wagner Act of 1935 that were sharply curtailed by Republicans twelve years later in the Taft-Hartley Act, adopted over President Truman's veto. Democrats created the Consumer Financial Protection Bureau as part of the

ON POLITICAL PARTIES

Partisan Conceptions of the Public Interest

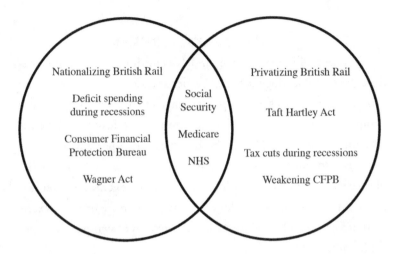

Dodd-Frank law in 2010, but Republicans subsequently eviscerated it. Left-of-center parties typically favor deficit spending during recessions, whereas right-of-center parties push tax cuts and fiscal discipline. Partisan conceptions of the public interest overlap where there is broad consensus, but they diverge on many issues.[44]

These differences are the stuff of electoral competition. They partly reflect politicians' beliefs about how the costs and benefits will affect their supporters, they partly reflect divergent ideological outlooks, and they partly reflect disagreement—and perhaps uncertainty—about which policies are in fact most effective. Programmatic competition is competition over these questions, in which both parties try to convince as many voters as possible that their approach has been best in the past and will continue to be best in the future. The cost of appealing to smaller groups of core supporters or sectional interests will likely be defeat, loading the dice against clientelism. But the parties will be Tweedledee and Tweedledum only when there is widespread agreement about what is best.

V. Schumpeter's Limitations

A version of the Tweedledee and Tweedledum objection is sometimes leveled at analogy between parties and firms, where it takes the form of objecting to the oligopolistic character of two-party political competition on the grounds that this promotes collusion.[45] This criticism misses the mark. Whereas both parties in two-party systems have incentives to run on platforms that can win as many voters as possible, we have seen that it is multiparty systems that generate incentives for coalition members to collude in ways that create negative externalities for others. The winner-take-all character of two-party competition militates against this.

There is, however, a different difficulty with Schumpeter's analogy. This does not have to do with likening voters to consumers, policies to goods and services, votes to profits, or political accountability to consumer sovereignty. These all enlighten up to a point, even if they grate on the sensibilities of participatory and deliberatively inclined democratic theorists. Rather, the difficulty is that there is no good political analogy for shareholders—no political equivalent of a residual claimant. This difference renders parties unusual, though not unique, organizational forms. Nonprofits like private American universities are illuminatingly similar. If Harvard sold all its assets and paid all its debts, it is unclear who would be entitled to what remained. This is why university governance is inherently contentious, with faculty, students, administrators, trustees, alumni, and others all vying for authority and often objecting to what they see as the excessive influence of others.[46] The governance of parties is contentious for the same reason.

Some will maintain that party members are the logical analog of a firm's shareholders, but that thinking—while superficially appealing—leads down an infelicitous path. To see what is at stake, consider the changes made in leadership election rules for Britain's Labour Party in 2015, based on a review led by Lord Collins. Previously, an "Electoral College" had given one-third weight to the Parliamentary Labour Party (PLP) plus Labour members of the European Parliament, one-third to individual party members, and one-third to trade unions and affiliated societies. This system had in 1981 replaced the long-standing arrangement whereby the members of the PLP selected their leader. The Collins reforms destroyed any meaningful role for the PLP in leadership selection. In the new system, eligibility to stand required support from only 15 percent Labour MPs (30 MPs in 2015), after which all members were eligible to vote. The 306 Labour MPs plus 20 Labour members of the European Parliament were a drop in the bucket of the 550,000 Labour Members who were eligible electors in a contest that Jeremy Corbyn won with 251,419 (59.5 percent) of the votes cast.[47]

Labour Party membership was open to anyone willing to pay the £3 fee. Unsurprisingly, membership is disproportionately attractive to activists who are well to the left, ideologically, of typical Labour voters and even further to the left of typical British voters. The result was that, notwithstanding efforts by Conservatives, Greens, and others to join solely for the purpose of influencing the outcome to Labour's disadvantage (members of other parties were eventually banned from participating), the PLP had a leader most of whose policies they could not support while retaining a realistic hope of reelection in their constituencies. Unsurprisingly, a year later, following mass resignations from the shadow cabinet, the PLP adopted a no-confidence resolution in Corbyn by 172–40, prompting another leadership contest. Labour's National Executive Committee raised the fee for voting eligibility to £25 in what turned out to be a vain attempt to limit the disproportionate influence of far-left activists, many of whom were middle class.[48] Corbyn was reelected by 62 percent, underscoring the reality that Labour had abandoned Britain's long tradition of strong, disciplined parties. In effect, as with the Tea Party's hostile takeover of the American Republicans via primaries and caucuses following Barack Obama's election in 2008, Labour was now controlled by activists on its ideological fringes. The extent of the damage was partly obscured in the 2017 general election because, even though it was Labour's third consecutive defeat, Theresa May blew a twenty-point lead and her parliamentary majority—taking the spotlight off Labour's inability to craft a winning program under Corbyn's leadership.[49] Any doubt about that was scotched eighteen months later when Corbyn led Labour to their worst defeat since 1935.[50]

VI. Party Strength and Party Purpose

Bizzarro et al. define strong parties as ". . . unified, centralized, stable, organizationally complex, and tied to long standing constituencies."[51] To this Simmons adds a requirement that representatives "outlive the political lives of their own coalescing members," so that they invest in policies that are good for the economy over time.[52] More simply put, strong parties operate as teams on which everyone is pursuing the same goal: to devise and implement strategies that can win and retain widespread voter support over time. Back benchers in strong parties delegate considerable authority, including the authority to discipline them, to leaders, but this is conditional on winning. As with coaches and quarterbacks, they do not last when they fail. They have enough rope to hang themselves. One symptom of the disorder of American parties is that leaders can survive without delivering victories, as with the House Republicans for decades before 1994 or when

ON POLITICAL PARTIES

Nancy Pelosi led Democrats to four successive defeats in the 2010s without being removed. Ineffective leaders displease back benchers, but the parties are so decentralized that coordinating to replace them is hard.[53] In April 2018, Republican Speaker Paul Ryan decided not to run for another term amid sagging popularity and intense conflict with his caucus that had dogged him since he had replaced the even more unpopular John Boehner.[54] Yet Ryan could not be dislodged, saddling the party with a lame duck leader for the seven-month runup to the 2018 midterms.[55]

Leaders should play major roles in selecting backbench candidates and in disciplining them to support a party's national program. The reason? Whereas candidates face powerful incentives to protect themselves in their districts, whether by delivering local private goods, or by catering to intense activists or well-funded groups that might otherwise primary them, national party leaders need back benchers who can both win in their districts and also support a winning platform. This gets harder as the distance between the median voter in the district and the party's median voter increases, and it will often involve hard judgment calls. But given the distribution of incentives, it is better for the national leadership to predominate in making those calls.[56] Think of it as Ulysses-and-the-sirens discipline. Back benchers submit to the leadership's discipline, but only in service of a cause that is in their longer-term interest.

Some will say that the candidates parties select and the platforms they pursue should be predominantly shaped—if not determined—by primary voters or party members, but that overlooks the problematic standing of these groups already discussed. Here it is worth recalling that, until the 1970s, presidential primaries in the United States were information-generating exercises through which candidates sought to demonstrate electoral viability. Presidential primaries did not achieve their almost sovereign authorizing status in a principal-agent relationship until the McGovern-Fraser Reforms restructured the Democratic Party in the early 1970s, creating a bottom-up model for selecting candidates and writing platforms that the Republicans would soon emulate. The changes were promoted as more democratic than proverbial smoke-filled rooms. In reality, they greatly weakened both parties in unintended ways, rendering them vulnerable to hostile takeovers of the sort Donald Trump staged in 2016.[57]

Congressional primaries have been around since the Progressive era, but the increased number of safe seats in recent decades has made them more consequential.[58] This weakens the authority of leaders over back benchers concerned about challenges in their districts. Hence the inability of House Republican leaders to craft a bill to repeal the Affordable Care Act that their members would support once they took control of the government in 2017, even though they had voted seventy times to repeal it when out of power.[59] This outcome also cautions us against interpreting increasingly polarized roll call votes in Congress as indicative of increased party strength or discipline. As Curry and Lee have documented, the great majority of legislation, including consequential legislation, requires bipartisan support in at least one chamber to become law, and this has not changed since the 1970s.[60] In principle, parties might be legislative cartels, as Cox and McCubbins contend.[61] In practice, they are too weak to govern that way in the United States Congress.

VII. Conclusion

The distinctive job of political parties is to facilitate competition over the state's legitimate monopoly of the use of coercive force. This kind of competition is best served, I have argued, by strongly disciplined parties that compete for voter support by offering programmatic policies that they expect will serve the interests of the widest possible swath of voters. Many will resist this view as insufficiently agent-centered, preferring to think of the voters as principals and the parties and politicians they elect as their agents. It is the apparent erosion, or outright collapse, of this principal-agent relationship that fuels perceptions that democratic politics is broken, prompting demands to unbundle platforms and assert greater voter control over parties and politicians. But the result is to diminish parties' capacity to govern effectively when in office—compounding voter alienation and prompting demands for self-defeating reforms that render parties vulnerable to populist takeovers.

Here I have sought to reject this principal-agent view. Schumpeter's market analogy is incomplete and partly misleading, but he was right that it is better to think of the relations between parties and voters as analogous to that between firms and consumers, rather than to firms and the interests of their shareholders. To the extent that they do the latter, they will deliver clientelist benefits to sectional interests, whether this turns out to be the wholesale clientelism that is extracted by single-issue parties in multiparty systems or the retail clientelism that operates in two-party systems when the parties are weak. If we want parties to cleave instead toward governing in the public interest, it is better to give them incentives to pursue their partisan conceptions in ways that will appeal to as many voters as possible over time.

Principal-agent views are superficially appealing because they speak to the idea that democracy is fundamentally about the people ruling themselves. But as Locke noted more than three centuries ago, the people can rule themselves only as a single collective entity if they are to rule themselves at all. Democratic theory does better when it starts by recognizing that power is a natural monopoly and then gets to work on how best to manage it both democratically and in the public interest, rather than insisting that the people should rule themselves without coming to grips with what that means in practice—or indeed whether it can mean anything at all.

This is a more plausible way to think about the relations between voters' interests and their preferences than the principal-agent view. After all, it's not as if in 2016 sixty-three million Americans were looking for a candidate who would promise to build a wall on the country's southern border. Rather, millions of working- and middle-class Americans were disaffected by the decades-long failure of both parties to address their stagnating economic fortunes, instead serving the interests and agendas of wealthy elites.[62] Trump saw an opportunity to mobilize their rage behind a populist agenda and acted accordingly.[63] That he promised to implement policies that would do little, if anything, for the people who elected him was beside the point. As even one of his greatest champions acknowledged, Trump's election was "a howl of rage, the end of decades of selfish and unwise decisions made by selfish and unwise leaders. Happy countries don't elect Donald Trump president. Desperate ones do. In retrospect, the lesson seemed obvious: Ignore voters for long enough and you get Donald Trump."[64] Politicians who ignore voters' interests must eventually confront their preferences. The result will seldom be pretty.

John Dewey once observed that although voters are the best equipped to know how well policies serve them, this does not make them the best designers of those policies. "The man who wears the shoe knows best that it pinches and where it pinches," he argued, but "the expert shoemaker is the best judge of how the trouble is to be remedied."[65] The analogy highlights the Luddite quality of much of the handwringing about voter ignorance. Voters know most about their interests, and especially when they are being ill-served, but they are not deficient for failing to know much about designing policies to vindicate those interests. The analogy also supplies ballast for resisting principal-agent views: politicians are no more agents of voters than cobblers are agents of walkers. And although Dewey himself had little to say about parties or electoral dynamics, his analogy underscores the importance of promoting systems in which designers of policies feel bound to learn as much as possible about what their supporters need, to address those needs better than their competitors, and to do it in ways that compromise their other interests, and the interests of other voters, as little as possible.

E. E. Schattschneider remarked long ago that the condition of political parties "is the best possible evidence of the nature of any regime."[66] Democratic regimes are healthier when parties aspire to govern in the public interest so as to win or retain power than when they become the ossified factions that the American founders rightly feared, or vehicles for those with intense preferences to indulge themselves while others bear the costs. There are no guarantees in politics, but strong parties, provided there are few of them, will more likely nurture that health better than the going alternatives. To paraphrase Churchill, they produce the worst kind of political competition except for the others that have been tried from time to time.[67]

PART THREE
Politics in Dark Times

7

Negative Liberty and the Cold War

(with Alicia Steinmetz)

The widespread euphoria that accompanied the end of the Cold War in many democracies has given way to alarming brands of xenophobic politics and a resurgence of authoritarian populism that calls to mind the 1930s. It might be true, as argued in the last three chapters, that democratic theorists have failed to provide adequate tools to combat these developments, but maybe the problems run deeper. Perhaps people cannot be persuaded to embrace better practices and institutions even when it is in their interest to do so and even when good arguments for doing so are on offer. We explore that possibility here by examining Isaiah Berlin's analysis of freedom and the debate it spawned during and after the Cold War.

Berlin's "Two concepts of liberty," delivered as his inaugural lecture for the Chichele professorship at Oxford on October 31, 1958, remains his most influential contribution to political philosophy. Published shortly thereafter as a pamphlet by the Clarendon Press, "Two concepts" became the armature for Berlin's *Four Essays on Liberty,* which appeared in 1969 and established him as one of the leading theorists—if not *the* leading theorist—of the subject writing in English in the twentieth century. Citation indexes stand as emphatic testimony of that status, but perhaps even more so is the reality that the terms *negative liberty* and *negative freedom,* which Berlin—like many successors—tended to use interchangeably, have become commonplace in the lexicon of ordinary usage. They are widely deployed to depict the freedom that is created and preserved when the state acts, if at all, principally to stop people from interfering with one another. "Two concepts" was presented as an analytical treatment of the differences between it and *positive* liberty, conceived as the freedom *to do* something that might be more or less fully specified, but Berlin was a manifest champion of the negative idea that has become so widely associated with his name.

Berlin was not, as he would be the first to say, negative liberty's original advocate.[1] Hobbes's discussion of "liberty by pretermission" in chapter 21 of *Leviathan* is a close relative at least. So are the robust zones for liberty of conscience and private action carved out in Locke's third *Letter Concerning Toleration* and Mill's *On Liberty,* and—if more ambiguously as we will see—in Kant's insistence that people should always be recognized as ends in themselves, not mere instruments for the use of others. Berlin was keen to establish that negative liberty has a substantial pedigree and provenance among these and other canonical thinkers as part of his case for its enduring appeal. He stood firm for it, but he did not stand alone.

Even negative liberty's critics affirm its importance. The revival of civic humanism since the 1970s rests, for instance, on self-conscious repudiation of a Berlinian construction of the alternatives. J. G. A. Pocock embraces a version of the dichotomy by counterposing his virtue-based paradigm to the characteristic liberal focus on legal protections for individuals.[2] Philip Pettit anchors his choice of a third conception of freedom in what he finds unsatisfying in the choice between the negative and positive alternatives.[3] Sensing, perhaps, negative liberty's enduring appeal, Quentin Skinner takes a different tack. His civic humanism centers on reclaiming negative liberty from Hobbes and his successors in a contest in which battles have been lost but Skinner is as yet unwilling to concede defeat in the longer war.[4]

For the civic humanists, it seems that negative liberty must be displaced, transcended, or coopted, but it cannot be ignored.

Nor were the civic humanists the first to throw down the gauntlet. In *Natural Right and History,* Leo Strauss took aim at the seventeenth-century shift in focus from natural law to the centrality of natural rights, which he read as heralding the modern fetish with individualism—a cousin if not a precursor of the negative idea.[5] From a different perspective, C. B. Macpherson viewed those same developments as ushering in an ideology supportive of the emerging capitalist market order.[6] In this he echoed Marx's polemical footnotes directed at Mill in *Das Capital* and elsewhere, where the individual's freedom to transact freely is seen to buttress—while it obscures—an exploitative economic order.[7] This last notion was carried into twentieth-century debates via Herbert Marcuse's "repressive tolerance."[8] In these and related formulations, negative freedom's staying power has more to do with ideological considerations than intellectual ones—or at least the two bleed into one another.

It is the staying power that interests us in this chapter. That endurance is all the more remarkable in view of the fact that the negative/positive dichotomy rests on questionable logical foundations. In 1967, Gerald MacCallum, Jr., made short work of it by pointing out that liberty is a relational concept that ranges over agents, restraining or enabling conditions, and actions.[9] That is, for any claim about freedom it is always possible to ask: "*Who* is free; *from what* restraint *or because of what* enabling conditions; *to do what?*" When people seem to disagree about the meaning of the term *freedom,* he noted, they are really disagreeing about how to characterize the relevant agent, the relevant restraining or enabling conditions, or the relevant action. Moreover, the restraining or enabling conditions can easily be redescribed as one another, as when one might characterize a prisoner as unfree because of the presence of chains or the lack of a key. Proponents of negative freedom, he argued, tend to focus attention on the first term in the relation—the agent—while describing the second in terms of impediments and leaving the relevant action implicit. Positive libertarians, by contrast, pay less explicit attention to agents, typically speak of the second in terms of enabling conditions, and focus explicit attention centrally on the actions to be performed.

There is a sense in which MacCallum was right, testified to by the fact that a good deal of the subsequent philosophical writing on freedom genuflects toward his seminal article. But there is also a sense in which his argument is too whiggish. The attacks on negative freedom, old and new, suggest that something more is at stake than analytical clear-headedness. They make it obvious that the negative freedom ideal carries substantial ideological freight regardless of philosophical considerations. This has been observed before, but the standard contention is that this has to do with the logic of individualism that undergirds the market behavior of *homo economicus*.[10] Instead, we advance the different—though perhaps complementary—thesis that Berlin's influential formulation is best understood through the lens of the Cold War. Both in his own mind and in those of his audience, including such figures as Karl Popper and Friedrich Hayek, who developed comparable accounts of liberty, and George Kennan, for whom the confrontation between positive and negative freedom was "the greatest contest of the age," Berlin's negative freedom was a bulwark against communism and particularly the Stalinist form it had taken by the 1950s.[11] Our evidence for this is taken largely from Berlin's letters that have been published since the turn of the century. Fascinating in their own right, the letters illuminate Berlin's experience of the ideological context of the 1950s, his agenda in defending negative liberty, and his contemporaries' reaction to that agenda.

We set out the main contours of the Cold War intellectual context, and Berlin's place in it, in section I. Like Popper's open society and Hayek's constitution of liberty, Berlin's negative liberty was billed and welcomed as a repudiation of the oppressive teleology built into Soviet communism. And like Kennan, Berlin saw negative liberty as an integral component of the bulwark that was needed to face down that threat. But unlike Kennan and the other Cold War liberals, Berlin believed that developing a technically sound philosophical defense of negative freedom and repudiating communism, while important, were not enough. He was skeptical that people are naturally inclined to opt for negative freedom, let alone to fight for it. As a result, he thought it necessary to develop a powerfully appealing, even romantic, defense of his favored conception of it that differentiated him from such negative libertarians as Popper and Hayek in that it also had a Herderian self-expressive dimension. This brought him, at times, uncomfortably close to positive libertarians like Rousseau—with whom he wrestled ambivalently for much of his life.

As we discuss in section II, Berlin agreed with Kennan that the Soviets took advantage of frailties in human psychology for nefarious ends, but he thought those frailties were a good deal older, and ran a lot deeper, than the Soviets' perverse exploitation of them. They are part of what it means to be human as he thought Rousseau understood and exemplified, and we discount them at our peril. Exploring Berlin's view of the human psychology that underlies both the need for freedom and its vulnerability leads us to a discussion of what he saw as Kant's successful modification of Rousseau's treatment of the matter in section III, and of his belief that Kant's account of autonomy is a viable—perhaps even the best—philosophical basis for the view of liberty that might win the high political ground. But perhaps ironically, Berlin was not confident that removing the external impediments to the negative liberty he prized would be enough for it to triumph. He saw it as a value that must be argued and even fought for, and, partly because of the reasons that give malevolent forms positive liberty their powerful psychological pull, he was unsure that this battle could be won. We agree with Berlin that insecurity makes people more likely to embrace politics that undermine their freedom, but we argue that it makes better sense to trace that insecurity to their circumstances rather than to inherent features of human psychology. Instead of giving up hope, this suggests an agenda of supporting policies that can reduce people's insecurity, better enabling them to resist policies that foster domination.

I. The Intellectual Context of the Cold War

The Cold War had a profound impact on all areas of public life. Academia was far from an exception, particularly in the United States where Berlin was to take up nearly twenty-five years of visiting appointments starting in 1949 with a position at Harvard's Russian Research Center. Toward the end of that year, Berlin gave a speech at Mount Holyoke College on "Democracy, Communism, and the Individual," whose substance and aftermath are particularly illuminating. This was a high-profile event, which included speakers such as Eleanor Roosevelt, Sir Alexander Cadogan, and Abba Eban, and Berlin seems, characteristically, to have risen to the public persona he wished to project for the occasion while shying away from the implications. Despite expressed fears that the *New York Times* reporter present at the event would print his words and that "very grave" consequences might follow for his various contacts in the USSR, Berlin delivered what Michael Ignatieff portrays as a "worthy but hardly incendiary sermon" and what Berlin himself described as being "somewhat Fascist Beast in character, on how a modus vivendi wasn't really possible between any democracy and 'them,' etc."[12]

The day after the event, a write-up of Berlin's speech appeared in the *New York Times* under the headline "Study of Marxism Backed at

Parley," in which Berlin's key purpose in the speech was described as "to impress upon [his] audience the importance of studying Marxism, and specifically of not placing a ban upon such studies."[13] Berlin felt he had been interpreted "as backing more and more Marxism in American universities and staunchly defending the Russian Revolution and all the other horrors" and (apparently now worrying less for his USSR informants than the possibility that he might be seen as a pro-Marxist), wrote a frantic letter to the *Times* clarifying his position, which was published under the headline "Attitude on Marxism stated: Dr Berlin amplifies his remarks made at Mount Holyoke."[14] Berlin attributed the misinterpretation of his aim and approach in the lecture to a private interview with the *Times* reporter, and he feared that his comments in this interview had given the reporter the impression that Berlin was a weak but true supporter of Marxism, hiding his defense of Marx within the language of a false objectivity. And yet, when one reads the speech, it is easy to see how the *Times* reporter could have interpreted Berlin in a way at odds with Berlin's stated agenda.

While the body of the speech may critique Marx, it is framed as an attack on eighteenth-century rationalism—and principally Rousseau—of which Marxism is described as a particular instance. Berlin's main argument suggested that "the root of communism . . . lay in the eighteenth-century belief—expressed in its most extreme form by Rousseau—that there was one right way for human beings to live," and that "Communism, Fascism and all other totalitarian orders" were an offshoot of that basic proposition.[15] But they were not the only offshoot. In his opening paragraph, Berlin submitted that both democracy and communism issue from this same central idea, and that where Marxism went wrong was in thinking that liberty and equality are completely compatible, even as the lesson of the nineteenth century was that they are not.

One can recognize here the pieces of what would become Berlin's celebrated distinction between positive and negative liberty, and of his contention that the former "[denied] that different ideals of life, not necessarily altogether reconcilable with each other, are equally valid and equally worthy," whereas the latter embraced that idea.[16] Yet in this early formulation, with Rousseau taking a central role, Berlin found that in a world with ears keenly attuned to how one would take a position on Marx, Marxism, and the USSR, his eighteenth-century culprit hardly registered an impact, and instead seemed to make him vulnerable to the appearance of defending Marx and Marxism.

In addition to his letter to the *Times,* Berlin also wrote to the provost of Harvard to assure him that he was not a secret communist, and to George Kennan at the State Department, asking him "to write a reassuring note to the FBI liaison officer at State."[17] The event clearly rattled Berlin profoundly. Even in his indignation he seems to have taken it to heart as a critique of his work and way of communicating it, for he wrote shortly afterward, "I feel that the rest of my life will be spent in démentis to people like the Provost of Harvard that I am an ambiguous snake of some sort."[18] Berlin seems nonetheless to have walked away from his first stint in the United States with a heartening lesson. In the same letter, he expressed admiration for Eleanor Roosevelt's speech at the Mount Holyoke event, writing, "I feel that she really did, almost single-handedly, make it possible for people here to be critical of the USSR and still not afraid of being condemned as Fascist Beasts—the opportunity for an anti-Soviet but 'progressive' attitude." He saw this accomplishment reflected in her clash with Soviet jurist Andrey Tanuar'evich Vyshinsky over civil liberties in the UN General Assembly, commenting that this clash's impact "really does seem to me to be important and very satisfying."[19]

These lessons provide an important orienting framework for understanding Berlin's subsequent intellectual trajectory, as well as the larger fabric of intellectual and social pressures within which Cold War political theory operated. On the one hand, there was powerful pressure to place one's thought in clear relationship to the Marxist East, which for Berlin at times would develop into a fight not just over ideas and the meaning of the history of ideas, but also the task and identity of political philosophy as such. On the other hand, there was a fear, even among liberals, that postwar malaise, social transformation, and a kind of temperate, perhaps unfocused commitment to pluralism were breeding the possibility for communism to gain root in Western Europe. People worried that the available arguments against communism were essentially negative and technical, and hardly inspiring.

This anxiety is manifest in an exchange between Berlin and Alan Dudley, head of the Information Policy Department in the Foreign Office, in the spring of 1948. In January of that year, Secretary of State Bevin had given a speech in which he sought "to stem the further encroachment of the Soviet tide . . . by creating some form of union in Western Europe," but in the process of distinguishing the West from the Soviet encroachment in the East, Bevin remarked on the importance of not just economic and political union, but also of a spiritual component. "If we are to have an organism in the West," he said in his conclusion, "it must be a spiritual union."[20] The Working Party on Spiritual Aspects of Western Union was set up in 1948 to explore what this unity would consist of, and it apparently found difficulties immediately in defining assertive aspects apart from anticommunist positions. Dudley consulted Berlin to ask if he could be of assistance in identifying "common factors in terms of attitudes towards a great variety of things (and ideas) ranging from art to social services," which Dudley thought must ultimately lie in "what philosophical ideas there are which are common to the West."

Berlin at first responds that he cannot identify any ideas in "technical philosophy" which belong specifically to the West more than the

East. "But you do not, of course, mean that. You mean to refer to general ideas, attitudes to this or that activity or form of life etc.," Berlin writes, and then quickly rules out some unwise avenues of approach to the question. First, he says Hegel, being key to both Marxism and "dominant English philosophy from, say, 1870 to say 1920," is a bad avenue of critique. He also suggests that pointing to the West as standing for "scientific objectivity, pursuit of truth by disinterested means" is a poor strategy since Marxist thought makes the same claims. Finally, Berlin suggests that any meaningful differences "seem to me to boil down to . . . conflicting views of social life," and breaks this down into two components.[21] The first of these he calls civil liberties, which he describes in a way recognizable as negative liberty, although he asserts that "there is no Eastern Democracy, as opposed to Western, any more than there is Eastern Liberty, Eastern Equality or Eastern Truth."[22]

The difference between the West and the "Marxists" is not exactly that one has civil liberties and the other does not. Rather, the former has the protection of civil liberties as a public ideal, a belief that without them, justice and liberty are not possible, while the latter believes that "men below a certain economic level are as helpless & unable to use their freedoms as people coerced by totalitarian states." Ultimately Berlin recommends that Dudley dispense with the attempt to distinguish West from East on the level of ideas, and suggests instead that it would be better to write "a clear & unwoolly" liberal manifesto.[23]

Yet these pressures continued to appear in the impetus for and reception to Berlin's developing work. It is evident, for example, from the correspondence which followed from the airing of Berlin's BBC 1952 Lecture series (*Freedom and Its Betrayal*), that Berlin felt a continuing obligation to mount a clear—and inspiring—vision and agenda against communism. These lectures took the form of a condensed, less complex, and more pointedly critical version of his earlier Flexner Lectures on the same topic (*Political Ideas in the Romantic Age*), the argument of which we will discuss shortly, but the basic project Berlin laid out was to look at six thinkers—Helvetius, Rousseau, Fichte, Hegel, Saint-Simon, and Maistre—who all wrote around the time of the French Revolution and shared two central things in common. The first was that they all seemed to Berlin to be concerned with human liberty, and some passionate defenders of it, but "in the end their doctrines are inimical to what is normally meant, at any rate, by individual liberty, or political liberty."[24] And second, Berlin thought they were all affected by the Newtonian revolution in establishing order in the realm of the sciences in such a way that they sought to find "some simple single principle" which could establish a similar degree of order within political life.[25] The broadcasts created something of a sensation, and they inspired an unprecedented editorial column published in *The Times* on December 6, 1952, called "The fate of liberty," whose topic was then taken up in the correspondence columns of the paper, to which Berlin himself contributed.

In a letter to Herbert Elliston referencing the *Times* editorial, Berlin reacts to the characterization of the purpose of his lectures as represented by journalist Thomas Utley. Utley had described the upshot of Berlin's argument as suggesting that "the need of the twentieth century is not so much for a new political faith (it has had too many) as for a firm foundation for political doubt."[26] Berlin agrees with the description that he indeed meant to suggest that there had been too many political faiths, but disagrees with the conclusion that this meant Berlin was calling for systematic doubt. Instead, he suggests, that he is calling for "more a kind of cautious empiricism" and mentions Popper and Hayek (although the latter with more reservations) as writers with kindred projects, although he specifies that this implies "a society in which the largest number of persons are allowed to pursue the largest number of ends as freely as possible, in which these ends are themselves criticized as little as possible and the fervor with which such ends are held is not required to be bolstered up by some bogus rational or supernatural argument to prove the universal validity of ends."[27]

Here again, Berlin struggles with how to articulate this in a way that is not just clear and distinct from (and critical of) the communist alternative, but also involves some spiritual force—if not quite political faith—of its own, that is, one that is not merely skeptical or hangs mainly on doubt and empirical uncertainty. He laments, "I do not see why it is not possible to believe in the various ends in which we do believe with as much fervor and self-dedication as Communists believe theirs."[28] But here, Berlin seems to describe the anxiety not merely as finding some (inspiring) way to describe the Western moral commitments in contrast to the Soviets, but also as worrying that in the process, the West might manifest the very same tendency that it seeks to combat in the enemy—"as people here think is happening in America, what with McCarran Acts etc., although I keep trying to persuade them that this is not so."[29]

This anxiety reflected an argument that was pressed in the political domain by George Kennan, someone who greatly admired Berlin and would eventually have considerable influence on Berlin's understanding of his own project.[30] Both men were appalled by Joseph McCarthy, whom Kennan saw as meriting at least as much opprobrium as the Marxism he was allegedly rooting out and Berlin deplored as "a sadist who enjoys tormenting the egg-heads who give him a sense of inferiority."[31] Apart from McCarthy's deleterious effect on American foreign policy and diplomacy, both men worried about his assault on the United States as an appealing alternative to the USSR, one whose allure depended on its embodying the negative freedom that McCarthy was undermining. In Kennan's case this was rooted in his view of what today is called the battle for hearts and minds. Rather than engage in the hopeless ideological debates with Soviet leaders, the way to prevail was to build manifestly flourishing democratic capitalist systems that the populations behind the iron curtain would envy. This meant resisting pressures to erode the quality of Western institutions, lest they start resembling those which they sought to contain.[32]

McCarthy embodied that threat. Kennan was so troubled by him that, in response to overtures in 1952 about the possibility of his returning to the State Department in the event of an Eisenhower victory, he insisted that this would be contingent on the future president and Secretary of State John Foster Dulles repudiating McCarthyism unequivocally.[33] Berlin agreed that the "frightful" McCarthy was destroying America's social and intellectual fabric and promoting paranoia. Indeed, Berlin himself was not immune to the threat. In March 1953 he worried that he might become the target of a probe at Harvard, and, a few months later, that he might be denied a U.S. visa.[34] Nor did he think McCarthy was a transient menace who could safely be ignored. As he wrote of to Alice James in June of 1953, "I do not for a moment believe in the doctrine of giving him enough rope—enough rope and he will hang everybody else."[35]

Kennan was optimistic about the longer-term prospects in the battle between the West and the Soviets. He was convinced that most people did not in the end submit to the Soviet model out of true ideological conviction, but rather "by a 'bandwagon effect': a sense that communism was 'the coming thing,' an unstoppable 'movement of the future.'"[36] As we will see shortly, Berlin would adopt a similar view, but he was considerably less sanguine that apparently thriving democracies would be enough on their own to combat the Soviet outlook, or that the Soviets were the only front where this baleful outlook could manifest itself.

The Elliston letter is frequently cited by others with a different interpretation in view—that Berlin was not an anxious but willing participant in the ideological battles of the Cold War, but rather a proud champion of a version of liberalism free from the fervency which grows out of ideological fault lines, a liberalism which could celebrate moderation and pluralism. Aurelian Craiutu argues, for instance, that "Berlin's anticommunism lacked the fervent zeal of those who saw themselves in an all-or-nothing crusade against communism and thirsted for absolute moral clarity and purity."[37] Similarly, Joshua Cherniss claims that Berlin must be read as principled and not just hand-wringing in his resistance to pressures to offer a clearer and more inspiring account of liberalism, asserting that "opposition to crusading was central to his outlook."[38] Our view is not incompatible with these readings of Berlin, but we contend that Berlin was not merely arguing against passionate, simplistic, or ideological political views. His underlying claim was that those views are compelling to people for a reason, and that cannot be discounted no matter how destructive they seem or how much one feels themselves to be immune to their pull. For even in Berlin's rejection of "monolithic . . . establishments," his language of choosing between a certain loss in "energy" or "drive" and being "hypnotised by the blood-curdling threats of the enemy into a frame of mind similar to [one's] own" reflects his conviction that people commit themselves to such causes for reasons that lie outside of the measured logic of tradeoffs.[39] Berlin's spirited insistence that we *must* choose operates alongside his darker acknowledgment that in reality people often embrace monolithic conceptions of politics because the mere possibility of choice does not inspire them.

This reading is further supported by Berlin's letter to Denis Paul in December 1952, written in response to a comment Paul had made on Berlin's lectures that they only left the audience with an impression that communism/fascism were bad, but that this only left listeners complacent, and additionally might do little to affect those in the

West who were sympathetic to socialist ideas. Berlin agreed that he should say more, but struggled with what to say, equivocating over whether economic planning in itself is a threat to political freedom. "I did try and make it clear that the notion of freedom which I approved of was what the English and French Liberals and Radicals were preaching in the early 19th century as opposed to the German brand, that it was a negative concept, that it was what you call elbow-room freedom, that it largely meant non-interference." But that in the end, when that preferred brand of freedom conflicts with other social purposes, "there is no clear solution." As a result, he concludes that "it is all a matter for compromise and balance and adjustment and empirical Popperism etc., and, in short, that the truth, when found, is not dramatic but possibly rather dreary."[40] Here Berlin appears simultaneously frustrated with Paul's critique and troubled by it, and even in defending his approach, he says, "But I daresay I really avoided crucial issues and should have said something else. I wish you would tell me what."[41]

Similarly, in his 1949 address on the intellectual life of American universities, Berlin does not conclude with a resolute and straightforward rejection of outlooks that promote protection "from the intellectual and moral burden of facing problems that may be too deep or complex to be dealt with by any patented method," but rather, a question which evinces genuine grappling with the complex forces that foster such mindframes: "what is to become of us?"[42] After all, even if Berlin thought anxiety might be necessary in a world of complex and contradictory moral and political institutions and commitments, and we might do well to reject those who promise easy cures to it (as if it is simply a disease to be treated), the fact of the matter is that anxiety is not a pleasant experience. Indeed, in the closing paragraphs of "Political ideas in the twentieth century" (1950), Berlin emphasizes the role of anxiety in moving a real increased need for social regulation into twentieth-century examples of fascism and totalitarianism, arguing, "The progress of technological skill makes it rational and indeed imperative to plan, and anxiety for the success of a particular planned society naturally inclines the planners to seek insulation from dangerous, because incalculable, forces which may jeopardize the plan."[43]

After "Political ideas in the twentieth century" was published in *Foreign Affairs* in April 1950, Berlin wrote a letter to Hamilton Fish Armstrong, in which he remarked on the reception of the article, and particularly the reaction he had received from Charles Bohlen, a U.S. diplomat and an expert on the Soviet Union: "he said he had talked most seriously with George Kennan about it, and they thought it was unfinished (!) and there should have been a long piece explaining why Communism cannot last and is contrary to human nature etc., and in effect formally refuting it and its claim to survive."[44] Berlin responds that he feels his position was quite clear throughout the piece, that the charge might move his exercise in analysis closer to propaganda, and in any case would have required a separate article likely taking the form of "a long coda full of exorcisms against the devil." He admits that he was not understood clearly by Professor W. Y. Elliot of Harvard, who criticized Berlin for making totalitarianism too attractive, but also that Elliot's opinion did not much matter to him. On the other hand, "that George Kennan," Berlin writes, "should also half think this seems to me more serious."[45] Berlin's resistance, in both principled and personal ways, to the ideological pressures issuing from Cold War politics does not mean he was not deeply affected by them. After all, even if Berlin did not give in to pressures to create propaganda, his understanding of the predicament was nonetheless informed by the evident existence of voices he admired that were actively calling for it. And yet, Berlin's response, perhaps unique among the Cold War liberals with which he is typically associated, was not simply to combat Soviet communism by championing a notion of freedom at variance with theirs, but also to seek to do so in a way that could account for what made this brand of communism, and other outlooks like it, attractive to its adherents.

II. The Psychology of Freedom

In 1935, while working on what would become his celebrated book on Karl Marx, a twenty-six-year-old Isaiah Berlin wrote to an undergraduate classmate of his named John Hilton complaining of his troubles. "I am trying desperately to write a book on Marx & find myself (a) unable to write at all for at least an hour after settling to, (b) when I begin I suddenly let loose a flood of words about Rousseau's influence on the romantic style, & then remember that the relevance needs proving."[46] Rousseau held a deep connection to Marx in Berlin's mind even in the earliest years of Berlin's scholarship, albeit an uncertain one, and it was a connection that would continue to trouble Berlin throughout his career.

But whereas Berlin's Russian would offer him a perspective on Marx denied to many of his English contemporaries, and through it lead him to both his hero Herzen and his perspective on Marx's place in Enlightenment thought via Plekhanov, Berlin's position on Rousseau would remain uncertain, increasingly disdainfully so. Nearly twenty years later, he would write to Jacob Talmon speaking again of the connection between Marx and Rousseau, and the troublesome position of the latter in his thought: "Now I must sit down to the hideous task of writing a book.[47] God knows, the awful shadow of Marx broods over the entire thing, and I do not know whether to put him in or keep him out, and I still feel terribly obscure and muddled about Rousseau."[48] Indeed, when Henry Hardy set out to challenge Berlin's reputation "as a man who talked much but wrote little,"[49] by cataloging his published works and collecting his unpublished ones, all of Berlin's major substantive treatments of Rousseau were in lecture form and remained unpublished, including what would become *Political Ideas in the Romantic Age, Freedom and Its Betrayal,* and *The Roots of Romanticism.*

Yet even as Berlin would exhibit great difficulty and reticence in committing his engagement with Rousseau to the written word, Rousseau would serve as an influential foundation and point of reference for his most famous insights. And while positive and negative freedom would permeate the language and structure of debates within political theory for the second half of the twentieth century, the debates that would play out concerning his interpretation and use of Rousseau seem to have been comparatively more heated at the same time that they were less influential. Berlin often explained the fervency with which people reacted to Rousseau as a sign of some special, powerful, and enduring insight even as he insisted that Rousseau was not all that innovative or unique at the level of "technical" philosophical ideas. What then made Rousseau such a crucial figure in Berlin's understanding of the history of political thought?

Berlin's fullest treatment of the relevant intellectual history was developed as a series of lectures for Bryn Mawr College, prepared and delivered between 1951 and 1952 during his second extended visit to the United States. These lectures, only four of which survived, were drawn from writings that would later become *Political Ideas in the Romantic Age.* In Henry Hardy's preface to that volume, he suggests that it "may be seen as Isaiah Berlin's *Grundrisse,* the ur-text or 'torso,' as Berlin called it, from which a great deal of his subsequent work derived."[50] Similarly, Ian Harris comments that this text "shows very clearly that . . . Berlin wrote a history that was formed by, and which was a vehicle for, his philosophical views."[51] Why Berlin never himself published these lectures remains a puzzle, especially because he would continue to refine the ideas and present them, again in lecture form, on BBC Radio's Third Programme in late 1952. And in the last decade of his life, he was supposedly still planning to write a book on romanticism, although at that point it was likely to look more like his A. W. Mellon Lecture series from 1965 on the topic (transcribed and published after his death under the title *The Roots of Romanticism*). In any case, his biographers and critics are nearly unanimous in suggesting that in *Political Ideas in the Romantic Age* one can see the development of arguments central to what, in 1958, would become the Chichele Inaugural Lecture.

The opportunity to present the Flexner Lectures at Bryn Mawr was fortuitous, arriving as it did at an important moment of transition in Berlin's intellectual trajectory. He was about to return to All Souls as a historian of ideas instead of in philosophy, which had previously been his appointment. When he accepted the offer to deliver the lectures, Berlin wrote Katherine McBride, the president of Bryn Mawr College, to propose a topic, which he provisionally described as "Six (or however many) types of political theory." He said his reason for choosing this project in particular was that "these seem to me to be the prototypes from which our modern views in their great and colliding variety have developed," and in a later letter, in which he shifted the proposed title to "Political ideas in the romantic age," he clarified that he wanted to avoid the term "origins" in the title because he felt that would force him to talk about thinkers "like Machiavelli, Hobbes, Locke, etc., who may be the fathers of all these things, but are definitely felt to be predecessors and precursors and, certainly as far as mode of expression is concerned, altogether obsolete."[52]

This description certainly tracks with Berlin's understanding of many of the authors he discusses, and Rousseau in particular. Throughout his writings and letters, Berlin would emphasize that, whatever might have been unique or original about Rousseau's view of liberty, his impact ultimately was a result, not of his innovation in ideas (which had mainly occurred earlier, via philosophical "technicians"), but rather of his "words and imagery."[53] What seemed to have grabbed and troubled Berlin about Rousseau was what he understood to be the impact of his language on the moral imagination of Western civilization. He writes years later, "he obviously said things, and said them in a fashion which, for the first time, touched chords, and brought into the open feelings and self-images which have, no doubt, in some sense always been there, but which no one had articulated so vividly and passionately."[54] Berlin thought Rousseau hit on something that both exposed and exploited a feature of human psychology with which liberalism had to contend. For this reason, perhaps the most revealing context for understanding how Rousseau would shape Berlin's famous division of liberty appears in a letter in which Berlin does not mention Rousseau at all.

In May 1950, George Kennan wrote to Berlin, commenting on the latter's "Political ideas in the twentieth century." Kennan offered a more psychological analysis of totalitarianism than Berlin had put forward, to which he added this emotional appeal against what he took to be the heart of the phenomenon:

> I really believe that this that the totalitarians have done—this taking advantage of the helpless corner of man's psychic structure—is the original sin. It is this knowledge which men were not supposed to develop and exploit. . . . For when a man's ultimate dignity is destroyed, he is killed, of course, as a man. This exploitation of his weakness is therefore only another form of taking human life arbitrarily and in cold blood, as a result of calculation and not of passion. . . . The success of civilization seems somehow to depend on the willingness of men to realise that by taking advantage of this Achilles' heel in man's moral composition, they shame themselves as

well as others; on their readiness to refrain from doing so; and on their sticking to the rational appeal which assumes—perhaps in defiance of the evident—that in the long run each man can be taught to rise above himself.[55]

When Berlin at last responded in February 1951, he began by saying that he had many times attempted to write back but had felt that he had not been capable of a worthy response, and even now felt that what he had to offer was chaotic and scattered. This sentiment might be chalked up to Berlin's tendency to self-deprecate, often protectively so, except for the intensity and length of the letter that followed, in which Berlin ranged over many topics, including the Holocaust, the Soviets, Hegel, and Marx, grouping them together under a common, central problem. "I must begin by saying that you have put in words something which I believe not only to be the centre of the subject," Berlin writes, "but something which, perhaps because of a certain reluctance to face the fundamental moral issue on which everything turns, I failed to say; but once forced to face it, I realise now that it is craven to sail round it as I have done, and moreover that it is, in fact, what I myself believe, and deeply believe, to be true."[56] Moreover, Berlin suggests that it is likely that a person's attitude on this question determines the entirety of their moral outlook.

The question that Berlin identifies at the heart of Kennan's observation comes down to nothing less than what it means to be a human being, and therefore, the true "evil" involved in denying a person that status. For Berlin, this turns on a specific interpretation of the Kantian imperative to treat people as "ends in themselves," based on the consciousness of choice, however narrowly constrained or tortuous that choice may be; and "that all the categories, the concepts, in terms of which we think about and act towards one another . . . all this becomes meaningless unless we think of human beings as capable of pursuing ends for their own sakes by deliberate acts of choice—which alone makes nobility noble and sacrifices sacrifices."[57] In this view, what made the Nazi (and Soviet) practices so horrifying was not just the deeds themselves, but more importantly the deception that accompanied them:

> Why does this deception, which may in fact have diminished the anguish of the victims, arouse a really unutterable kind of horror in us? The spectacle, I mean, of the victims, marching off in happy ignorance of their doom amid the smiling faces of their tormentors? Surely because we cannot bear the thought of human beings denied their last rights—of knowing the truth, of acting with at least the freedom of the condemned, of being able to face their destruction with fear or courage, according to their temperaments, but at least as human beings, armed with the power of choice.[58]

Berlin thought even in desperate, impossible circumstances, even facing degrading, certain death, a human being could still make choices about how to respond to his or her fate, and what mattered was not that one's deeds would be witnessed or remembered by others (as it would for Arendt), but rather that, from one's own perspective, "the possibility of goodness . . . is still open." Without this ability and willingness to choose, Berlin suggested, "there are no worthwhile motives left: nothing is worth doing or avoiding, the reasons for existing are gone," and there remained no framework for moral evaluation of self or other, and therefore, no moral identity as such.[59]

For Marx and Hegel, Berlin argues, the moral question "what is good?" has a correct answer, and therefore being irrational coincides with being immoral. In this view, success comes to define the good and failure comes to define the wicked. In contrast to the Hegelian/

Marxist view, the morality of the nineteenth century, and "in particular in the romantic period," suggests that a person's motive to serve an idea or "bear witness to something which he believes to be true" separate from whether one agrees with the aims or how one evaluates the consequences, is something always to be admired. Berlin uses Don Quixote to bring out the contrast. From a Hegelian or Marxist perspective on morality, Quixote is both absurd and immoral, whereas for the liberal, Quixote can be admired even when he is somewhat ridiculous.

Yet while Berlin thought this moral outlook lay "at the heart of all that is most horrifying both in utilitarianism and in 'historicism' of the Hegelian, Marxist type," he hardly thought it was limited to that.[60] He agreed with Kennan that the phenomenon was psychological in origin, but he resisted Kennan's view that it was some perversion or manipulation specific to the Soviets. Instead Berlin saw it "as an extreme and distorted but only too typical form of some general attitude of mind from which our own countries are not exempt."[61] For this reason, Berlin also doubted that the West would win this ideological war through moral purity and commitment to its principles and institutions alone, or that its triumph would be absolute, and that it would not turn into "inverted Marxists" in the process of triumphing. The battle for the modern soul was larger, deeper, and older than the conflict between the West and the Soviets.

III. Freedom's Insecurity

Berlin's exchange with Kennan over psychology and freedom provides a useful framework for viewing what Berlin's concern with freedom really was—and why its division into positive and negative varieties would have seemed so illuminating and useful to both him and his contemporaries. He saw positive freedom, or at least the variants of it that were likely to gain traction in real politics, as posing dangerous threats to the freedom of choice that he prized. The danger was not merely that proponents of positive freedom typically traffic in monistic conceptions of the good life which must be embraced for anyone to be genuinely free. In politics, the more serious danger was these monistic conceptions would be imposed on others in the name of making them "genuinely" free.[62]

But a simple blanket condemnation of freedom's positive varieties would not be a viable avenue of attack. Berlin was convinced that the vision of freedom at the heart of liberalism had both positive and negative aspects, and thus could not be meaningfully reduced into its fully negative form without losing a considerable part of its moral force. Indeed, what Berlin found so puzzling and enchanting about the romantics, and Rousseau in particular, was that they seemed, through exactly the same central moral insight, to be the locus of both liberal democratic moral sensibilities and the moral justification driving the Soviet political project. Berlin sees both as admiring dramatic visions of people sacrificing themselves to an idea higher and greater than themselves, but for the former, this can only happen on the individual level through conscious choice, whereas for the latter, it can instead be enacted and justified through, if not positively requiring, a collective political project.[63]

In Rousseau, Berlin finds this tension over the moral identity of the human being—and the logic that serves both strands—at its muddled, contradictory apex. Rousseau's conception of freedom was original because it was absolute, and because, in a way similar to how Berlin himself would come to understand liberty, it was precisely what made the human being human. "His concept of freedom was not at all clear," Berlin argues, "but it was very passionate: human freedom was to him what the possession of an immortal soul was for orthodox Christians, and indeed it had an almost identical meaning for him.... To rob a man of his freedom was to refuse him the right to say his word: to be human at all; it was to depersonalise him, to degrade or destroy his humanity, in other words those characteristics to maintain and promote which was the sole justification of any action; justice, virtue, duty, truth, the morally good and bad, could not exist unless man was a free being capable of choosing freely between right and wrong, and therefore accountable for his acts."[64] It was the passion, intensity, and absoluteness in how Rousseau conceived of freedom which made him unwilling to make the tradeoff that other liberal forefathers were willing to make: to limit or curtail freedom of the individual in any way for the sake of social existence.

Because Rousseau's conception of freedom was so absolute, Berlin argued, limiting liberty in any way was essentially cutting into the individual's very humanity. Even the most basic of social contracts, insofar as it involved this tradeoff, could never be justified. Therefore, Berlin argued, Rousseau required that any solution to the difficulties of social and political organization must necessarily include "the total preservation of absolute human freedom—the freedom from invasion of one human personality by another, the prohibition of all coercion and violence, of the crushing of one human will by another or the maiming of one will to make it serve another's egoistic purposes."[65]

The flip side of embracing such an absolute conception of freedom is that any political authority, if it is to be coherent with protecting that freedom, must also be absolute. Rousseau's solution in the general will was, for Berlin, "the mysterious, the unique point of intersection of the two scales of value. Men must freely want that which alone is right for them to want, which must be one and the same for all right-minded men."[66] As for why Berlin thought Rousseau's solution required consensus on one correct solution, rather than a process of persuasion and approximation, his explanation seems to be that Rousseau shared the view common to eighteenth-century thinkers of there being a correct solution, but he thought the solution could be found through introspection rather than empirical observation. Whereas Helvetius and Condorcet expected that natural sciences would provide the definitive answer, Rousseau thought the correct answer could be found by those able to "hear the voice of nature."[67] And because, Berlin argued, nature for Rousseau implied uniformity, it was precisely nature herself who guaranteed that all who listened correctly would converge on the same answer.

Rousseau thus evinced two failings that ultimately led liberty's most avid defender to become its worst enemy, but only one of these seemed to Berlin a viable object for attack. His issue with Rousseau is, on one hand, the intensity of desire for freedom, and on the other hand, the idea that in being truly free we must necessarily arrive at the same, universal answer (Berlin emphasizes this second feature more heavily in *Freedom and Its Betrayal* than he does in *Political Ideas in the Romantic Age*). But the intensity is exactly what Berlin saw as lying at the heart of the Western moral imagination, and to attack it threatened to leave one without solid moral ground on which to stand. Intensity of commitment with regards to liberty was something that had to be both protected and checked. It was therefore the second failing of Rousseau, a failing Berlin saw as common to thinkers in the romantic age, that was the true target of his critique. Liberty for Berlin, like Rousseau, was basic to the human condition. And indeed, Berlin could describe events like the Holocaust as depriving people of their humanity, not only or even primarily because they were interfered with by others, but because they were deprived of the ability to act and make choices in light of this interference. Deception, a perversion of communication about and recognition of one's situation, was the ultimate liberty-denying evil.

Berlin was keenly aware of the danger that this argument could morph into an unappealing claim about higher and lower human natures. In the way that one can argue that those deceived victims of the Holocaust might have chosen to act differently had they known the truth about how they were being manipulated and sacrificed, it might be argued that all of us might choose to act differently if structural conditions were different, or if we knew more or had a different education. But Berlin worried that this insight, taken to its logical conclusion, would lead to a situation where the choices one makes were taken for granted, and the only questions that remained were questions of means—what the best way to get there was. Criticizing the Soviets was, for Berlin, a practice that threatened two possible unsavory outcomes. The first was a Kennanite fear that the West would, in the process of seeking to combat the enemy, fall into the same search for the "correct" answer and become the very thing it was fighting. The second was that the enterprise would collapse into debates merely over empirics, when Berlin thought nothing less than the moral soul of Western civilization was at stake.

This presents a paradox: Berlin seems to have wanted to defend the absolute value of human liberty, at the same time that he thought the only way this liberty could be defended required viewing it as a choice among others. But how can liberty be an absolute value and also be available for the logic of political tradeoffs?[68]

This paradox might have been resolvable as a philosophical matter for Berlin, and indeed, his own attempts to wrestle with Kant's legacy show how he thought this possible. Berlin contends that Kant's vital innovation was to sharpen Rousseau's distinction between humanity's "rational and 'animal' nature" by granting us some metaphysical distance from nature such that our moral identity cannot be reduced or collapsed entirely into whatever unity is believed to exist in our empirical nature: "That is Kant's specific contribution and the basis of the romantic doctrine of man, who stands, in Herder's words, intermediate between nature and God, beasts and angels, touching at one extremity the mechanical world of the sciences, and at the other the spiritual realm revealed only in moments of the special illumination peculiar to spiritual beings."[69] In other words, our spiritual nature (and the domain of our freedom) could only be revealed in the act of choice; and even if it was supposed to be a rational choice for Kant, it could never be dictated to us without infringing on the specifically human quality of our action.[70] Indeed, Berlin's conception of what it means to treat others as "ends in themselves" emphasizes the respect for choice over self-actualization: "that every human being is assumed to possess the capacity to choose what to do, and what to be, however narrow the limits within which his choice may lie, however hemmed in by circumstances beyond his control."[71] Respect for choice certainly does not promise self-mastery, but it also does not preclude this possibility.

But the psychological problem remained. For Berlin, the danger with regard to freedom seemed to be that its double nature makes it easy to rally people for some political goal in the name of freedom, even if in the process of realizing that goal it might seem necessary or expedient to sacrifice their capacity for individual choice. Freedom rallies us, but choice often confronts us as a burden. This is not simply because choices usually appear to us only in uncertain light, where information is incomplete, and the impact of our action is as yet unknown. It is also because choices are often quite tragic, and their tragic nature issues specifically from the fact that not all good things go together, everyone cannot be made happy at once, and perhaps, everyone cannot truly be free at once. The great challenge and great importance of freedom, he writes, "is that it is involved in the necessity for these hideous choices, the making of which liberals should certainly regard as an end in itself."[72] In short, what some varieties of positive liberty, particularly in the Marxist form, offer is emancipation from having to make those of tragic choices, which Berlin saw as a possibility that could be particularly attractive and powerful in a world otherwise caught in the frequently inefficient and often unromantic demands of pluralism.

This raises the question whether Berlin was concerned with freedom as such or whether his true target was our psychological vulnerability of which he saw Rousseau as both a culprit and a victim. Writing to Karl Popper in 1959, several months after "Two concepts" first appeared, Berlin insisted that "the whole of my lecture, in a sense, is an attempt at a brief study . . . of the way in which innocent or virtuous or truly liberating ideas ([know yourself] or sapere aude or the man who is free although he is a slave, in prison, etc.) tend (not inevitably!) to become authoritarian & despotic and lead to enslavement and slaughter when they are isolated & driven ahead by themselves."[73] Did Berlin think this phenomenon was unique and limited to freedom, or did he think freedom merely constituted a clear, identifiable example of a larger feature of human psychology? The answer seems to fall between these options: Berlin thought the psychological vulnerability was larger than freedom, but freedom was a particularly dangerous and malleable trigger of that vulnerability.

Indeed, as attested to by an essay on freedom that Berlin wrote at the age of eighteen for the Truro Prize at St. Paul's School, he seems to have thought of the threat for freedom to transmute into its opposite as more of a general epochal condition than as a feature unique to Soviet communism. The assignment was to assess this claim: "In the present century, more than ever before, it is true that men called themselves free but are everywhere in chains." The youthful Berlin agreed, characterizing our modern condition as one of two great camps, far removed from each other, but "equally bound with chains." On the one hand, there were those who, "be they Russian Communist, American industrialist, or Italian Fascist, work to achieve an essentially collectivist State, whose dominant characteristics shall be equality and impersonality, who must be opposed to individual freedom as being, in a *mechanical* world, a disruptive, because centrifugal, force." And on the other side would be those who "strive at all costs to preserve their personal spiritual ego, even though it should mean a total abdication of their rights as citizens of any human polity and a willful self-blinding to their actual condition."[74]

But years later, in the midst of the Cold War, to claim that Anglo-American democracy and Soviet communism were, philosophically speaking, two sides of the same coin would have been a difficult proposition, even if some of what Berlin said seems to imply this. Berlin was too often asked to distinguish, distance, and criticize. Western Europe seemed to stand, wearied, in some condition of political, economic, but also *spiritual* existential threat as the Soviets encroached on Eastern Europe. In any case, the lasting impact of "Two concepts" speaks to the idea that it at least touched a nerve or hunger in the broader intellectual culture, regardless of Berlin's own intellectual trajectory. When Karl Popper first read the work, he wrote to Berlin, "I am delighted by your clear distinction between what you call negative and positive freedom; in your own confession of faith—even though it is only implicit, it is no less open and forceful—for negative freedom; by your exposition of the dangers of the ideology of positive freedom."[75] Yet traces of Rousseau remained in Berlin's conviction that freedom is a primary value. However much he objected to this desire in others, it seems that Berlin wanted to believe in something simply and passionately, without reservation. It was almost as if his commitment to freedom both required and prohibited such abandonment.

Two years before his death, Berlin wrote to Michael Walzer that he truly believed that there were two types of liberty other than those of positive and negative liberty. One type of liberty, the kind that the positive and negative varieties mostly fit into, is the kind of liberty that exists as a value among other possible values that a society might choose to promote or curtail. "But," he clarifies, "there is another more basic sense of liberty, which is the ability to choose telle quelle—as such."[76] He suggests this distinction between basic human liberty and liberty as a political value arises largely because he thinks others do not tend to value liberty in a primary or absolute sense: "I was terribly impressed by a passage in my hero Herzen's book *My Past and Thoughts,* in which he says that men do not really all seek liberty—security, yes, but liberty? . . . all men seek security, only some seek liberty. And even if Rousseau denounces the former as a disgraceful choice of slavery, they still are as they are. I cannot pretend that human beings as such (even if I do) put liberty as a primary value, with a special status. I think that simply as a fact is not the case."[77] Perhaps then, it was so important to Berlin that people be "free from" rather than "free to" precisely because, in the end, he did not trust the majority of people to choose freedom at all.

As Henry Hardy notes, the passage which Berlin incorrectly attributes above to *My Past and Thoughts* seems to appear instead in *From the Other Shore* (1850), where Herzen writes, "The masses want to stay the hand that impudently snatches from them the bread they have earned—that is their fundamental desire. They are indifferent to individual freedom, to freedom of speech; the masses love authority."[78] But the insecurity that Berlin feared was as much, if not more, a state of mind as it was any particular political or material condition; and the type of insecurity that worried him most was the human vulnerability to manipulation, to being shaped by some grand planner or inspiring vision of political order. This threat could appear at any time, but in particular during those times when it was easiest to feel lost, displaced, or torn by conflicting impulses. Writing to a friend shortly after the publication of *Four Essays on Liberty* in 1969, Berlin remarks that he doubts his message will register with the students of the present, lamenting, "I have a feeling that the Gods of yesterday have failed the young, that just as the Soviet Union can no longer be believed in with that utter and guileless faith which so many found so easy to hold in the 1930s, so that the Welfare State, prosperity, security, increasing efficiency etc. do not attract those young who feel the need to sacrifice themselves for some worthy ideal . . . and that they are desperately searching for some form of self-expression which will cause them to swim against some sort of stream and not simply drift in a harmless way, too comfortably, with it."[79] Negative liberty was, for Berlin, a rare and precious human accomplishment that humanity might prove incapable of sustaining.

Berlin was wrong to suppose that his work would fail to register with the new students of political philosophy, as negative liberty's staying power attests, but his insight runs deeper than its predictive power. In the 1930s, he suggests, there were enemies, yet there was also hope. But by 1969, Berlin worried that the lack of concrete prospects, of figures and projects to rally around and adversaries to fear, was perhaps a more dangerous breeding ground. Between the ills of fear and ennui in the surrounding political landscape as he perceived it, Berlin concluded that fear may be the better option. After all, fear can be tempered, met with calls for moderation and skepticism; but ennui only stirs the longing to find a cause for which to sacrifice oneself.

IV. Conclusion

Our main interest in this chapter has been in the staying power of negative liberty in contemporary political theory. We have revealed this staying power to have been buttressed by the Cold War, both for Berlin and for those who attended to his arguments in the 1950s and 1960s. Evidence adduced from his correspondence, forays into the media, and other ancillary writings supports this contention. Berlin was acutely sensitive to being perceived or portrayed as soft on Marxism in any of its forms, and he was gratified when voices on the left began criticizing the USSR. He shared the antipathy of Cold War liberals like Popper, Hayek, and especially Kennan for the Soviet Union's virulent oppression, and he welcomed the elective affinities that they and others discerned between his views and theirs.

Nonetheless, Berlin's account was distinctive. Ironically perhaps, in view of Kennan's reputation as a hardboiled political realist, Berlin found Kennan's outlook too sanguine. Kennan believed that the Soviet experiment was bound to fail because its economic model was unsustainable and its imperial ambitions would lead it to become overextended. All the West had to do was contain it behind the iron curtain, rebuild visibly prospering Western democracies, resist the McCarthyist temptation to emulate authoritarian practices in the ostensible defense of freedom, and wait.[80] Patience and resolution would be enough for the West to prevail.

Berlin was not convinced. Despite sharing Kennan's attitude toward the Soviets and his hostility to McCarthyist impulses in the West, Berlin was doubtful that Kennan's recipe was a sufficient guarantor of the kind of freedom—geared to protecting pluralism—that they both prized. He agreed that fear and insecurity made people all too easily manipulated by the Soviets, but, because he saw that fear and insecurity as deeply rooted features of the human condition rather than artifacts of the Cold War confrontation, Berlin saw no reason to believe that malevolent variants of positive freedom would cease to be threats in the future.

By the same token, Berlin could never have endorsed Hayek's view that "spontaneous order" would be the blossoming byproduct of human interaction if government simply got out of the way.[81] Indeed, one helpful consequence of bringing the Cold War lens to bear on Berlin's account of negative liberty is to dispatch the distortions that result from reducing it to a possessive individualist ideological creed. In this respect, Berlin is a useful ally in Skinner's quest to rescue negative freedom from Hobbes and his successors, if not in a civic humanist idiom.

Berlin saw people's instinct for freedom as halting and fragile, not a coiled spring that would regain its natural form if only the compressing impediments were removed. Commentators like Gina Gustavsson emphasize Berlin's worry that people who see freedom as self-mastery can become dangerous partisans of positive liberty, committed to obliterating freedom in the name of preserving it.[82] Here we have sought to illuminate the corollary of this concern that worried Berlin just as much: that champions of negative freedom would continue to find it difficult, and perhaps even impossible, to get traction for their view because it lacked positive liberty's mesmerizing potential.

Monistic conceptions of human purposes that give positive freedom this allure threaten human freedom, but when push comes to shove people might not care—particularly when their sense of security is in doubt. Berlin believed that we have to take that possibility seriously, revealing a Hobbesian streak—at least—in his view of the human psyche. The Hobbesian solution was no more available to Berlin than was Rousseau's oxymoronic dictum that people should be forced to be free. What appealed to Berlin about Rousseau was his passion for freedom, but Berlin doubted that it could be pressed into the service of sustaining negative freedom through the temptations and vicissitudes of real politics. Berlin's pessimistic view of human political psychology thus ultimately led him to a pessimistic assessment of the prospects for human freedom. Threats to freedom are rooted in human insecurity, and Berlin feared that they would likely become more serious in circumstances where that insecurity increases.

The flip side of Berlin's pessimistic prognosis, however, was his positive call for philosophers to take political ideas seriously not despite, but because of their rough edges and internal tensions and contradictions. In that spirit, it is worth asking whether, and to what extent, his analysis holds true today. From our post–Cold War and post-2016 vantage point, Berlin's distinctive defense of negative liberty has a mixed legacy. On the one hand, Berlin's concerns seem prescient and well-founded in light of the resurgence of identity politics, ethno-nationalism, and many people's willingness to support leaders who show open contempt for negative liberty and the institutions on which it depends. The collapse of the Soviet Union did not lead to a spontaneous flowering of Enlightenment values, and liberal-democratic institutions have proved to be far from secure. Instead, fundamentalisms that submerge the human agency that Berlin valued in totalizing ideologies have flourished to a degree that would likely have surprised even him. In this respect, Berlin was right to warn against philosophical and political complacency among defenders of negative liberty.

On the other hand, Berlin's conviction that ideologies and movements advocating negative liberty had, in general, proved less politically dangerous historically than those aligned with positive liberty appears less sound today. In the older democracies, negative liberty seems to have become the ideological ballast of what Berlin himself might have identified as positive liberty–type movements. Berlin's defense of negative liberty assumed that the welfare state was a lasting achievement. He thought the New Deal had played an important role in buttressing freedom in the United States, praising it as "the most successful, admirable experiment promoting both justice and prosperity in a society" and "what on the whole saved America from socialism."[83] Yet today a variety of different movements wield the rhetoric of negative liberty against social services, industry regulation, and collective bargaining rights. Whereas Berlin's understanding of negative liberty was never antigovernment, recent movements that present themselves as protectors of personal liberty espouse a virulent antipathy for government regulation and a deep distrust of elites and experts that can all too easily ignite populist and even antidemocratic politics. Such developments suggest that Berlin's benign picture of negative liberty and his insistence that positive liberty is the only variant that threatens human freedom rested on contingent features of his world, not different analytical parsings of the term *freedom*.

MacCallum's original critique, however whiggish it might be, is therefore still worth endorsing. Just as there is little sense in throwing out the whole of the Enlightenment Project instead of reworking it toward the more chastened approach defended in the first part of this book, the moral of Berlin's story should not be that it leads us to reject either positive liberty or negative liberty on the testimony of their more extreme formulations, but to see that his dichotomous thinking rests on a category mistake. There is no correct definition of freedom by which we can determine someone to be free or unfree simpliciter because freedom is a relational concept. We learn more about the threats to freedom by considering the real-world restraints and enabling conditions affecting those relational components than we do by debating over different "kinds" of freedom. It may be, then, that Berlin's more meaningful legacy is not in the staying power of his "Two concepts." Rather, it is his warning that people are more easily mobilized in support of illiberal and antidemocratic causes when they feel insecure, and that theorists whose job it is to attend to political ideas do best in looking to understand the causes of this insecurity. But instead of searching for the causes of these developments in armchair speculations about human psychology, it makes better sense to look for them in the declining capacity of governments in many democracies to protect the basic interests of large numbers of their populations, who have consequently become vulnerable. Populist demagogues thrive when people face employment insecurity, downward mobility for themselves and their children, and the prospect of poverty in old age. A better Berlinian moral of his story is that unless the champions of liberty become successful advocates for diminishing the insecurity that feeds people's susceptibility to populist appeals, all bets are off.

8

Transforming Power Relations: Leadership, Risk, and Hope

(with James Read)

Political communities marred by long-standing, bitter conflicts find them extremely difficult to resolve, even if most members of the community suffer their effects and want them resolved. Such conflicts are chronically self-reinforcing: violent eruptions reproduce incentives for parties, leaders, and ordinary individuals to perpetuate the dynamic. They resemble Thomas Hobbes's hypothetical state of nature, and the prisoner's dilemma of game theory. The "Troubles" in Northern Ireland, the racial conflicts in South Africa, the Israeli-Palestinian conflicts today—others could be added—display the incentives and behaviors that perpetuate that cycle.

Hobbes insisted that only an all-powerful sovereign could break the cycle and bring civil peace.[1] But communities suffering chronic conflict lack an effective sovereign, or perhaps worse, harbor a state-asserting sovereign authority which itself propels the conflict because it is perceived as illegitimate by much of the population. The South African apartheid state, for example, possessed a powerful military, an effective bureaucracy, and strong support among white South Africans. But it was powerless to impose a solution to a conflict driven in large part by the very character of that state.

Nor is partition an assured solution. Territorially separate states can sometimes minimize conflict by disengaging. That is more difficult where communities in conflict share territory. In Yugoslavia the worst atrocities occurred after partition. Overturning South Africa's "Homelands" policy, a forced racial partition on extremely unequal terms, was a chief aim of the anti-apartheid movement. Even to agree on fair terms of partition, and ultimately separate states (an outcome generally favored in the Israeli-Palestinian case), requires a degree of intercommunal cooperation difficult to achieve given the conflict's bitter history.

Democratic franchise is not itself a solution without democratic institutions regarded on all sides as fair and legitimate. Communities marked by chronic conflict might not lack democratic practices altogether. Often they are flawed democracies that appeal to a democratic legitimacy which the system itself conspicuously fails to embody.[2] Leaders of battling groups are not monarchs able to arrange a pact and impose it on their subjects. They are accountable to separate constituencies, which retain the power to replace them and block any agreement the constituency has not been persuaded to support. In commencing a risky reform process in 1990, for example, South African President F. W. de Klerk anticipated a future in which all South Africans would enjoy political rights in some form. But his reforms would have been stillborn if, in the early 1990s, he had lost majority support among white South Africans. Democratic institutions at their best hold leaders accountable to the community as a whole. But flawed democratic institutions often reinforce the conflicts that prevent agreement on better democratic institutions.

It is tempting to categorize some conflicts as inherently zero-sum, one side's gain the other's loss, and dismiss as illusory any lasting, mutually acceptable settlement. Today the Israeli-Palestinian conflict is often thus described. Both sides make exclusive claims to the same territory, invoke irreconcilable religious identities to support those claims, and resort to violence that the other can neither forgive nor forget. Perpetual war seems inevitable. But similar claims were made about South Africa in the 1980s. Few observers then believed that white South Africans, whose military power remained unmatched on the African continent, would accept any state ruled by a black majority. To characterize a conflict as inherently zero-sum because of rival parties' supposedly irreconcilable interests and values is to overlook how events themselves, and actions of leaders with a hand in those events, can reshape people's preferences and beliefs about the conflict.

We make the case in section I that risk-embracing acts of political leadership, marked by what we call strategically hopeful action, are needed to extract positive-sum outcomes from apparently zero-sum conflicts. These acts clear the way for agreement on institutions that are cured of the flaws that undermined the old order's legitimacy. We elaborate on this argument in section II via a case study of the leadership by Nelson Mandela and F. W. de Klerk that made possible (though by no means guaranteed) the South African democratic transition. This leads to a general discussion of hopeful leadership in section III by reference to models of conflict and cooperation in the work of Robert Axelrod, Thomas Schelling, and Josep Colomer. In section IV we show how strategically hopeful leadership embodies a variable-sum understanding of power, and in section V we discuss the leadership records of the Northern Ireland settlement and the Israeli-Palestinian conflict in light of the preceding analysis.

I. Strategically Hopeful Action

By strategically hopeful action we mean a certain kind of calculated risk-taking in the face of imponderably complex circumstances, the aim of which is to replace a destructive status quo with a new and better dispensation. The paradoxical overtones of "strategically hopeful" are intentional: the phrase blends aspects of political action typically kept separate. The action must be strategic, because attempts to resolve chronic conflicts without hardheaded calculation would be merely wishful thinking, and in some circumstances dangerously reckless. The action must be hopeful because it requires willingness to bolster historical adversaries and take personal risks for a better future when key determinants of that future are, at best, imponderable. Displaying hope adds a performative ingredient at a time when it is essential. In periods of rapid political and institutional flux (like South Africa in the early 1990s), it is impossible for any leader to foresee, much less control, the wider flow of events. But a skilled leader can estimate the likely response of an adversary to an unexpected opening and act to improve its chance of being constructive. Among other skills this requires empathy, the capacity to imagine oneself in another's place and comprehend how the conflict looks from their perspective.

We illuminate strategically hopeful action by drawing from the indefinitely iterated prisoner's dilemma featured in the work of Robert Axelrod. But in contrast to Axelrod's unitary rational actors, we highlight the strategic dilemmas confronting individual leaders facing chronic conflict while retaining the support of refractory constituencies. Bitter communal conflicts resemble prisoner's dilemmas (PD) because most people on both sides would gain, compared to the miserable status quo, were they able to cooperate. But, without mutual trust, no party has good reasons to cooperate; thus potential mutual gains go unrealized. This will hold both for single-round PDs and for iterated PDs where the stakes are high and the number of rounds are known beforehand.

Actual conflicts are often of uncertain duration, generating more interesting possibilities. If A knows she will face B again in an indefinitely iterated interaction, then it might be in A's interest to cooperate, hoping *B* will reciprocate; and in *B*'s interest to reciprocate because if he defects, A will retaliate in the following round. This is the essence of "TIT FOR TAT" (TFT): cooperate on the first round, then mimic the other player.[3] But *A* takes a risk by cooperating first. If instead of reciprocating, *B* exploits *A*'s cooperation by defecting, *A* then defects on the next round, *B* defects again in turn, and the result is a self-reinforcing, mutually costly cycle. In contrast to a one-shot prisoner's dilemma, where the dominant strategy is always to defect, the indefinitely iterated PD offers genuine choices.

Axelrod found that TFT won in computer simulations of iterated dilemmas, beating a wide range of alternative strategies. Ironically, although TFT offers the highest average payoff, in any given round it never scores better than the other player, and always scores lower than an opponent who responds to cooperation by defecting. But players employing "nasty" strategies score badly against other "nasty" players: each drags the other down. TFT won "not by beating the other player, but by eliciting behavior from the other player which allowed both to do well."[4]

Real-world communal conflicts rarely permit a fresh beginning and exhibit instead an oft-repeated history of mutual violence and distrust. Axelrod recognized that with simple TFT, "once a feud gets started, it can continue indefinitely."[5] In later work Axelrod investigated strategies for restoring cooperation when it has broken down. These include "generous" TFT (occasionally cooperating in the face of an opponent's defection) and "contrite" TFT (cooperating in response to defection that was in response to your own previous defection).[6] Such restorative strategies can work if they are employed about 10 percent of the time, not more; otherwise they will be exploited.[7] They are useful here because they allow us to pinpoint the potential contributions of leaders to cooperative outcomes, and to highlight the risks they must be willing to take. Because generous TFT will be exploited if used too frequently, leaders who employ it assume a significant risk—for they must commit 100 percent to the move once chosen.

Moreover, in long-standing conflicts like those of South Africa, Northern Ireland, and Israel-Palestine, it is misleading to speak of "restoring" cooperation (as in Axelrod's model) because cooperation might never have existed. Strategically hopeful leaders must instead construct intercommunal cooperation for the first time and create an enduring constituency for it. And even if most people on both sides prefer peace to war, there typically remains a determined minority on each side that prefers war to any negotiated settlement. Such hardliners must be marginalized if they cannot be convinced or coopted. This is among the most difficult and essential tasks of a strategically hopeful leader. If one cannot be confident that hardliners (in the adversary's camp as well as one's own) can no longer be effective spoilers, then one cannot know what strategic game is being played. For among hardliners it is a zero-sum conflict, not a prisoner's dilemma.

Axelrod did not address the role of leaders; his actors could be whole communities, or even distinct species "cooperating" over the span of evolutionary time.[8] His narrative of the tacit "live and let live" ethic (which emerged across trench lines mutually to limit casualties in World War I) shows that leaderless cooperation can sometimes reduce the death toll.[9] But it did not end the war. One can imagine a comparable ethic occasionally emerging in neighborhoods of East Jerusalem, without resolving the larger conflict.

Individual leaders can initiate new, tentatively cooperative approaches more readily than can whole communities, but in the process accept a different degree of risk than the community does. Besides political failure and repudiation, such leaders risk assassination by extremists on both sides. The community can take a longer view: if one leader fails, it can elevate another; if a cooperative initiative fails, the community can pivot back to a warlike approach. Communities in long-term conflict thus mirror Axelrod's indefinitely iterated PD. But individual leaders may have only one major chance at intercommunal cooperation; if it fails, they could be finished. Their predicaments more closely resemble single-round PDs: the safe money bets the other way. To press forward with a cooperative opening, despite the odds, is a mark of strategically hopeful leadership. In effect, such leaders internalize the costs of solving collective-action problems that will otherwise continue plaguing their constituencies.

Game theorists typically assume utility-maximizing actors with fixed preferences who are indifferent to one another.[10] Axelrod makes more illuminating psychological observations. He reports that in real-world approximations of the iterated PD, "the very experience of sustained mutual cooperation altered the payoffs of the players, making mutual cooperation even more valued than it was before." Thus the successful experience of mutual cooperation can itself predispose people to view interactions in variable-sum rather than zero-sum terms. But the reverse also occurred: failed attempts at cooperation evoked "a powerful ethic of revenge" and reinforced tendencies to view conflicts as zero-sum, even when successful cooperation would have produced mutual gains.[11]

To have any chance of bridging long-standing divisions, strategically hopeful leaders must first judge for themselves that the conflict is potentially positive-sum. They have to believe, and persuade others to believe, that all parties lose if the conflict continues unabated (even if they lose unequally), and that all stand to gain if the conflict can be resolved. Yet they recognize that accumulated bitterness and past failures at cooperation have led many to perceive it as zero-sum—resolvable only by victory for one side and defeat for the other. Game theoretic models mask this judgment problem when utilities over outcomes are assigned to actors. The payoff schedule of a PD indicates that both actors are better off if they cooperate; the problem is that neither can trust the other. Strategically hopeful leaders confront the trust problem, but they also face another, equally difficult challenge: convincing skeptics on both sides that any potential outcome will leave both parties better off. The mutual cooperation outcome in the PD interaction, if never realized, may disappear altogether from participants' consciousness, making it appear a game of pure conflict. Thus strategically hopeful leaders must not only play the game strategically; they must also persuade others about which strategic game is being played.

Strategically hopeful leaders must also know how to circumvent preconditions. Parties locked in chronic conflict typically insist on mutually incompatible preconditions for negotiations. Preconditions highlight and often magnify the prisoner's dilemma because each side insists on securing concessions before negotiations that could only be obtained with great difficulty through negotiations; in the unlikely event that its preconditions were met, it would have no further incentive to negotiate. Waiving one's own preconditions looks like waving the white flag. Strategically hopeful leaders must somehow sidestep their constituency's preconditions without acceding to their adversary's, and risk failing if "the enemy" refuses to meet them halfway. Strict preconditions—like demands to end violence or decommission—also enable hardliners to kill negotiations by deliberately violating those preconditions.

Strategically hopeful leaders recognize their bridge-building attempts will fail unless preferences on both sides change. If leaders instead seek to maximize the satisfaction of prevailing preferences—which in practice means the preferences of the constituency to whom they are immediately accountable—then peace efforts are doomed. In times of regime transition, when stakes are high, institutions in rapid flux, and the outcome uncertain, political preferences become interdependent to a significant degree: the aims of each side become importantly conditioned by signals from the other side. It is here that strategically hopeful leadership can have its greatest impact. A cooperative opening that, against the odds, achieves early if limited success can change each side's perception of the other side's intentions. Changes in what is perceived to be possible alter in turn what is possible, to a degree unforeseeable to many before the process began. The assumption before 1994 that white South Africans would never relinquish their monopoly on political power turned out, given the right circumstances, to be unfounded.

The dynamic of interdependent preferences cuts both ways. On one hand it encourages hope for a new opening. However risky and difficult the first step, if it induces a constructive response, this can alter the preferences and perceptions of others, generate a surplus of good will, and make subsequent moves possible that previously were not. But the same effect works in reverse: any serious misstep risks modifying preferences in negative directions, making future cooperation harder than before. Strategically hopeful leaders recognize that, if they fail, their failure constricts the options of their successors.

Strategically hopeful leaders implicitly see power as variable-sum. Political power is frequently, perhaps even normally, gained at another's expense: one candidate wins an election, another loses. More fatefully, in the cases that concern us here, the success of reformist leaders depends upon facing down their own radical flanks, whose members will see reformists' gain of power as their own loss and vice versa. To perceive power as variable-sum does not mean that literally everyone gains, or that gains are equally shared, only that gains can exceed losses or losses exceed gains. Even during the horrific meltdown of the former Yugoslavia in the 1990s (where, it is often remarked, "everyone lost," and whose path South Africa might have followed), every atrocity produced its own relative winners and losers.[12] A variable-sum understanding of power requires looking past the more obvious political gains and losses and taking into consideration the wider community's collective power over its own future, which can be enhanced or diminished by leaders' success or failure in risk-taking efforts at cooperation.

Strategically hopeful leaders must recognize that their own power to secure a resolution acceptable to their constituency depends upon preserving, and where necessary reinforcing, the power of the "enemy" leader across the table. They must resist the temptation to weaken an antagonistic rival and divide the opposition; otherwise their rivals will be unable to persuade their own constituencies to support an agreement. Here one's own power stands or falls with the power of one's counterpart on the other side. This is easy to recognize in principle, but acting upon it is difficult.

We turn next to two decisions, one taken by Nelson Mandela in 1985 and the other by F. W. de Klerk in 1992, that exemplify strategically hopeful leadership. Neither leader possessed comprehensive, impartial understanding of the events in which they participated. Both were limited in what they could see and even more limited in what they could control. Nor were they saints, untainted by ordinary political ambition. Yet their political ambitions led them, at decisive moments, to risk their careers and perhaps their lives on making cooperative moves across the divide when the usual political incentives, and the advice of trusted colleagues, prescribed the opposite. Different leaders might well have chosen differently, with very different consequences for the country.

Some rational choice analyses of leadership treat leaders as political entrepreneurs who solve collective-action problems in exchange for personal "profit" (appropriating revenues, distributing patronage, continuing in office).[13] This describes many politicians, but fails to illuminate strategically hopeful efforts to resolve long-standing, bitter conflicts when all previous attempts have failed. Even success here may ultimately spell the end of a political career, as it did for F. W. de Klerk and David Trimble; and failure will end a career even sooner. Strategically hopeful leaders recognize the human cost of continued battle. Their ambition is perhaps to be remembered as one of those who resolved it.

II. Two Leaders, Two Gambles

In 1985 Nelson Mandela (then in Pollsmoor Prison) decided to initiate secret talks with representatives of the National Party government, without the knowledge or approval of the African National Congress (ANC) executive committee—neither its leaders in exile, nor those likewise imprisoned at Pollsmoor with whom he was in regular communication. Mandela did not propose formal negotiations with the government; he invited "talks about talks." Yet even this step was exceedingly risky, both for the ANC and for Mandela personally. The ANC's policy was that negotiations could begin only after the government satisfied various preconditions, none of which had been met: revoking the legal ban on the ANC and other anti-apartheid groups, releasing all political prisoners, and allowing open political opposition. On the contrary, the government's repression of anti-apartheid activity was increasing (Prime Minister P. W. Botha would declare a new state of emergency in 1986). The government's own preconditions excluded negotiations unless and until the ANC permanently renounced violence and dismantled its military wing, Umkhonto we Sizwe.

Mandela recognized that military overthrow of apartheid was "a distant if not impossible dream."[14] But the *idea* of armed struggle, even on a limited scale, was enormously important to the ANC rank-and-file and could not easily be relinquished. By 1985 the Soviet Union had ended the support it once provided to the ANC and the

South African Communist Party.[15] This would have increased the ANC's motivation to negotiate with the government, but also heightened the risk in doing so, because eagerness to talk might telegraph the ANC's diminished military capability and worsen its bargaining position. Under the circumstances, for Mandela to invite talks could betray ANC weakness in an increasingly high-stakes struggle. The government might accept Mandela's invitation with the ulterior aim of trapping him and dividing ANC leadership at a crucial moment.[16]

Nevertheless Mandela decided to go forward, and to keep it secret from his ANC colleagues until he was committed:

> If we did not start a dialogue soon, both sides would be plunged into a dark night of oppression, violence, and war. . . . Both sides [would] lose thousands if not millions of lives in a conflict that was unnecessary. [The government] must have known this as well. It was time to talk.
>
> This would be extremely sensitive. Both sides regarded discussions as a sign of weakness and betrayal. Neither would come to the table unless the other made significant concessions. . . . Someone from our side needed to take the first step.
>
> I chose to tell no one of what I was about to do. . . . I knew that my colleagues upstairs would condemn my proposal, and that would kill my initiative even before it was born. There are times when a leader must move out ahead of his flock, go off in a new direction, confident that he is leading his people the right way. Finally, my isolation furnished my organization with an excuse in case matters went awry: the old man was alone and completely cut off, and his actions were taken by him as an individual, not a representative of the ANC.[17]

Once his initiative was underway, Mandela informed his ANC colleagues. Their responses were sharply divided, but most were guardedly willing to permit Mandela to continue an action they would not have approved in advance.

Mandela's strategic observations could be summarized as follows:

1. The South African conflict was potentially variable-sum. Though many on both sides perceived it as zero-sum, in fact both stood to gain from a political settlement and both would lose terribly in an escalating racial war.
2. Nevertheless, if present trends continued, the lose-lose outcome ("dark night of oppression, violence, and war") would occur, because "both sides regarded discussions as a sign of weakness and betrayal." Mandela was describing a classic prisoner's dilemma.
3. A leader must resolve this impasse, "move out ahead of the flock," hoping this will enable people to perceive, and act on, the positive-sum possibilities. But this is risky because the leader cannot control the process he/she sets in motion; the other side may indeed suspect weakness and escalate its demands.
4. In taking this step Mandela internalized much of the risk, thereby diminishing it for other anti-apartheid activists. He realized that his initiative might backfire, finishing him as a top ANC leader. Indeed he discerned bargaining leverage with the government in the fact that, if "matters went awry," his colleagues could limit the damage by renouncing the initiative of an irrelevant old man. Mandela might "move out ahead of his flock," but he knew the "flock" was free to denounce him and refuse to follow.

Mandela's 1985 decision to "talk to the enemy" was one vital step in replacing apartheid with racially inclusive democracy.[18] Equally crucial and risky was the decision taken in 1992 by President

F. W. de Klerk, the man who had released Mandela from prison two years earlier. Unlike Mandela's 1985 move, which occurred far from public view, de Klerk's gamble took place in the glare of publicity.

De Klerk belonged to P. W. Botha's cabinet during the 1980s, but had not participated in, and initially was not informed of, the government's talks with the still-imprisoned Mandela. Before his presidency de Klerk appeared a typical conservative Afrikaner politician displaying little reformist behavior. But he became privately convinced that apartheid had failed and that only fundamental reform "could pull South Africa back from the edge of the chasm on which we were teetering."[19] Botha had admitted as early as 1979 that South Africans must "adapt or die," but was unwilling or unable to follow through. And even if Botha had committed to reform, there were then no ANC leaders with whom he could have negotiated. In contrast, from the outset of de Klerk's presidency in 1989 (by which time he would certainly have known of the Mandela talks) he judged Mandela to be someone with whom "it would be possible for us to do business."[20] In February 1990 de Klerk surprised South Africa and the world by lifting the ban on the ANC, the South African Communist Party, and the Pan Africanist Congress (PAC) unconditionally. He announced plans to release all political prisoners including Mandela, and to begin negotiations toward democracy.[21]

But by 1992 de Klerk's reform effort was greatly endangered. Political violence had escalated, especially between ANC supporters and followers of Mangosuthu Buthelezi's ethnically Zulu Inkatha Freedom Party (IFP) in Natal. Negotiations on a new constitutional settlement had collapsed. There was an apparently unbridgeable gulf between the ANC's demand for full majority rule and the government's insistence on permanent constitutionally guaranteed veto rights for all minorities (the white minority included). Instead of trusting the government to lead the reform process, as de Klerk hoped, the ANC had stepped up its campaign of mass action. Though it had announced a "suspension" of the armed struggle in 1990, it had not dismantled its military wing. The economy was imploding. Personal relations between de Klerk and Mandela had soured. Mandela accused de Klerk of complicity in government-instigated violence, a charge the latter vehemently denied; de Klerk in turn suspected Mandela of concocting such charges to maximize his bargaining leverage.[22] The country appeared headed for the abyss.

De Klerk's standing among the white electorate, to whom he owed his presidency and thus any opportunity to engage in reform, was eroding dangerously. In late 1991 and early 1992 the Conservative Party, which was intensely opposed to de Klerk's reforms, began winning by-elections in former National Party strongholds. The election results were widely interpreted as a rejection of the National Party's reform proposals on the part of white voters, who were at that point still the only voters who mattered.[23] "The mandate that I had received in 1989 from the white electorate was visibly slipping away from me and the National Party."[24] According to conventional wisdom, de Klerk at this point should have moved to the right, shoring up his political base and salvaging his party's governing status—even at the cost of scaling back or postponing his plans to dismantle apartheid. Many of de Klerk's supporters, advisors, and cabinet members urged this course.

Instead, on February 20, 1992, de Klerk surprised the public and many in the National Party leadership by calling a snap referendum among white voters on the question: "Do you support the continuation of the reform process that the state president started on 2 February 1990 and which is aimed at a new constitution through negotiations?" De Klerk typically sought consensus in his party and cabinet, but in this one case he acted unilaterally: "If I had put my decision to the vote the majority of the caucus would have opposed what they then regarded as an over-hasty and risky decision."[25] He made clear that if the referendum failed he would resign. He campaigned vigorously for the March referendum, winning an impressive 68.7 percent yes vote.

De Klerk later explained his reasoning in calling the referendum: people were expressing their fears and dissatisfactions in the by-election results, but when confronted squarely with the issue of the country's future they would rise to the occasion and embrace the need for change. There was no polling data on the subject. He was relying on his intuitive sense of what moved his compatriots and why.[26]

De Klerk survived one risky move only to face another. The referendum had not ratified any particular post-apartheid settlement. It had merely authorized him to continue a process whose ultimate outcome he could not fully control. He would likely have been finished politically if, after winning the referendum, he had failed to secure an agreement with the ANC that was also acceptable to a critical mass of white South Africans. And in 1992 the two sides' constitutional demands were still fundamentally opposed. De Klerk and the National Party had promised during the referendum campaign that they would never give up constitutionally guaranteed power sharing, while the ANC rejected any such provision as apartheid in another form. Only in late 1993 did de Klerk relinquish entrenched power sharing, settling instead for constitutional guarantees on property rights, civil freedoms, and a two-thirds majority to alter the constitution. The white minority's willingness ultimately to accept in 1994 what they still appeared implacably to reject in 1992—black majority rule over which whites possessed no guaranteed veto rights—illustrates the fluid character of political preferences as events unfolded. (Whether de Klerk knew in 1992 that he was promising white voters more than he could later deliver is an open question.)[27]

De Klerk recognized he could not impose a constitutional settlement unilaterally. He needed the cooperation of Mandela and his supporters in the ANC—this after the National Party government and the ANC had been through decades of bitter conflict in which countless people had been uprooted, imprisoned, tortured, and killed. Unlike his predecessor, de Klerk was not only willing to cross this Rubicon, but to plunge into it and start swimming when he had no guarantee that anyone on the other bank—the ANC and its radical allies—would help him across if he began to drown.[28]

Both Mandela and de Klerk recognized the interdependent character of the negotiated transition: neither could succeed without the cooperation of the other. Both viewed the situation as variable-sum (they and their respective constituencies stood to gain or lose together, but each also hoped to gain more or lose less than the other). Both knew there were hardliners on both sides who saw the conflict as irreducibly zero-sum, anticipating a violent showdown. De Klerk observed of Mandela: "We realized that we both bore the ultimate responsibility for ensuring that there would be a negotiated settlement and we were both committed to carrying out this responsibility."[29] Mandela correspondingly recognized de Klerk's "genuine and indispensable contribution to the peace process," remarking that, "To make peace with an enemy one must work with that enemy, and that enemy becomes one's partner."[30] Both believed that failure to cooperate would produce horrifying losses for all—"a dark night of oppression, violence, and war," "a prolonged struggle so bitter and destructive that there would be little left for anyone to inherit."[31]

Yet both also recognized conflict over the terms on which these common interests would be met. De Klerk and Mandela acted "in the full knowledge that we were opponents with divergent goals."[32] In addition to conflicts among the constituencies they represented and deeply divergent constitutional proposals, there was little personal trust between Mandela and de Klerk during the negotiations process. Yet both were willing to take significant personal risks to bridge the racial divide, hoping but not knowing that the other would reciprocate.

The South African transition was far from bloodless. Between February 1990, when Mandela was released from prison, and April 1994, when the ANC won South Africa's first democratic election, more than fourteen thousand South Africans died in political violence.[33] By some conventional measures the struggle over apartheid during the period 1985–94 crossed the threshold of civil war; the early 1990s conflict between ANC supporters and Inkatha in Natal certainly did.[34] Political violence motivated Mandela and de Klerk to persist in negotiations because both feared matters would become much worse if they failed to cooperate. Other leaders in their position might well have acted differently, with radically different consequences.

III. Leadership, Strategic Interaction, and the Prisoner's Dilemma

Mandela and de Klerk realized that resolution of the conflict depended on an interdependent decision: neither could impose a unilateral solution, but each instead had to offer something that could become acceptable both to the adversary and to their own constituencies. The tragedy of interdependent decision is that outcomes worse for all may result because leaders cannot agree on terms of cooperation.

There is an enormous literature on leadership, scholarly and popular. But little of it addresses the problem that concerns us here: how leaders democratically accountable to one constituency in a long-standing communal conflict can initiate cooperation across the divide, then persuade their own constituency to start crossing a bridge that is still under construction. Analyses of democratic leadership that presuppose effectively functioning institutions widely perceived as legitimate, like the large literature on presidential leadership, do not reach our case.

Rational choice theories of leadership often feature what William Riker calls "heresthetics" or "the art of political manipulation"—leaders strategically deploying words and actions to structure decisions to their advantage, to get their way without having to persuade anyone to modify their preferences.[35] For example, by manipulating the order in which a set of alternatives is voted on, one can win a decision—without altering preferences—that would have been lost had the voting order been different. Both Mandela and de Klerk were, among other things, skilled "political manipulators" in Riker's sense: at key moments both took risks that their colleagues would have opposed had they been consulted beforehand but were guardedly willing to support afterward. But Mandela's and de Klerk's short-term "agenda manipulation" was directed to longer-term ends that could only be realized if other key elites and substantial numbers of their constituents were persuaded, through both word and act, to modify their political preferences.

The notion that leaders merely manipulate fixed preferences provoked an initially useful, but now excessive counterreaction in the enormous literature on "transforming" leadership pioneered by James MacGregor Burns.[36] In contrast to merely "transactional" leaders, "transformative" leaders are said to create new possibilities by modifying the character and preferences of followers. Transformative leadership theories identify an important element missing from rational choice accounts, but too often treat transformation as a quality inhering in a charismatic leader, or emerging from that leader's interactions with committed followers. At least equally important for understanding acts of communal bridge-building are leaders' strategic interactions with rival leaders, and with their constituencies—for whom an adversary's charisma might actually be a threatening liability. In the South African transition, Mandela's transformative capacities depended upon de Klerk's responses and vice versa, and on the fragile support of skeptical constituencies—as both leaders fully understood. For these reasons we find theories of strategic interaction, even when they exclude or underplay leadership, more useful to the problem at hand than much of the leadership literature. But it needs to be supplemented by greater attention to the way leadership shapes the outcomes of strategic interactions. Axelrod's iterated prisoner's dilemma has been discussed; here we examine Thomas Schelling and Josep Colomer.

Despite its vintage, Schelling's *Strategy of Conflict* remains among the most fruitful examinations of the type of decision problem considered here.[37] Schelling makes a fundamental distinction between zero-sum (or "constant sum") conflicts, where "more for one participant inexorably means less for another"; and variable-sum, or "mixed motive" conflicts, in which "there are common as well as conflicting interests among the participants" and "mutual dependence as well as opposition." Strategy in a variable-sum game must take account, not only of "the division of gains and losses between two claimants," but also of "the possibility that particular outcomes are worse (better) for both claimants than certain other outcomes. . . . There is a common interest in reaching outcomes that are mutually advantageous." Neither participant can fully control the outcome; instead, "the ability of one participant to gain his ends is dependent to an important degree on the choices or decisions that the other participant will make."[38] Cooperation might fail because whoever first indicates willingness to cooperate signals potential weakness, inviting exploitation by the other side or because one or both sides are unable credibly to commit to positions from which they will not later be tempted or pressured to move. For negotiations to succeed, expectations on both sides "must somehow converge on a single point at which each expects the other not to expect to be expected to retreat."[39]

Either party can jeopardize the possibility of an agreement by weakening the other too much. Mandela illustrates Schelling's point when he writes that, despite the frictions, "I never sought to undermine Mr. de Klerk" because "the weaker he was, the weaker the negotiations process."[40] Mandela did on occasion push ANC demands close to the limits of what de Klerk could accept, but never forgot that de Klerk had his own constituencies to satisfy.

Schelling's variable-sum model aptly describes the South African racial power contest as perceived by both Mandela and de Klerk. Both agreed that through cooperation each side stood to gain—at least compared to the likely outcome without cooperation. Both recognized the interdependent character of the decision: if either refused to sign, or agreed to a pact they could not persuade their constituency to support, then both constituencies would lose, as would the leaders themselves, politically and personally. Each recognized that the other also recognized these things.

But Mandela and de Klerk also understood something Schelling does not discuss: whether a conflict is perceived as zero-sum or variable-sum may itself be at stake in what leaders do and say. Schelling takes as given that a conflict is either zero-sum or variable-sum, which in turn is a function of the respective, independently derived preferences on each side. This initial classification is decisive because "the intellectual processes of choosing a strategy in pure conflict and choosing a strategy of coordination are of wholly different sorts."[41] But Schelling does not explain how participants decide whether they believe the conflict to be zero-sum or variable-sum. Mandela's inviting "talks about talks" with the government in 1985 was risky because, though he perceived the conflict as potentially variable-sum, he did not know whether his colleagues or the National Party government would agree. For Mandela to frame the conflict as involving potential shared gains was a hopeful act.

Even if leaders on both sides view a conflict as potentially variable-sum, cooperation might fail because their respective constituencies—who retain the power to block agreements and replace their leaders—might instead prefer a fight to the finish. Mandela noted that many anti-apartheid activists in the early 1990s demanded "a victory on the battlefield, not the negotiating table" and he noticed signs at rallies reading, "MANDELA, GIVE US GUNS" and "VICTORY THROUGH BATTLE NOT TALK."[42] De Klerk was equally aware of the white right who anticipated a violent showdown.[43] Both faced a twin challenge: first to manage a difficult bargaining process with adversaries, then to persuade a critical mass of the rank-and-file on both sides to support an agreement.

Unlike more formalized rational choice approaches, Schelling does not stipulate invariant preference functions. But his bargainers maximize their share of a fixed supply of gains from cooperation. He ignores the ways in which actors with interdependent preferences can expand (or shrink) the available surplus depending on their behavior in successive rounds of bargaining. This is the performative dimension of cooperation: when successful, it creates a new reality.[44]

Schelling also downplays the moral dimension of leadership: negotiations between warring underworld gangs, or kidnappers and victims, do not differ in strategic logic from any other bargaining situation in which conflict and cooperation intermix.[45] Schelling's undemanding leadership assumptions reach their limits in explaining anything as difficult as the South African settlement. What Mandela asked white South Africans to give up—their monopoly on political power, in exchange for an uncertain future under majority rule—went well beyond the kind of concessions featured in *The Strategy of Conflict*. It is unsurprising that many people on all sides saw the conflict as zero-sum, and in particular that white South Africans anticipated harsh treatment from an empowered black majority they had oppressed for so long. White South Africans still retained decisive military and economic superiority, and some on the right would have gladly pushed de Klerk aside to spearhead a violent contest. Both de Klerk and Mandela kept a close eye on the South African military throughout a transition that the military could have halted had it chosen to do so.[46]

Yet in the end white South Africans turned over power to a black-majority government led by Nelson Mandela, who promised them no more—but also no less—than to live as equal citizens in a multiracial democracy. That "South Africa belongs to all who live in it, black or white" was affirmed in the ANC's Freedom Charter of 1955. But few South Africans of any race had personally experienced this kind of political community. One of Mandela's accomplishments was to make this vision believable, both to its advocates after nearly a century of frustration, and to white South Africans who feared that majority rule meant oppressor and oppressed exchanging positions.

Mandela understood this fear and addressed it. "I have fought against white domination, and I have fought against black domination. I have cherished the ideal of a democratic and free society in which all persons live together in harmony and with equal opportunities."[47] But it was his actions that made the statement believable, just as de Klerk's turning on the white right and plunging into the Rubicon established his credibility. Taking these risks enabled them to persuade their supporters to rethink the conflict in variable-sum terms. Once they did, they could focus on their enduring common interests beneath the more obvious conflicts.

Schelling does not specifically discuss democratic transitions. Josep M. Colomer's *Strategic Transitions: Game Theory and Democrati-*

zation is immediately directed to the problem at hand.[48] Colomer examines possible coalitions among six types of strategic actors: radical democratic opposition; moderate democratic opposition; radical softliners (reformists in the regime); moderate softliners (less committed reformists); moderate hardliners; and radical hardliners.[49] His model emerges from democratic transitions in the former Soviet bloc, but with some modification can also illuminate South Africa, Northern Ireland, and other cases.

Colomer seeks to explain why confrontation between regime and democratic opposition sometimes produces stable compromises, and other times triggers "frontal conflict" whereby both sides risk "becoming an absolute loser."[50] Like Schelling, Colomer presupposes variable-sum interdependent decision: neither regime nor democratic opposition is powerful enough unilaterally to determine outcomes, and failure to cooperate leads to consequences worse for both. Following Axelrod, Colomer takes the prisoner's dilemma as the starting point and seeks to explain how "cooperation can develop even among antagonists."[51] But Colomer argues that critical transitions more closely resemble single-shot PDs because "actors' opportunities to repeat interactions in a process of regime change may be remote."[52]

To explain how cooperation might emerge from a single-shot PD, Colomer endows actors with the capacity for foresight. Mutually destructive outcomes result from "short-term-looking decisions . . . made in ignorance of other actors' choices." But rational actors should be able "to foresee not only the immediate consequences of their choices but also the consequences of the other actors' reactions, their further counter-reactions, and so on."[53] Colomer's prescient actors do not make simultaneous, blind choices as in the classic PD. Instead they "enter into open, dynamic interactions in which they make choices precisely in the expectation of other actors' reaction, as is typically the case in political exchanges."[54] Rejecting the assumption that moves once taken cannot be reversed, Colomer introduces retractable moves—for example, "if the hard-liners reject an intermediate formula proposed by the opposition, the latter can resume mobilizations and protests."[55] Colomer's model thus builds flexibility into single-shot PDs; mutual defection is not inevitable.

Colomer's introduction of foresight—the principal innovation of his model—simultaneously reveals a limitation: there is no specific role for leadership. If foresight was equally distributed among human beings and operative in all strategic interactions, PDs would always be resolved and civil wars would seldom occur. Most people most of the time operate with limited and inflexible cognitive capacities.[56] Colomer's actors represent strategic positions (like "moderate democratic opposition"), not individual leaders, even when he illustrates those positions with proper names like Gorbachev and Havel.[57] If the classic PD underestimates the cooperative possibilities, Colomer's revision, while insightful, downplays the difficulty of exercising foresight in periods of rapid and extraordinarily complex change.

Nor does the model provide for the different degree of risk run by individual leaders as compared to collectivities during such periods. Colomer assumes, for example, that actors' strategies will be weighted by a preference for peace over war: "A transition by agreement is less risky for the actors involved than a civil war."[58] This is true as a general proposition (otherwise negotiated solutions would be impossible). But for individual leaders it is often much riskier, politically and personally, to initiate a cooperative opening where there has been a long history of conflict and distrust than to do nothing. What would be ultimately risk-minimizing for the group, if it can be achieved, may be risk-augmenting for the leader who makes the first move. The foresight required under such circumstances is more complex than the general recognition that both groups lose if they fail to cooperate.

IV. Zero-Sum and Variable-Sum Power

The prisoner's dilemma is a parable of powerlessness. The prisoners lack power to realize their common interests because they can neither alter the rules, nor trust one another to cooperate under those rules. With respect to utility, the PD is potentially variable-sum: mutual cooperation yields the highest aggregate utility and mutual defection the lowest. But with respect to power, their interaction appears zero-sum. For the only aspect of the interaction lying within each prisoner's control is deciding whether to cooperate or defect. Cooperation leaves one powerless and vulnerable. Defection promises each prisoner a small degree of power, though of course at the other's expense.

An iterated PD creates a wider range of options. If each actor must take future retaliation or cooperation by the other into account, defection is no longer obviously a dominant strategy. An invitation to mutual cooperation is sometimes successful, though it offers no guarantee. This expanded range of strategies suggests an alteration of the power relations among the actors. This latter possibility has not received much discussion, perhaps because the concept of power is not explicitly employed in formal game theory, though assumptions about power are implicit in the structure of the game.[59] If, under the classic one-shot PD, each actor's power comes at the expense of the other and aggregate power is fixed at a low level, then it should follow that, under an iterated PD where reciprocity and trust can potentially emerge, the power of each actor does not necessarily come at the other's expense, and the power available to both actors is potentially variable, not fixed. This hypothesis requires that we examine the concept of power itself.

The meaning of power has long been contested.[60] Hobbes defined it as one's "present means to obtain some future apparent good."[61] This definition of power is not inherently zero-sum; in principle we might secure our own good by cooperating with others in realizing theirs. But where interests conflict, or where shared interests go unrealized because trust is absent (as in the state of nature), power for Hobbes becomes zero-sum in practice. Thus elsewhere Hobbes provides the classic zero-sum description of power: "Because the power of one man resisteth and hindereth the effects of the power of another: power simply is no more, but the excess of the power of one above that of another. For equal powers opposed, destroy one another, and such their opposition is called contention."[62]

For Hobbes, one's power is demonstrated through victory in a head-to-head contest. This premise is shared by the realist school of international relations theory, who perceive an anarchic realm in which war-winning capacity counts above all.[63] But Hobbes's idea is also echoed in the way many political scientists define power even under the operation of peaceful democratic rules. According to Nelson Polsby—speaking here as a "pluralist" in the "three faces of power debate"—in studying power we should focus above all on who wins and who loses in a "direct conflict between actors," because this is the best measure of their respective "capacities to affect outcomes."[64] The "radicals" in this faces-of-power debate pointed out that conflict and domination were not always readily visible. But they did not question the assumption that power always comes at another's expense; indeed they drove that premise further.[65]

Conflict and inequality are always relevant to understanding political power. The more problematic assumption is that A's capacity to "affect outcomes" is a direct function of B's lack of capacity to affect those same outcomes. This doubtless describes many power relations, but not the negotiations between Mandela and de Klerk. If those interactions were conflictual and "subtractive" in some respects, they were cooperative and "additive" in others. Conflict and cooperation fused in the same complex relation; both shaped the outcome. To comprehend as power only the conflict and ignore the cooperation—

as though cooperation were passive, something other than power—is to misunderstand the power relationship itself.

The assumption that power is inherently zero-sum has not gone unchallenged. Power has alternatively been defined as the cooperative capacity to achieve collectively shared aims (Talcott Parsons) or the general capacity of human beings to "act together" (Hannah Arendt). But Parsons's and Arendt's arguments, though insightful, are flawed by their treating power as almost wholly cooperative, thus neglecting the element of conflict that preoccupies other theorists of power.[66] Some challenges to the zero-sum view do incorporate both conflict and cooperation, but fail to develop alternative variable-sum descriptions in much detail.[67] The zero-sum view of power, despite its one-sidedness, has produced rich descriptions of political life.[68] The variable-sum alternative view, to be fully persuasive, must pass this same test.

The political interactions between Mandela and de Klerk, and between the constituencies they led, suggest that a variable-sum theory of power can persuasively describe significant dimensions of political life—without neglecting inequality, domination, the potential for violence, and the persistence of conflict. Both Mandela and de Klerk understood the struggle in variable-sum, not zero-sum terms. When Mandela reminded South Africans that "I have fought against white domination, and I have fought against black domination," he was challenging a zero-sum picture of power: that liberation for either community entailed domination for the other. Mandela's hopeful view—one shared with de Klerk, despite their divergent constitutional visions—was that black South Africans could be liberated without dominating whites (or any other group of this multiracial society).[69]

But Mandela and de Klerk also realized that many South Africans on all sides saw one group's gain as the other's loss; such zero-sum perceptions threatened to produce negative-sum outcomes. Both were aware of the conflicting aims of their respective constituencies and of their personal conflicts as rival leaders. Yet both also recognized that each had to keep the other strong enough to retain the support of their constituencies for any negotiated settlement, and for this reason could not push an advantage too far. They can be imagined as actors in a prisoner's dilemma who, by taking risks to generate trust, have found a way out of the prison. In the classic prisoner's dilemma, the powerlessness of each ensures the defection of both. Mandela and de Klerk overcame this dilemma because their interactions generated new power on both sides.

The variable-sum view of power sketched out above does not "refute" the common assumption that political power is gained at another's expense, for two reasons. First, where power is cooperatively generated, there remain important respects in which power gains for some entail power losses for others. In a stable democracy, rival parties compete for a fixed number of powerful offices even as they cooperate to maintain the power of the democratic system itself. In South Africa, the reversal-of-domination scenario feared by white South Africans did not occur, in part because de Klerk and Mandela cooperated to prevent it. In this sense the variable-sum model best captures events even though white South Africans had to relinquish significant political power for black South Africans to gain new political power.

Furthermore, because it remains a self-fulfilling prophesy, the zero-sum hypothesis cannot be dismissed. If one behaves as though power is radically zero-sum, one can indeed make it zero-sum. Had either Mandela or de Klerk been replaced by leaders who understood the contest in zero-sum terms and acted accordingly, an escalation of racial war would have been the likely outcome. A zero-sum strategy, once decided upon, will prove itself correct because the adversary responds in kind. A strategically hopeful opening, by contrast, might fail. There is no best strategy but instead a morally charged choice among contingent strategies.

V. Unionists and Nationalists, Israelis and Palestinians

The South African constitutional resolution was not replicated in Northern Ireland or Israel. Those conflicts differ in their histories, the ideologies invoked, the role of outside actors, and the design of settlements realized or proposed. But there are significant parallels.

First, all three are (or were) high-intensity, self-reinforcing conflicts with no end in sight. Second, none of the parties to these conflicts could win a decisive victory and impose a unilateral solution. But reformers in the government and moderates in the opposition could potentially negotiate settlements that would command enough support to endure. Finally, all three conflicts can be understood either as zero-sum or variable-sum, depending on how one frames them and whether one regards the preferences of the principal actors as fixed or dynamic. There was nothing about the South African conflict that made it inherently more amenable to resolution than the other two. Apartheid was obviously incompatible with nonracial democracy. Northern Irish nationalism contradicts Northern Irish unionism. Israelis and Palestinians advance irreconcilable historical and religious claims to exclusive possession of the same land. If human beings were mere replicas of the ideologies they espouse, then all these conflicts would be inescapably zero-sum. In fact, people who live through chronic conflicts often suffer greatly, and most appear to place more value on physical and economic security and personal liberty than on pursuing ideological stances to their ultimate conclusion.[70]

Protracted, self-reinforcing conflicts will continue unless a leader of at least one of the parties stakes a career on altering the dynamic. Even so, the odds of failure are high; there are many more ways for negotiations to fail than to succeed. And leaders who successfully bridge the abyss against the odds may receive few political rewards for doing so, as Northern Ireland demonstrates.

The 1998 Good Friday (or Belfast) Agreement should be considered a qualified success because it ended most of the political violence, and all significant players remain committed to employing only peaceful means in pursuit of political goals.[71] (Peace efforts stalled whenever parties demanded preconditions and advanced when these were waived.)[72] The fundamental question—whether Northern Ireland shall remain with the United Kingdom or join the Republic of Ireland—remains unresolved, and Protestant and Catholic communities remain highly politically and culturally segregated.[73] But all major parties, including those most committed to a united Ireland, have accepted "the principle of consent": that "Northern Ireland should remain in the UK as long as a majority of Northern Ireland's citizens support this status," and that any unification with Ireland requires majority support of Northern Ireland's people in a referendum.[74] The agreement was facilitated by external actors—Britain, the Republic of Ireland, the United States—but would have been impossible without risk-embracing political leaders from both sides of Northern Ireland's communal divide. Yet those leaders occasionally lost their nerve or dragged their feet in ways that weakened the example they set.

In Northern Ireland, the political incentives for communal reconciliation have always been slim. Unionist firebrand Ian Paisley expressed the once-prevailing view in both camps: "A traitor and a bridge are very much alike, for they both go over to the other side."[75] In the decades preceding the 1998 agreement, Unionist leaders like Terence O'Neill and Brian Faulkner who reached across communal lines found their political careers abruptly cut short. For Nationalists and Republicans (who seek to unite Northern Ireland to the Republic of Ireland) the political rewards for compromise have been equally meager.[76] The most significant Nationalist bridge-builder has long been John Hume of the Social Democratic and Labour Party (SDLP), who since the 1960s advocated what ultimately became central principles of the 1998 agreement: commitment to exclusively peaceful measures, the legitimacy of both Northern Ireland political traditions, and the principle of consent.[77] But Britain's violent repression in 1972 energized the Irish Republican Army (IRA) at the expense of Hume's peaceful approach. Republican leaders who agreed, even provisionally, to a partitioned Ireland invited the fate of Michael Collins in 1922. Gerry Adams, the Sinn Féin leader who eventually turned the republican movement toward politics and (gradually) away from violence, knew that in doing so he risked assassination.[78]

Yet by 2007 Paisley and his Democratic Unionist Party (DUP) were willing to cross a bridge (the 1998 agreement) whose builders they had denounced as traitors, and accept power sharing with Sinn Féin and Gerry Adams, who in entering government tacitly accepted a divided Ireland, at least for the present. The 2007 electoral success of the DUP and Sinn Féin came at the expense of the parties and leaders who did the most to make the 1998 agreement possible. In the 1980s Hume, recognizing that lasting peace was impossible without the participation of Sinn Féin, risked his reputation by entering into initially secret talks with Gerry Adams, hoping to persuade Republicans to declare a ceasefire.[79] The IRA ceasefire was so long delayed that Hume's eventual success appeared to be a failure at the time. Hume insisted that Sinn Féin be treated as a legitimate party to the Good Friday settlement—perhaps recognizing that a successful peace agreement would boost Sinn Féin's political fortunes at the expense of Hume's own party, as indeed happened.[80]

Unionist support for the agreement depended critically on the Ulster Unionist Party (UUP) and its leader David Trimble. Trimble's party and political career afterward suffered eclipse for his efforts, in part because the IRA's long delay in disarming left him hanging.[81] But Trimble's own limitations as a leader contributed. In 1997 he made the risky decision to enter negotiations that could have gutted his support base, and he kept the UUP at the table despite significant opposition within his own party and right-wing charges that he was betraying his own people.[82] But during the May 1998 referendum on the agreement, Trimble's resolve wavered. In contrast to F. W. de Klerk, who called the 1992 referendum and personally led the successful campaign for a yes vote, Trimble—though he continued to voice support for the agreement—stayed largely on the sidelines during the campaign, apparently in response to the heat he had taken earlier. Supporters of the agreement repeatedly advised Trimble "to become more forthright and to engage in more active campaigning," and in the final weeks before the vote Trimble did become more active.[83] The yes vote ultimately succeeded among Protestants, but just barely, and many of the yes votes were shaky.[84]

Trimble's political future was uncertain in any case, but his episodes of hesitation did nothing to restore his political fortunes, and clouded the legacy of his more courageous moments. The same is true of Adams's unwillingness or inability to persuade the IRA to disarm in the years immediately following the 1998 agreement. The IRA's long-delayed decommissioning in 2005 appeared grudging, not an act of communal reconciliation.[85] Trimble and Adams deserve credit for the risks they took. But in the end John Hume, who first attempted a bridge to Unionists, then risked his reputation and his party's electoral future to persuade Sinn Féin to cross that bridge, set the strongest example for Northern Ireland's future leaders.

Today, the Israeli-Palestinian conflict appears impossibly difficult to resolve, despite its continuing urgency. Both sides view any hint of compromise as signaling weakness, and insist on preconditions each knows in advance the other will reject. Repeated failures to secure peace have reinforced a penchant to regard as some primordial antagonism what has in fact resulted from contingent choices and repeated failures of leadership. Here we focus on one notable missed opportunity.

In 1993, Israeli Prime Minister Yitzhak Rabin decided for the first time to talk to the Palestinian Liberation Organization (PLO) and its chairman Yasser Arafat, who was then the most powerful Palestinian leader and essential to any deal. Arafat was no Nelson Mandela. He headed a corrupt and ineffective organization, and his leadership status among Palestinians was often shaky. He lacked Mandela's strategic judgment. But Arafat had taken a historic and politically risky step when he publicly acknowledged the State of Israel in 1988. In the mid-1990s Arafat, whatever his faults, seemed willing and able to secure Palestinian support for an agreement that appeared potentially viable.[86]

By 1995, both Rabin and Arafat were well positioned to manage hardliners on their respective flanks and consummate an agreement, the main elements of which had been hammered out in secret negotiations in Oslo and announced in the fall of 1993. Rank-and-file support was strong in both communities for the two-state solution envisaged at Oslo. Rabin was a war hero whose dedication to Israel's security was not in doubt. Arafat committed to policing the West Bank to secure Israel from Palestinian attacks. Both were personally invested in the process and recognized a common interest in preventing terrorism. Had the process continued, they might have reached a provisional agreement delivering benefits that would have replenished their political capital for further negotiations.

Rabin's assassination in November 1995 by an Israeli right-winger opposed to the peace process was a stunning blow. But tragedy might have been turned to opportunity had Rabin's successor, Shimon Peres, been willing to take greater political risks. Peres could have called a snap election in the wake of the assassination and won an endorsement from the Israeli public for continuing the peace process, analogous to de Klerk's 1992 referendum. At the time, public opinion on both sides strongly favored a two-state solution and outrage at Rabin's assassination had all but the most fanatical Israeli right on the defensive.[87] Major issues remained unresolved, but this was also true in South Africa in 1992. One round of successful negotiations shifts perceptions of what might be possible in the next round, which in turn changes what is possible.

But Peres missed the opportunity, tacking instead to the right. He permitted the assassination of Hamas militant Yahva Ayyash in January 1996, reinforcing the cycle of violence and closures on the West Bank and Gaza. Peres responded to attacks from Southern Lebanon by bombing Lebanese refugee camps. A wave of suicide bombings in spring of 1996 hardened the Israeli stance in negotiations. Palestinian radicals thus helped secure the victory of the Israeli right. Peres alienated Israeli supporters of the negotiations and lost the May 1996 election to Benjamin Netanyahu who was openly hostile to the Oslo accords. Arafat's political support among Palestinians had been decisively weakened by his failure to secure an agreement. When President Clinton summoned Arafat and Israeli Prime Minister Ehud Barak to Camp David in 2000, Arafat was offered a deal similar to what he would have accepted five years earlier, but it was too late; Palestinian support for the deal had evaporated—as had support among Israelis.[88] Arafat was no longer able to secure Palestinian consent to anything Barak could have offered. Mandela and de Klerk both realized, despite their conflicts, that each needed to keep the other strong enough to close the deal. Recognition of this strategic reality has been in chronically short supply in the Israeli-Palestinian conflict.

Rabin's fate demonstrates that political risk-taking can literally be fatal. Other leaders involved in the Israeli-Palestinian conflict have shown little appetite for the kind of strategically hopeful action that made the South African transition possible. Leaders on both sides (which since the 2006 elections in Gaza and the West Bank have included Hamas) have not placed high enough priority on resolving the conflict or taken the risks necessary to advance its prospects for success. Indeed, both sides have countenanced policies likely to worsen them. But further entrenching the status quo is not risk-free either. Leaders who refuse to take risks to recast festering conflicts thereby increase the costs and dangers faced by someone else, somewhere else, sometime in the future.

VI. Conclusion

We have argued that strategically hopeful action by leaders willing to take calculated risks is necessary for transforming political orders characterized by chronically violent communal conflict. One vital characteristic of such leaders is their capacity, despite the bitter history, to view a conflict widely seen as zero-sum to be potentially positive-sum.

We do not claim that strategically hopeful leadership is sufficient; factors outside a leader's control may cause even a carefully calculated, risk-embracing effort to fail. And sometimes, as with the Israel-Palestine conflict since the mid-1990s, the chances might be vanishingly slim. But we do argue that strategically hopeful leadership is necessary: without it chronic conflicts will remain impossible to resolve, even if the stars align in every other respect. Routine leadership cannot resolve the conflict because ordinary political incentives favor action that reinforces the status quo.

If our analysis challenges leaders to take risks for peace, it also challenges social scientists and political theorists to look differently at leadership, interdependent decision, conflict, and power. Leadership theories that feature profit-maximizing elites who manipulate fixed preferences, or conversely attribute extraordinary transformative powers to individual leaders, miss vital dimensions of Mandela's and de Klerk's joint accomplishment. Theories of mixed-motive interdependent decision, exemplified here by Axelrod, Schelling, and Colomer, better reach the problem at hand. But they fail to explore the dynamic possibilities opened by leaders willing to take unusual risks, in the hope that others will reciprocate rather than exploit them. Our understanding of political power would be deepened by attention to the peculiar blend of conflict and cooperation in power interactions of the sort that facilitated South Africa's transition.

When Mandela was released from prison in 1990, many long-festering world conflicts appeared on the verge of resolution—in Eastern Europe with the fall of communism, in Latin America, and elsewhere. South Africa's 1994 settlement seemed to ride this "wave of history." But global optimism of the early 1990s soon gave way to some ghastly nightmares, as in the former Yugoslavia at the same moment Mandela and de Klerk were heading off disaster in South Africa. A cascade of optimism will not substitute for leaders willing and able to take risks at critical junctures, as the sobering evolution of the Arab Spring in the early 2010s underscores. In retrospect it is clear that Mandela and de Klerk did not merely ride a wave. They bet on one another when they had good reasons not to, displaying hope that reshaped possibilities in the present and created new ones for the future. This enabled them to dismantle apartheid without destroying their country in the process, an achievement that is deserving of our attention today no less than it was in 1994.

Notes

Introduction

1. Alasdair MacIntyre, *After Virtue: A Study in Moral Theory* (Notre Dame, IN: University of Notre Dame Press, 1981); Richard Rorty, *Philosophy and the Mirror of Nature* (Princeton, NJ: Princeton University Press, 1981).

2. Leo Strauss, *Natural Right and History* (Chicago: University of Chicago Press, 1951).

3. Frederick Jameson, *The Prison House of Language: A Critical Account of Structuralism and Russian Formalism* (Princeton, NJ: Princeton University Press, 1975); Thomas Nagel, *The View from Nowhere* (Oxford: Oxford University Press, 1986); Don Herzog, *Without Foundations: Justification in Political Theory* (Ithaca, NY: Cornell University Press, 1985).

4. Max Weber, "Science as a Vocation," in *The Vocation Lectures*, ed. David Owen and Tracy Srrong, trans. Rodney Livingstone (Indianapolis, IN: Hackett Publishing, 2004 [1917]), pp. 1–31.

5. See Richard Portes, "I think the people of this country have had enough of experts," London Business School, May 9, 2017, www.london.edu/think/who-needs-experts (accessed December 4, 2022). Likewise with the mainstreaming of relentless attacks on expert knowledge and the promotion of quack cures during the Covid pandemic. See Vera Bergengruen, "How 'America's frontline doctors' sold access to bogus Covid-19 treatments—and left patients in the lurch," *Time*, August 26, 2021, https://time.com/6092368/americas-frontline-doctors-covid-19-misinformation (accessed December 4, 2022).

6. Immanuel Kant, *Groundwork of the Metaphysic of Morals*, ed. Allen Wood (New Haven: Yale University Press, 2002 [1785]), pp. 9–62.

7. John Rawls, *A Theory of Justice*, rev. ed. (Cambridge, MA: Harvard University Press, 1999). Rawls originally published *A Theory of Justice* in 1971, but he had been developing the central ideas in journal articles for over a decade before that. He continued refining, and—indeed—revising, them in articles and lectures, leading to the

publication of a substantially revamped second and final edition in 1999. On his "political, not metaphysical" turn, see also his *Political Liberalism* (Cambridge, MA: Harvard University Press, 1993), pp. 3–46, 89–172, 372–434.

8. "Welfare does not have any ruling principle because it depends on the will's material aspect, which is empirical and thus incapable of becoming a universal rule." Immanuel Kant, "The contest of faculties" [1798], in *Political Writings*, ed. H. S. Reiss (Cambridge: Cambridge University Press, 2001), pp. 183–84.

9. Amartya Sen, *The Idea of Justice* (Cambridge, MA: Harvard University Press, 2009).

10. John Dunn, *Western Political Theory in the Face of the Future* (Cambridge: Cambridge University Press, 1979), p. 26.

11. Frances Fukuyama, "The end of history?" *National Interest* 16 (1989): 3–18. He later expanded it into the best-selling book: *The End of History and the Last Man* (New York: Free Press, 1992).

12. Russell Dalton, "Political support in advanced industrial democracies," in *Critical Citizens: Global Support for Democratic Governance*, ed. Pippa Norris (Oxford: Oxford University Press, 1999), pp. 57–77; Richard Wike, Laura Silver, and Alexandra Castillo, "Many across the globe are dissatisfied with how democracy is working," Pew Research Center Report, April 2019, www.pewresearch.org/global/2019/04/29/many-across-the-globe-are-dissatisfied-with-how-democracy-is-working (accessed August 2, 2022).

13. Joseph Cappella and Kathleen Jamieson, "New frames, political cynicism, and media cynicism," *Annals of the American Academy of Political and Social Science* 546 (1996): 71–84; Milan Svolik, "Polarization versus democracy," *Journal of Democracy* 30, no. 3 (July 2019): 20–30; and Matthew Graham and Milan Svolik, "Democracy in America? Partisanship, polarization, and the robustness of support for democracy in the United States," *American Political Science Review* 104, no. 2 (2020): 392–409.

14. See Frances Rosenbluth and Ian Shapiro, *Responsible Parties: Saving Democracy from Itself* (New Haven: Yale University Press, 2018); Christian Salas, Frances Rosenbluth, and Ian Shapiro, "Political parties and the new politics of insecurity," in *Who Gets What? The New Politics of Insecurity*, ed. Frances Rosenbluth and Margaret Weir (Cambridge: Cambridge University Press, 2021), pp. 237–58.

15. See Michael Graetz and Ian Shapiro, *Death by a Thousand Cuts: The Fight over Taxing Inherited Wealth* (Princeton, NJ: Princeton University Press, 2005), pp. 85–98.

16. Kenneth Arrow, *Social Choice and Individual Values* (London: Chapman & Hall Publishing, 1951).

17. See Mark Tushnet, "A political perspective on the theory of the unitary executive," *Journal of Constitutional Law* 12, no. 2 (2010): 313–29.

18. Linda Greenhouse, "Should we reform the Court?" *New York Review of Books*, April 7, 2022, p. 14.

19. Carole Pateman, *Participation and Democratic Theory* (Cambridge: Cambridge University Press, 1974); Benjamin R. Barber, *Strong Democracy: Participatory Politics for a New Age* (Berkeley: University of California Press, 1984).

20. Amy Gutmann and Dennis F. Thompson, *Democracy and Disagreement* (Cambridge, MA: Harvard University Press, 1996), and *Why Deliberative Democracy?* (Princeton, NJ: Princeton University Press, 2009); James Fishkin, *The Voice of the People: Public Opinion and Democracy* (New Haven: Yale University Press, 1995); *When the People Speak: Deliberative Democracy and Public Consultation* (Oxford: Oxford University Press, 2009); *Democracy When the People Are Thinking: Revitalizing Our Politics through Public Deliberation* (Oxford: Oxford University Press, 2018); Hélène Landemore, *Democratic Reason: Politics, Collective Intelligence, and the Rule of the Many* (Princeton, NJ: Princeton University Press, 2012), and *Open Democracy: Reinventing Popular Rule for the Twenty-First Century* (Princeton, NJ: Princeton University Press, 2020).

21. Christian Salas, Frances Rosenbluth, and Ian Shapiro, "Political parties and the new politics of insecurity," in *Who Gets What? The New Politics of Insecurity*, ed. Frances Rosenbluth and Margaret Weir (Cambridge: Cambridge University Press, 2021), pp. 237–58.

22. Robert Nozick, *Anarchy, State, and Utopia* (New York: Basic Books, 1974).

23. James Madison, Alexander Hamilton, and John Jay, *The Federalist Papers*, ed. Ian Shapiro (New Haven: Yale University Press, 2009 [1787–88]), p. 264.

24. Madison, Federalist 10, *Federalist Papers*, p. 52.

25. Robert A. Dahl, *A Preface to Democratic Theory* (Chicago: University of Chicago Press, 1956), pp. 104–5, and *Dilemmas of Pluralist Democracy* (New Haven: Yale University Press, 1982), pp. 4–54.

26. Madison, Federalist 51, *Federalist Papers*, p. 264.

27. Ibid.

28. For proposals see Rosenbluth and Shapiro, *Responsible Parties*, pp. 199–212.

29. Gerard MacCallum, Jr., "Negative and positive freedom," *Philosophical Review* 76, no. 3 (1967): 312–34.

30. "Ils y doivent travailler devant la majestueuse égalité des lois, qui interdit au riche comme au pauvre de coucher sous les ponts, de mendier dans les rues et de voler du pain." Anatole France, *Le lys rouge* (Paris: Pourpre, 1946 [1894]), p. 118.

31. Michael Graetz and Ian Shapiro, *The Wolf at the Door: The Menace of Economic Insecurity and How to Fight It* (Cambridge, MA: Harvard University Press, 2020), pp. 10–36, 260–80.

32. Joan Kahn et al., "Growing parental economic power in parent–adult child households: Coresidence and financial dependency in the United States, 1960–2010," *Demography* 50, no. 4 (August 2013): 1449–75; Emily Wiemers and Susan Bianci, "Competing demands from aging parents and adult children in two cohorts of American women," *Population and Development Review*, March 17, 2015, www.ncbi.nlm.nih.gov/pmc/articles/PMC4649941/ (accessed March 30, 2023).

33. Ann Maria Santacreu, "Long-run economic effects of changes in the age dependency ratio," Federal Reserve Bank of St. Louis Economic Synopses, 2016, no. 17, https://research.stlouisfed.org/publications/economic-synopses/2016/09/02/long-run-economic-effects-of-changes-in-the-age-dependency-ratio (accessed February 9, 2023).

34. Brian Bubb and Richard Pildes, "How behavioral economics trims its sails and why," *Harvard Law Review* 127 (2014): 1607–36.

35. Katherine Kramer, *The Politics of Resentment: Rural Consciousness in Wisconsin and the Rise of Scott Walker* (Chicago: University of Chicago Press, 2016); Arlie Hochschild, *Strangers in Their Own Land: Anger and Mourning on the American Right* (New York: New Press, 2016).

36. Graetz and Shapiro, *Wolf at the Door*, pp. 112–79, 260–80.

37. Iris Kesternich et al., "The effects of World War II on economic and health outcomes across Europe," *Review of Economics and Statistics* 96, no. 1 (2014): 103–18.

38. Eric Hobsbawm, *The Age of Extremes: The Short Twentieth Century, 1914–1991* (New York: Vintage Books, 1994), pp. 257–319.

39. See Robert A. Dahl, *On Democracy*, 3rd ed., with a new introduction and two additional chapters by Ian Shapiro (New Haven: Yale University Press, 2020), pp. xv–xxvi, 180–210.

40. Albert O. Hirschman, *A Bias for Hope: Essays on Development and Latin America* (New Haven: Yale University Press, 1971). Rousseau's comment was, "The better constituted the State, the more public business takes precedence over private business in the minds of Citizens. . . . In a well-conducted city everyone flies to the assemblies; under a bad Government no one likes to take a step to go to them." Jean-Jacques Rousseau, *The Social Contract*, in Jean-Jacques Rousseau, *The Social Contract and Other Writings*, ed. Victor Gourevich (Cambridge: Cambridge University Press, 2002 [1762]), p. 113.

41. See Elisabeth Wood, *Forging Democracy from Below: Insurgent Transitions in South Africa and El Salvador* (Cambridge: Cambridge University Press, 2000).

42. "In South Africa, trust in political leaders plunges to near-record low," Afrobarometer, May 17, 2016, https://afrobarometer.org/sites/default/files/press-release/south-africa/saf_r6_pr3_South_Africa_trust_in_officials_17052016.pdf (accessed March 16, 2022); Tim Cocks, "More welfare or less? South Africa's ANC confronts apartheid's legacy," Reuters, March 14, 2022, www.reuters.com/world/africa/more-welfare-or-less-safricas-anc-confronts-apartheids-legacy-2022-03-14 (accessed March 16, 2022).

43. United Nations Human Development Report, *The Next Frontier: Human Development and the Anthropocene* (New York: United Nations, 2020).

44. "South Africa unemployment rate," Trading Economics, 2021 data, https://tradingeconomics.com/south-africa/unemployment-rate (accessed March 16, 2022).

45. "South African corruption report," Risk and Compliance Portal, www.ganintegrity.com/portal/country-profiles/south-africa, May 2020 (accessed March 16, 2022); Neil Arun, "State capture: Zuma, the Guptas, and the sale of South Africa," BBC News, July 15, 2019, www.bbc.com/news/world-africa-48980964 (accessed March 16, 2022).

46. "South Africa economic outlook," African Economic Outlook 2021, African Development Bank Group, www.afdb.org/en/countries/southern-africa/south-africa/south-africa-economic-outlook (accessed March 16, 2022).

47. See Ian Shapiro and Kahreen Tebeau, eds., *After Apartheid: Reinventing South Africa* (Charlottesville: University of Virginia Press, 2011), pp. 1–17.

48. See Kurt Weyland, *Assault on Democracy: Communism, Fascism, and Authoritarianism in the Interwar Years* (Cambridge: Cambridge University Press, 2021), and "How populism dies: Political weaknesses of personalistic plebiscitarian leadership," *Political Science Quarterly* 137, no. 1 (2022): 9–42; Agnes Cornell et al., "The real lesson of the interwar years," *Journal of Democracy* 28, no. 3 (July 2017): 14–28; and Agnes Cornell et al., *Democratic Stability in an Age of Crisis: Reassessing the Interwar Period* (Oxford: Oxford University Press, 2020).

49. Hirschman, *Bias for Hope*, pp. 26–37.

50. For elaboration, see my introduction to *The Selected Writings of Thomas Paine* (New Haven: Yale University Press, 2014), pp. xi–xxxiv.

Chapter One. Against Impartiality

1. The earliest known representation of justice as blind appears to be Hans Gieng's 1543 statue of the Gerechtigkeitsbrunnen (fountain of justice) in Bern, Switzerland.

2. Ludwig Wittgenstein, *Philosophical Investigations,* trans. G. E. M. Anscombe (Oxford: Basil Blackwell, 1953), pp. 27–28.

3. John Locke, *Two Treatises of Government and a Letter Concerning Toleration,* ed. Ian Shapiro (New Haven: Yale University Press, 2003 [1681]), p. 30.

4. For elaboration of the idea of basic interests, see Ian Shapiro, *Democratic Justice* (New Haven: Yale University Press, 1999), pp. 85–90.

5. Robert Cover, *Justice Accused: Antislavery and the Judicial Process* (New Haven: Yale University Press, 1975).

6. William Godwin, *Enquiry concerning Political Justice* (Harmondsworth: Penguin Books, 1976 [1793]), pp. 168–74. Godwin became sufficiently uncomfortable with his example that in later editions he replaced his mother with his father, brother, or another benefactor.

7. Neil MacCormick, "Justice as impartiality: Assenting with anti-contractualist reservations," *Political Studies* 44, no. 2 (June 1996): 305–6.

8. Brian Barry, *Justice as Impartiality* (Oxford: Oxford University Press, 1995), p. 11.

9. On motivation for agreement, see Sharon Krause, "Partial justice," *Political Theory* 29, no. 3 (June 2001): 315–36.

10. Thomas Scanlon, *What We Owe Each Other* (Cambridge, MA: Harvard University Press, 1998), pp. 105–6.

11. Barry, *Justice as Impartiality,* pp. 168–69.

12. Ibid., p. 169.

13. Ibid., pp. 84–85.

14. Barry concedes that religious and sexual tolerance "can, of course, be derived from some conceptions of the good," but he insists that his own defense of them depends only on the appeal to fairness built into the Scanlonian test. Ibid., p. 94. For reasons set out on below, this is not plausible.

15. Ibid., pp. 91–92.

16. Barry says that the permissibility of abortion cannot turn on harm to the fetus "because the issue at stake is precisely whether the foetus is a human being." Ibid., pp. 91–92. Though not material to the point under discussion, Barry is mistaken that the abortion question turns on whether a fetus is a person. On the one hand, Judy Thompson pointed out long ago that conceding that someone is a person does not oblige you to keep him or her alive. "A defense of abortion," *Philosophy and Public Affairs* 1, no. 1 (Fall 1971): 47–66. On the other hand, someone committed to minimizing suffering might be unconvinced that a fetus is a person, yet still oppose abortion once the fetus can experience significant pain.

17. Barry, *Justice as Impartiality*, pp. 98–99.

18. This might qualify me for what many will see as the dubious distinction of being the only person on earth who is less sympathetic to multicultural accommodation than was Barry. See Brian Barry, *Culture and Equality: An Egalitarian Critique of Multiculturalism* (Cambridge: Polity Press, 2001), pp. 168–74.

19. Ibid., p. 174.

20. Ibid., pp. 174–75.

21. This is suggested by Barry's discussion of the related subject of religious establishment: "We must, of course, keep a sense of proportion. . . . Strict adherence to justice as impartiality would, no doubt, be incompatible with the existence of an established church at all. But departures from it are venial so long as nobody is put at a significant disadvantage, either by having barriers put in the way of worshiping according to the tenets of his faith or by having his rights and opportunities in other matters (politics, education, or occupation, for example) materially limited on the basis of his religious beliefs." Ibid., p. 165.

22. Michael Walzer, *Spheres of Justice: A Defense of Pluralism and Equality* (New York: Basic Books, 1983), pp. 3–30.

23. Barry, *Justice as Impartiality*, pp. 86–88.

24. Ibid., pp. 142–43.

25. Brian Barry, "A commitment to impartiality: Some comments on the comments," *Political Studies* 44, no. 2 (June 1996): 332.

26. John E. Roemer, "Equality of resources implies equality of welfare," *Quarterly Journal of Economics* 101, no. 4 (November 1986): 751–84; Ian Shapiro, *The Evolution of Rights in Liberal Theory* (Cambridge: Cambridge University Press, 1986), pp. 213–14, 283–84.

27. Andrew Reeve, "Impartiality between what? Lifestyles, conceptions of the good, and harm," *Political Studies* 44, no. 2 (June 1996): 314–18.

28. Barry, "Commitment to impartiality," pp. 332–33.

29. Philippe Van Parijs, *Real Freedom for All: What (If Anything) Can Justify Capitalism* (Oxford: Clarendon Press, 1995).

30. Rawls held that differences in capacity, whether due to nature or nurture, are morally arbitrary, but not differences that result from how we use capacities. This is unconvincing: the capacity to deploy capacities is itself distributed in morally arbitrary ways. See Ian Shapiro, *Democracy's Place* (Ithaca, NY: Cornell University Press, 1996), pp. 67–75.

31. See Barry, *Justice as Impartiality*, p. 98. Barry qualifies the claim discussed in the text by saying that it should be up to the legislature to set the overall level of provision "within certain limits." Unfortunately, he does not say what these limits are, who should determine them, or how. I suspect that, as with my earlier discussion of race

and gender in connection with the *Bob Jones* case, if pressed, Barry would have ended up insisting that medical care should at least be provided in circumstances where refusal to do so would render people vulnerable to domination by others. That is, nondomination would have displaced impartiality as the principle doing the real work.

32. Barry, "Commitment to impartiality," p. 332.

33. The Constitutional Court refused to order the dialysis that was being sought, throwing its hands up in the face of scarcity. See *Soobramoney v. Minister of Health* (November 27, 1997), p. 13, www.escr-net.org/usr_doc/Soobramoney_Decision.pdf (accessed September 26, 2015).

34. See Barry, *Justice as Impartiality*, pp. 95–98.

35. With respect to public services, citizens should decide through democratic politics what the level of provision should be and justice bears "primarily on the way in which the money is raised and the way in which the services are distributed among the claimants." But Barry insists that "there is no similarly conventionalist element in justice as it concerns the distribution of income and wealth." Ibid., p. 98.

36. Ibid., pp. 96–97.

37. See Shapiro, *Democracy's Place*, pp. 16–52.

38. Brian Barry, *Why Social Justice Matters* (Cambridge: Polity Press, 2005), pp. 7–9.

39. Tony Judt, *Postwar: A History of Europe since 1945* (New York: Penguin Books, 2006), p. 384.

40. On the role of war in reducing inequality, see Walter Scheidel, *The Great Leveler: Violence and the History of Inequality from the Stone Age to the 21st Century* (Princeton, NJ: Princeton University Press, 2017).

41. T. H. Marshall described a progression from civil rights in the eighteenth century to political rights in the nineteenth to social (welfare) rights in the twentieth. See T. H. Marshall, "Citizenship and social class," in *Class, Citizenship, and Social Development: Essays by T. H. Marshall* (Garden City, NY: Doubleday, 1964).

42. Judt, *Postwar*, p. 385.

43. "Democracy is the worst form of Government except all those other forms that have been tried from time to time." Winston Churchill, speech on the Parliament bill, House of Commons, November 11, 1947, http://hansard.millbanksystems.com/commons/1947/nov/11/parliament-bill (accessed January 19, 2015).

44. Robert A. Dahl, *A Preface to Democratic Theory* (Chicago: University of Chicago Press, 2006 [1956]), pp. 12–26.

45. For a review of the various resourcist theories on offer, see Ronald Dworkin, *Sovereign Virtue: The Theory and Practice of Equality* (Cambridge, MA: Harvard University Press, 2002), pp. 65–119.

46. John Hart Ely (born in 1938), Ronald Dworkin (born 1931), and Bruce Ackerman (born 1943), all published accounts of justice that affirmed values close to those of the Warren Court as the impartial dictates of justice. John Hart Ely, *Democracy and Distrust: A Theory of Judicial Review* (Cambridge, MA: Harvard University Press, 1980); Ronald Dworkin, *A Matter of Principle* (Cambridge, MA: Harvard University Press, 1985); and Bruce Ackerman, *Social Justice in the Liberal State* (New Haven, CT: Yale University Press, 1981). The Warren Court turned out to be no more of a new normal than European Social Democracy.

47. For the flavor, see Dworkin's many contributions to the *New York Review of Books*, www.nybooks.com/search/?q=ronald%20dworkin&size=n_10_n (accessed March 30, 2023).

48. *Dred Scott v. Sandford*, 60 U.S. 393 (1857), held that blacks, whether free or slave, were not citizens and therefore lacked standing to sue in federal court. *Plessy v. Ferguson* 163 U.S. 537 (1896) coined the euphemism "separate but equal" to sanctify racial segregation in schools and public facilities. *The Slaughter-House Cases*, 83 U.S. 36 (1873) crafted a narrow reading of the Fourteenth Amendment, immunizing the states' police powers, and *The Civil Rights Cases*, 109 U.S. 3 (1883) held that its enforcement provisions did not empower Congress to outlaw racial discrimination by private individuals and organizations—only state and local governments.

49. Melvin Urofsky, *The Warren Court: Justices, Rulings, and Legacy* (Santa Barbara, CA: ABC-CLIO, 2001), p. 264.

50. See Kevin T. McGuire and James Stimson, "The least dangerous branch revisited: New evidence on Supreme Court responsiveness to public preferences," *Journal of Politics* 66, no. 4 (November 2004): 1018–35; Michael Giles, Bethany Blackstone, and Rich Vining, "The Supreme Court in American democracy: Unraveling the linkages between public opinion and judicial decision-making," *Journal of Politics* 70, no. 2 (April 2008): 293–306; and Barry Friedman, *The Will of the People: How Public Opinion Has Influenced the Supreme Court and Shaped the Meaning of the Constitution* (New York: Farrar, Strauss & Giroux, 2010).

51. Patrick Devlin, "Morals and the criminal law," 1959 British Academy Maccabean Lecture, reprinted in *The Enforcement of Morals* (Oxford: Oxford University Press, 1965), p. 15.

52. *Bowers v. Hardwick*, 478 U.S. 186 (1986) upheld as Georgia's proscription of homosexual conduct between consenting adults. It was reversed by *Lawrence v. Texas*, 539 U.S. 558 (2003), which granted constitutional protection to same-sex sexual activity legal in all U.S. jurisdictions.

53. *Roe v. Wade*, 410 U.S. 113 (1973). See Robert Burt, *The Constitution in Conflict* (Cambridge, MA: Harvard University Press, 1992), pp. 344–52; Ruth Bader Ginsburg, "Speaking in a judicial voice," *New York University Law Review* 67, no. 6 (December 1992): 1185–209.

54. Recent scholarship has emphasized that abortion was less divisive at the time the 7–2 opinion in *Roe* was handed down than it would subsequently become. See Michael Graetz and Linda Greenhouse, *The Burger Court and the Rise of the Judicial Right* (New York: Simon & Schuster, 2016), pp. 146–48.

55. *Dobbs v. Jackson Women's Health Organization*, 597 U.S. ___ (2022).

56. Gerald A. Rosenberg, *The Hollow Hope: Can Courts Bring About Social Change?* 2nd ed. (Chicago: University of Chicago Press, 2008).

57. See Robert A. Dahl, *A Preface to Democratic Theory* (Chicago: University of Chicago Press, 2006 [1956]), pp. 105–12, and "Decision-making in a democracy: The Supreme Court as national policy-maker," *Journal of Public Law* 6, no. 1 (Spring 1957): 279–95.

58. See Mark Tushnet, *Taking the Constitution Away from the Courts* (Princeton, NJ: Princeton University Press, 1999); and Ran Hirschl, *Towards Juristocracy: The Origins and Consequences of the New Constitutionalism* (Cambridge, MA: Harvard University Press, 2007).

59. Ran Hirschl, "The political origins of judicial empowerment through constitutionalization: Lessons from four constitutional revolutions," *Law and Social Inquiry* 25, no. 1 (2000): 91–147.

60. Thomas Piketty and Emmanuel Saez, "The evolution of top incomes: A historical and international perspective," *American Economic Review, Papers, and Proceedings* 96, no. 2 (2006): 200–205.

61. See *Buckley v. Valeo* 424 U.S. 1 (1976) and *Citizens United v. Federal Election Commission* 558 U.S. 310 (2010). For discussion, see Ian Shapiro, *Politics against Domination* (Cambridge, MA: Harvard University Press, 2016), pp. 93–99; and Graetz and Greenhouse, *Burger Court*, pp. 243–68.

62. See Shapiro, *Politics against Domination*.

63. James Buchanan and Gordon Tullock, *The Calculus of Consent: Logical Foundations of Constitutional Democracy* (Ann Arbor: University of Michigan Press, 1962).

64. Brian Barry, *Political Argument*, 2nd ed. (Herefordshire: Wheatsheaf, 1990 [1965]).

65. See ibid., pp. 242–85, 312–16. See also Douglas W. Rae, "Decision-rules and individual values in constitutional choice," *American Political Science Review* 63, no. 1 (March 1969): 40–56, and "The limits of consensual decision," *American Political*

Science Review 69, no. 4 (December 1975): 1270–94; and Michael Taylor, "Proof of a theorem on majority rule," *Behavioral Science* 14, no. 3 (May 1969): 228–31.

66. Brian Barry, *Why Social Justice Matters* (Cambridge: Polity Press, 2005), pp. 180–83; Ian Shapiro, "Why the poor don't soak the rich," *Daedalus* 131, no. 1 (Winter 2002): 118–28.

67. Barry, *Why Social Justice Matters*, pp. 235–37.

68. Aristotle, *Nicomachean Ethics*, in *The Complete Works of Aristotle*, vol. 2, ed. Jonathan Barnes (Princeton, NJ: Princeton University Press, 1984 [ca. 350 B.C.]), p. 1733.

69. Alexander Bickel, *The Least Dangerous Branch: The Supreme Court at the Bar of Politics* (New York: Bobbs Merrill, 1962).

70. Alexis de Tocqueville, *Democracy in America*, ed. J. P. Mayer (New York: Perennial Classics, 1969 [1835]), pp. 246–60.

Chapter Two. On Sen versus Rawls on Justice

1. Amartya Sen, *The Idea of Justice* (Cambridge, MA: Harvard University Press, 2009), pp. 376–79; Alasdair MacIntyre, *After Virtue* (Notre Dame, IN: University of Notre Dame Press, 1984).

2. Sen, *Idea of Justice*, p. 101.

3. Jean-Jacques Rousseau, *The First and Second Discourses*, trans. and ed. Roger Masters and Judith Masters (New York: St. Martin's Press, 1959 [1754]), p. 129.

4. Amartya Sen, "Justice—and India," Third Annual Penguin Lecture, Calcutta, India, August 5, 2009.

5. Sen, *Idea of Justice*, pp. 101–2.

6. Rawls's focus on relatively favorable conditions was meant to restrict the focus to societies that have reached a level that he described as "moderate scarcity." He assumed that people are not so overwhelmed by hunger that they cannot reason, and he exempted from consideration failed states or societies facing chronic poverty or famines—which he supposed should be evaluated by reference to different distributive principles than those he defended in *A Theory of Justice*, rev. ed. (Cambridge, MA: Harvard University Press,1999).

7. Sen, *Idea of Justice*, pp. 18–19.

8. Ibid., p. 205.

9. W. D. Hamilton, "The genetical evolution of social behaviour," *Journal of Theoretical Biology* 7 (1964): 1–52.

10. See Brice Rich, *To Uphold the World: A Call for a New Global Ethic from Ancient India* (Boston: Beacon Press, 2010), pp. 136–82.

11. Sen, *Idea of Justice*, pp. 75–77.

12. I am inclined to agree with Madison in Federalist no. 10 that institutions are best designed on the assumption that "enlightened statesmen will not always be at the helm." Alexander Hamilton, James Madison, and John Jay, *The Federalist Papers*, ed. Ian Shapiro (New Haven: Yale University Press, 2009), p. 50.

13. Sen, *Idea of Justice*, pp. 68, 79–80.

14. Ibid., p. 11.

15. Rawls, *A Theory of Justice*, p. 226.

16. Ibid., pp. 134–35.

17. Sen, *Idea of Justice*, pp. 103–4.

18. Rawls, *Theory of Justice*, pp. 70–73; Ian Shapiro, *The Evolution of Rights in Liberal Theory* (Cambridge: Cambridge University Press, 1986), pp. 218–34.

19. Rawls, *Theory of Justice*, pp. 8, 68, 215, 302, 309.

20. Ibid., pp. 234–42.

21. Sen, *Idea of Justice*, p. 6n.

22. This is not Sen's example, but it might as well have been. See Kenneth Arrow, "Some ordinalist-utilitarian notes on Rawls's theory of justice," *Journal of Philosophy* 7 (1974): 245–63, at p. 254; Ronald Dworkin, *Sovereign Virtue: The Theory and Practice of Equality* (Cambridge, MA: Harvard University Press, 2000), p. 49; G. A. Cohen, "On the currency of egalitarian justice," *Ethics* 99 (1989): 906–44, at pp. 923–24; John Rawls, *Political Liberalism* (New York: Columbia University Press, 1993), p. 185.

23. Sen, *Idea of Justice*, p. 396.

24. Ibid., pp. 14, 201.

25. Ibid., pp. 13–14.

26. Drawing on the welfare economics literature on compensation from Kaldor and Hicks to Scitovsky and Samuelson, Nozick argued from libertarian premises that the fear generated by "independents," who reject the prevailing order, is an externality that can be mitigated if they could be compensated for the rights violation involved in removing their capacity to threaten, but everyone else would still be better off than they would have been living in fear of the uncoerced independents. Robert Nozick, *Anarchy, State, and Utopia* (New York: Basic Books, 1974). For discussion see Shapiro, *Evolution of Rights in Liberal Theory*, pp. 169–76.

27. Sen, *Idea of Justice*, pp. 235–37.

28. Ibid., p. 243.

29. Ibid., pp. 396–97.

30. See Charles E. Lindblom, *The Intelligence of Democracy* (New York: Free Press, 1965).

31. Sen, *Idea of Justice*, pp. 1–3.

32. Cass Sunstein, "Incompletely theorized agreements," *Harvard Law Review* 108 (1995): 1733–72. Sen differentiates his stance from Sunstein's (and, presumably, Rawls's, discussed below) on the grounds that Sunstein is concerned with alternative theories that converge on the same conclusion, whereas Sen focuses on different "perspectives" that can "be accommodated internally *within* a capacious theory" (*Idea of Justice*, 397n, Sen's italics). In fact, in his examples of plural grounds (impeaching Hastings and the Iraq war) Sen adduces considerations that could emanate from either or both. As already noted, the same is true of the flute trilemma.

33. Rawls, *Political Liberalism*, pp. 9–11, 133–72.

34. Sen, *Idea of Justice*, pp. 2, 12–15, 200–201, 353–54.

35. Ibid., p. 101.

36. In fact, establishing the height of mountain peaks definitively can be difficult. See Chris Baranluk, "The mountains whose height still remains a mystery," BBC documentary, March 18, 2016, www.bbc.com/future/article/20160318-the-mountains-whose-height-still-remains-a-mystery (accessed November 13, 2022).

37. The viable defense of Rawls's first principle, if there is one, is that it embodies the most extensive possible system of liberties compatible with a like liberty for all, not that it is neutral. For discussion, see Ian Shapiro, *The Moral Foundations of Politics* (New Haven: Yale University Press, 2003), pp. 131–32.

38. Sen, *Idea of Justice*, p. 45.

39. Adam Smith, *The Theory of Moral Sentiments* (London: Henry Bohn, 1853 [1759]), p. 161.

40. Sen, *Idea of Justice*, pp. 124–35.

41. Ibid., pp. 367–68; see also p. 259 and pp. 285–86.

42. See chapter 1, p. 38.

43. Sen, *Idea of Justice*, pp. 71–72.

44. Ibid., pp. 404–5.

45. Ibid., p. 407.

46. See *Furman v. Georgia* 408 U.S. 238 (1972), at 360–69. See also Marshall's dissent in *Gregg v. Georgia* 428 U.S. 153 (1976).

47. Sen, *Idea of Justice*, p. 89.

48. See Justice Scalia's remarks to Justice Breyer at the U.S. Association of Constitutional Law Discussion at American University, www.freerepublic.com/focus/news/1352357/posts. Opposition to Harold Koh's nomination included a "Coalition to preserve American sovereignty" letter by the Ethics and Policy Center to the U.S. Senate Committee on Foreign Relations. See David Weigel, "Letter to Kerry and

Lugar," *Washington Independent,* April 9, 2009, http://washingtonindependent.com/37916/letter-to-kerry-and-lugar (accessed September 20, 2011).

49. He might have added that democracies do better than nondemocracies at protecting human rights—indeed that democracy is more important from this point of view than much trumpeted (at least by American constitutional theorists) role of independent courts and bills of rights. See Robert A. Dahl, *A Preface to Democratic Theory,* exp. ed. (Chicago: University of Chicago Press, 2006), pp. 152–72; Ian Shapiro, *The Real World of Democratic Theory* (Princeton, NJ: Princeton University Press, 2011), pp. 68–79.

50. Classical liberals like John Stuart Mill and Alexis de Tocqueville feared that a universal franchise would lead to majority tyranny through which the masses would expropriate the assets of the few. This led Mill to advocate a second vote for university graduates and Tocqueville to embrace standard republican constraints on majoritarian politics. In his later years a chastened Karl Marx noticed the same possibility from a different point of view, leading him to endorse the "parliamentary road to socialism" in hopes that the working class would do through the ballot box what they had failed to do at the barricades. The median voter theorem developed by Harold Hotelling, Anthony Downs, and others also predicts that imposing majority rule on a distribution of income and wealth of the sort that we observe in the capitalist democracies will lead to significant downward redistribution. For a review of the literature on why this does not occur in fact see Ian Shapiro, *The State of Democratic Theory* (Princeton, NJ: Princeton University Press, 2003), pp. 104–45.

51. Sen, *Idea of Justice,* pp. 321–28.

52. This does not mean they won't make a mess of it, as the George W. Bush administration did in response to Hurricane Katrina's devastation of New Orleans in 2005. But when that happens, they will widely be seen as inept more than as malevolent (though not universally so, as with Kanye West's declaration following Katrina that George Bush didn't care about black people. See Maxwell Strachan, "The definitive history of 'George Bush doesn't care about black people': The story behind Kanye West's famous remarks," *Huffpost,* September 9, 2015, www.huffpost.com/entry/kanye-west-george-bush-black-people_n_55d67c12e4b020c386de2f5e (accessed November 13, 2022).

53. See John Coffee, "The political economy of Dodd Frank: Why financial reform tends to be frustrated and systemic reform perpetuated," *Cornell Law Review* 97 (2012): 1019–204.

54. Sen, *Idea of Justice,* pp. 131, 395–96.

55. Ibid., pp. 398–99.

56. David Brion Davis, *Inhuman Bondage: The Rise and Fall of Slavery in the New World* (New York: Oxford University Press, 2006), pp. 250–322.

57. Kaufmann and Pape point out that from the 1835 through 1857 elections, the gap between the two major parties' share of the vote was significantly smaller than the Dissenter share of the electorate, and that although the Dissenters favored free trade and most of the other reform causes associated with the Whig-Liberals, they were unwilling to trade them off against abolition—even to the point of toppling the Whig government of Viscount Melbourne in 1841. See Chaim Kaufmann and Robert Pape, "Explaining costly international moral action: Britain's sixty-year campaign against the Atlantic slave trade," *International Organization* 53 (1999): 631–68, at pp. 660–61.

58. The exceptions were Ceylon, St. Helena, and some territories possessed by the British East India Company.

59. Seymour Drescher, *Econocide: British Slavery in the Era of Abolition,* 2nd ed. (Chapel Hill: University of North Carolina Press, 2010), pp. 113–86.

60. See Gavin Wright, "Slavery and the rise of the nineteenth-century American political economy," *Journal of Economic Perspectives* 36, no. 2 (Spring 2022): 123–48.

61. Steven Deyle, *Carry Me Back: The Domestic Slave Trade in American Life* (New York: Oxford University Press, 2005), pp. 14–39.

62. Most Tories opposed abolition, but they felt more immediately threatened by mounting demands for Catholic emancipation, expanding the franchise, abolishing rotten boroughs, reducing Royal prerogatives, and social legislation on behalf of the expanding industrial workforce. Pragmatists like Pitt were persuaded by moderate Whigs who wanted tactical concessions to staunch these more radical demands (Kaufmann and Pape, "Explaining costly international moral action," pp. 650–53).

63. Roger Anstey, "Religion and British slave emancipation," in *The Abolition of the Atlantic Slave Trade,* ed. David Eltis and James Walvin (Madison: University of Wisconsin Press, 1981), pp. 37–62, at 38–41; Kaufmann and Pape, "Explaining costly international moral action," pp. 650–53.

64. This is not to say that single issue redistributive coalitions will always be progressive or otherwise justice-enhancing. See Michael J. Graetz and Ian Shapiro, *Death by a Thousand Cuts: The Fight over Taxing Inherited Wealth* (Princeton, NJ: Princeton University Press, 2005).

Chapter Three. On Nondomination

1. Plato, *The Republic,* trans. G. M. A. Grube, rev. C. D. C. Reeve (Indianapolis, IN: Hackett Publishing, 1992), pp. 102–3, 119; John Rawls, *A Theory of Justice,* 2nd ed. (Cambridge, MA: Harvard University Press, 1999), p. 3.

2. Ian Shapiro, *Democratic Justice* (New Haven: Yale University Press, 1999), pp. 85–86.

3. I say that vulnerability to domination is operationalized *principally* by reference to the notion of basic interests because domination can occur in other ways as well—as when someone threatens to blackmail a closet homosexual or someone who is having a secret affair. No doubt there are other reasons to outlaw blackmail, but a commitment to nondomination would proscribe it as well.

4. Ian Shapiro, *The Real World of Democratic Theory* (Princeton, NJ: Princeton University Press, 2011), pp. 255–56.

5. See Amartya Sen, "Inequality re-examined," Occasional Paper no. 2 (The Economic Growth Center, Yale University, 1989), p. 15. See also Sen's book of the same title (Cambridge, MA: Harvard University Press, 1992). For criticism, see John Kane, "Justice, impartiality, and equality: Why the concept of justice does not presume equality," *Political Theory* 24, no. 3 (August 1996): 375–93. For Sen's response, see "On the status of equality," *Political Theory* 24, no. 3 (August 1996): 394–400, and, for Kane's rebuttal, see John Kane, "Basal inequalities: Reply to Sen," *Political Theory* 24, no. 3 (August 1996): 401–6.

6. See Friedrich A. Hayek, *The Mirage of Social Justice* (Chicago: University of Chicago Press, 1976).

7. Robert Nozick, *Anarchy, State, and Utopia* (New York: Basic Books, 1974).

8. Sen, "On the status of equality," pp. 39–56.

9. Kane, "Basal equalities," pp. 403–5.

10. In the final formulation of his principles Rawls opts for the standpoint of the worst-off as the standpoint of justice, but this is only because of the assumption that if the person most adversely affected by a policy would choose it, then so would everyone else. In this way, the standpoint of the worst-off functions as a proxy for the standpoint of all. Questions can be raised about the plausibility of these moves. See Ian Shapiro, *Evolution of Rights in Liberal Theory* (Cambridge: Cambridge University Press, 1986), pp. 226–30.

11. Rawls, *Theory of Justice*, p. 74.

12. John Harsanyi, "Can the maximin principle serve as a basis for morality? A critique of John Rawls's theory," *American Political Science Review* 69, no. 3 (1975): 594–606.

13. In one of the earliest systematic statements of laissez-faire in torts, Oliver Wendell Holmes argued in lecture III of *The Common Law* [1881] (Cambridge, MA: Harvard University Press, 2009) for a benchmark presumption that losses should lie where they fall.

14. Ian Shapiro, "Justice and workmanship in a democracy," in *Democracy's Place* (Ithaca, NY: Cornell University Press, 1996), pp. 64–69, 73–75.

15. Ronald Dworkin, "What is equality?" part 2, "Equality of resources," *Philosophy and Public Affairs* 10, no. 4 (Fall 1981): 283–345.

16. See Ian Shapiro, *The State of Democratic Theory* (Princeton, NJ: Princeton University Press, 2003), pp. 128–39.

17. Dworkin is partly aware of this difficulty. The case he considers is one in which someone has an incapacitating obsession that he wishes he did not have. Dworkin deals with this by arguing that such cravings should be thought of as handicaps and thus handled via a hypothetical insurance scheme. Dworkin asks us to speculate about whether, ex ante, people with a given finite supply of resources to spend on insurance would have insured against turning out to have the handicap in question. See "What is equality?" part 2, pp. 283–90. I have noted the difficulties with this scheme in *Democracy's Place*, pp. 70–71. It is in any case irrelevant to the point being made here, which is that the obsession may itself incapacitate a person from forming the relevant second-order desire to make Dworkin's hypothetical insurance solution work.

18. G. A. Cohen, "On the currency of egalitarian justice," *Ethics* 99 (July 1989): 933.

19. See Cohen, "Equality of what? On welfare, goods, and capabilities," in *The Quality of Life,* ed. by Martha Nussbaum and Amartya Sen (Oxford: Oxford University Press, 1993), pp. 14–15.

20. Quoted from Hurley's contribution to a joint symposium with Richard Arneson, "Luck and equality," *Proceedings of the Aristotelian Society,* supp. vol. 75 (2001): 56. As she elaborates: "Considerations of responsibility do not direct us to take equality as the default position: they neither specify nor justify doing so. The immediate consequence of this point is that luck-neutralizing per se does not require us to neutralize only one kind of relation that is a matter of luck and not another. . . . People are not responsible for equal amounts of manna, or any other particular amounts; they are not responsible for it at all." Ibid., pp. 56–57. Generally, see her *Justice, Luck, and Knowledge* (Cambridge, MA: Harvard University Press, 2003), pp. 146–80.

21. Rawls, *Theory of Justice,* p. 226.

22. Why the case against slavery should be detached from claims about its economic benefits has been eloquently put by Robert William Fogel in *Without Consent or Contract: The Rise and Fall of American Slavery* (New York: W. W. Norton, 1994), pp. 388–417.

23. Rawls, *Theory of Justice,* p. 242. Kant was well aware of this, insisting that "welfare does not have any ruling principle" because it depends "on the will's material aspect, which is empirical and thus incapable of becoming a universal rule." Immanuel

Kant, *The Contest of Faculties,* reprinted in *Kant's Political Writings,* ed. Hans Reiss, trans. H. B. Nisbet (Cambridge: Cambridge University Press, 1970), pp. 183–84.

24. Michael Walzer, *Spheres of Justice: A Defense of Pluralism and Equality* (New York: Basic Books, 1984), pp. 3–30.

25. Karl Marx, *Capital,* trans. Ben Fowkes, vol. 1 (Harmondsworth: Penguin Books, 1976), pp. 270–82.

26. Iris Marion Young, *Justice and the Politics of Difference* (Princeton, NJ: Princeton University Press, 1990), pp. 15–65; Nancy Fraser, "From redistribution to recognition? Dilemmas of justice in a 'postsocialist' age," *New Left Review,* no. 212 (July–August 1995): 68–93.

27. See Nancy Fraser, "Rethinking recognition," *New Left Review* 3, no. 3 (May–June 2000): 107–20, and "Feminist politics in an age of recognition: A two-dimensional approach to gender justice," *Studies in Social Justice* 1, no. 1 (Winter 2007): 23–35.

28. See John Rawls, "The priority of right and ideas of the good," in *Collected Papers,* ed. Samuel Freeman (Cambridge, MA: Harvard University Press, 1999), pp. 457–61, and *Theory of Justice,* pp. 354–55. Rawls does invoke the idea of disestablishment in this context but, for reasons elaborated in the next paragraph, it seems to me to capture the essence of his claim.

29. Rawls, "The priority of right," p. 460.

30. Rawls, *Theory of Justice,* pp. 220, 266.

31. Rawls, "The priority of right," p. 459.

32. Rawls, "Justice as fairness: Political not metaphysical," *Collected Papers,* p. 390.

33. Rawls, "The priority of right," p. 459.

34. A similar difficulty arises in Charles Larmore's defense of neutrality. He argues that when people disagree about something that is an obstacle to the agreement they are trying to reach, both should prescind from the beliefs that the other rejects to see if there is neutral common ground "with the hope of either resolving the dispute or bypassing it." He calls this "moral norm of equal respect" neutral in that it is "compatible with a wide range of views about the good life on which reasonable people disagree." *Patterns of Moral Complexity* (Cambridge: Cambridge University Press, 1987), pp. 53, 65–66. But as James Fishkin has noted, there is no reason to believe that this neutrality-as-common ground principle will yield any particular political conclusions—let alone those that Larmore claims for it—such as religious toleration or something like Rawls's difference principle. See Fishkin's review in *Political Theory* 17, no. 1 (February 1989): 153–56. Even if it did, this would not amount to a justification of it, as Larmore concedes in his response to Fishkin: "Although I try to

explicate the content of equal respect, I offer no justification of this norm itself. I have no idea of how such a justification would proceed." Charles Larmore, "Liberal neutrality: A reply to James Fishkin," *Political Theory* 17, no. 4 (November 1989): 580–81.

35. Nietzsche's defense of the will to power is not, in any case, an account of the desire to dominate others so much as to behave with indifference toward them. Indeed, he blamed the advent of democracy for the political and social domination—such as barbaric criminal punishments—that he identified around him. He had contempt for the individualism of his day, but this was because he saw it as a perversion of the romantic individualism, marked by the single-minded pursuit of greatness, which he treasured. Friedrich Nietzsche, *The Genealogy of Morals*, in *The Birth of Tragedy and the Genealogy of Morals*, trans. Francis Goldberg (New York: Anchor Books, 1956), pp. 158–229. Arguably this takes self-absorption to the point of narcissism, which is perhaps one reason why Nietzsche so often appeals to teenagers when they first dabble in philosophy but seems puerile to more mature minds.

36. Alasdair MacIntyre, *After Virtue*, 2nd ed. (Notre Dame, IN: University of Notre Dame Press, 1984), pp. 181–203; Walzer, *Spheres of Justice*, pp. 10–20.

37. In this there is a parallel with Rawls's metric of justice inasmuch as he endorses interpersonal judgments about primary goods, but not about the uses people make of those goods in their life plans. See *Democratic Justice*, chaps. 2 and 3.

38. Martin Heidegger, *Being and Time*, trans. John Macquarrie and Edward Robinson (New York: Harper and Row, 1962).

39. In particular I am leery of any conception of freedom that requires a prior commitment to agreement and shared goals. Philip Pettit, *A Theory of Freedom* (Oxford: Oxford University Press, 2001), pp. 67ff. See also his *Republicanism: A Theory of Freedom and Government* (Oxford: Oxford University Press, 1997), discussed below.

40. In fairness to Pettit, he does not deny that there might be defenses of nondomination other than the one he supplies. His argument, after all, is in the first instance a theory of freedom, not one of nondomination—so one could read him as saying that embracing his account of freedom as discursive control is sufficient to justify nondomination as he understands it, but not necessary.

41. Max Weber, *Economy and Society*, ed. Guenther Roth and Claus Wittich (Berkeley: University of California Press, 1968 [1914]), p. 53.

42. See John Rawls, "Justice as fairness: Political not metaphysical," *Philosophy and Public Affairs* 14, no. 3 (Summer 1985): 223–51; and Cass R. Sunstein, "Incompletely theorized agreements," *Harvard Law Review* 108 (1995): 1733–72.

43. For all intents and purposes Habermas's use of the term *legitimacy* is equivalent to what I mean by justice.

44. On the ideal speech situation, see Jürgen Habermas, "Wahrheitstheorien," in *Wirklichkeit und Reflexion,* ed. Helmut Fahrenbach (Pfüllingen: Neske, 1973), pp. 211–65, and "Reflections on the linguistic foundations of sociology," in Jürgen Habermas, *On the Pragmatics of Social Interaction* (Cambridge, MA: MIT Press, 2001), pp. 1–104. For subsequent formulations see Jürgen Habermas, *Between Facts and Norms: Contributions to a Discourse Theory of Law and Democracy* (Cambridge, MA: MIT Press, 1998), and "Rightness versus truth: On the sense of normative validity in moral judgments and norms," in Jürgen Habermas, *Truth and Justification* (Cambridge, MA: MIT Press, 2003), pp. 237–76.

45. See my *The Moral Foundations of Politics* (New Haven: Yale University Press, 2003), pp. 109–41.

46. Jürgen Habermas, "Religion in the public sphere: Cognitive presuppositions for the 'use of reason' by religious and secular citizens," in Jürgen Habermas, *Between Naturalism and Religion: Philosophical Essays* (Cambridge: Polity Press, 2008), pp. 114–48; and Jürgen Habermas, " 'The political:' The rational sense of a questionable inheritance of political theology," in *The Power of Religion in the Public Sphere,* ed. Jonathan Van Antwerpen (New York: Columbia University Press, 2011), pp. 15–33.

47. Jürgen Habermas, *The Structural Transformation of the Public Sphere: An Inquiry into a Category of Bourgeois Society,* trans. Thomas Burger (Cambridge, MA: MIT Press, 1991).

48. See Kevin Olson, "Deliberative democracy," in *Jürgen Habermas: Key Concepts,* ed. Barbara Fultner (Durham, NC: Acumen Press, 2011), pp. 140–55.

49. See Maeve Cooke, "Violating neutrality? Religious validity claims and democratic legitimacy," in *Habermas and Religion,* ed. by Craig Calhoun, Eduardo Mendieta, and Jonathan Van Antwerpen (Cambridge: Polity Press, 2013).

50. See *State of Democratic Theory,* pp. 33–34, for elaboration. See also Albena Azmanova, *The Scandal of Reason: A Critical Theory of Political Judgment* (New York: Columbia University Press, 2011), chap. 2.

51. Michel Foucault, *The Archeology of Knowledge and the Discourse on Language,* trans. M. Sheridan Smith (New York: Vintage Books, 1982); *Madness and Civilization: A History of Insanity in the Age of Reason,* trans. Richard Howard (New York: Vintage Books, 1988); *Discipline and Punish: The Birth of the Prison,* trans. Alan Sheridan (New York: Vintage Books, 1995); *The History of Sexuality,* trans. Robert Hurley (New York: Vintage Books, 1990); Jürgen Habermas, *Legitimation Crisis,* trans. Thomas McCarthy (Boston: Beacon Press, 1975); *The Theory of Communicative Action I,* trans. Thomas McCarthy (Boston: Beacon Press, 1984); and "Three normative models of democracy," *Constellations,* no. 1 (1995): 1–10.

52. See *Democratic Justice,* chap. 3, for elaboration.

53. For elaboration see Ian Shapiro, *Political Criticism* (Berkeley: University of California Press, 1990), chap. 3.

54. On the changing laws of marital rape in the United States, see Diana E. H. Russell, *Rape in Marriage,* 2nd ed. (Bloomington: Indiana University Press, 1990); and Rebecca M. Ryan, "The sex right: A legal history of the marital rape exception," *Law and Social Inquiry* 20, no. 4 (Fall 1995): 941–1001.

55. Quentin Skinner, *Hobbes and Republican Liberty* (Cambridge: Cambridge University Press, 2008), p. 216.

56. Thomas Hobbes, *Leviathan, or the Matter, Forme & Power of a Commonwealth Ecclesiastical and Civill,* ed. Ian Shapiro (New Haven: Yale University Press, 2010 [1651]), pp. 133, 129.

57. Ian Shapiro, *The Evolution of Rights in Liberal Theory* (Cambridge: Cambridge University Press, 1986), pp. 39–40, 276–77.

58. Charles Taylor, "What's wrong with negative liberty," in *The Idea of Freedom,* ed. Alan Ryan (Oxford: Oxford University Press, 1979), p. 179.

59. Isaiah Berlin, "Two concepts of liberty," in *Four Essays on Liberty* (Oxford: Oxford University Press, 1990), pp. 118–72.

60. Jean-Jacques Rousseau, *The Social Contract,* trans. Maurice Cranston (Baltimore: Penguin Books. 1968 [1762]), p. 64.

61. Quentin Skinner, "The idea of negative liberty: Philosophical and historical perspectives," in *Philosophy in History,* ed. Richard Rorty, J. B. Schneewind, and Quentin Skinner (Cambridge: Cambridge University Press, 1984), pp. 204–19.

62. Skinner, *Hobbes and Republican Liberty,* p. 211. A comparable conception informs the picture affirmed by J. G. A. Pocock and others, who offer "civic humanist" readings of the motivations of the American revolutionaries, one that embodies the ideal of the independent yeoman farmer. J. G. A. Pocock, *The Machiavellian Moment: Florentine Political Thought and the Atlantic Republican Tradition* (Princeton, NJ: Princeton University Press, 1975). See also Gordon Wood, *The Radicalism of the American Revolution* (New York: Alfred A. Knopf, 1992); and Bernard Bailyn, *The Ideological Origins of the American Revolution* (Cambridge, MA: Belknap Press of Harvard University Press, 1967).

63. Gerald MacCallum, Jr., "Negative and positive freedom," in Peter Laslett, W. G. Runciman, and Quentin Skinner, eds., *Philosophy, Politics and Society,* 4th series (Oxford: Basil Blackwell, 1972); Ian Shapiro, "Gross concepts in political argument," in *The Flight from Reality in the Human Sciences* (Princeton, NJ: Princeton University Press, 2005).

64. Shapiro, *Evolution of Rights*, pp. 14–19.
65. Skinner, "Idea of negative liberty," p. 196n8.
66. MacCallum, "Negative and positive freedom," p. 182n9.
67. This is not an exact analogue of the Hobbesian account, in which the subject, though dependent for his freedom on the sovereign's silence, is not owned by him.
68. Literally: "the majestic equality of laws, which forbid the rich as the poor to sleep under bridges, to beg in the streets, or to steal bread." Anatole France, *Le lys rouge* (Paris: Pourpre, 1946 [1894]), chap. 7.
69. It is not entirely clear to me what this ultimate basis for this presumption is in Pettit's account. On my view it derives from the fact that there is no perfect democratic decision rule, which carries the implication that even the best democratic procedures will leave some people feeling not only aggrieved, but legitimately aggrieved.
70. Pettit holds that having the power to interfere arbitrarily with another is by itself domination, whereas I say that it creates the possibility for domination. As I explain below, this difference partly accounts for Pettit's schizoid attitude toward the state.
71. Pettit, *Republicanism*, p. 58.
72. Ibid., p. 57.
73. Ibid., p. 113.
74. Ibid., p. 115.
75. I doubt that they are true, at least not without very substantial qualifications of what Pettit says here. It is far from obvious, for example, that countries lacking nuclear weapons would become more secure if every other country got them. If Iran develops nuclear weapons, it might be more likely to be attacked by Israel than if it does not, and the likelihood of attack would not decrease at a diminishing marginal rate with the number of weapons it creates. It is more a step function. Arms races can be counterproductive in defusing potential conflicts. I suspect that the relationship between relative power and security is sometimes U-shaped, and that it becomes indecipherably complex once we move from the kind of two-player situations Pettit analyzes here (pp. 114–17) to interactions among multiple players who are engaged in numerous overlapping bilateral as well as multilateral power relations. See Scott Sagan, *The Limits of Safety: Organizations, Accidents, and Nuclear Weapons* (Princeton, NJ: Princeton University Press, 1995); and Alexandre Debs and Nuno Monteiro, *Nuclear Politics: The Strategic Causes of Proliferation* (Cambridge: Cambridge University Press, 2016).
76. Pettit, *Republicanism*, p. 118.
77. Ibid., pp. 118–19.

78. See *Democratic Justice,* chaps. 5 and 6.

79. This power-based resourcism puts my argument squarely into the resourcist camp of Rawls, Dworkin, and Sen, and others, but my focus differs from theirs in that I think the resources needed to vindicate basic interests should be guaranteed to people not as to enable them to achieve some conception of welfare or the good life, but rather to protect them from vulnerability to domination by others.

80. Pettit, *Republicanism,* pp. 90–91.

81. Locke, First Treatise of Government, § 42, in *Two Treatises of Government and a Letter concerning Toleration,* ed. Ian Shapiro (New Haven: Yale University Press, 2003), p. 30.

82. I am indebted to Rebecca Trupin for this example.

83. This is not to defend everything Bush, Sr., did in Iraq in 1991. In particular his decision to encourage the Shiite uprising in the south then abandon it was at a minimum a tragic lapse of judgment that led to the avoidable slaughter of countless thousands of Iraqis. See "War in the Gulf: Bush statement," *New York Times* (February 16, 1991), www.nytimes.com/1991/02/16/world/war-gulf-bush-statement-excerpts-2-statements-bush-iraq-s-proposal-for-ending.html (accessed February 9, 2023).

84. See my discussion in *Politics against Domination* (Cambridge, MA: Harvard University Press, 2016), pp. 152-62.

85. Pettit, *Republicanism,* p. 186.

86. Ibid., p. 195.

87. Ibid., pp. 196–97.

88. Walter Berns, "The morality of anger," in *Capital Punishment: A Reader,* ed. Glenn H. Stassen (New York: Pilgrim Press, 1998), pp. 15–25.

89. Pettit, *Republicanism,* p. 198.

90. Ibid., p. 210.

91. Some might claim that the dangers of such social movements as the Tea Party were less evident in 1997 when Pettit published *Republicanism.* In addition to the antitax movement discussed in the text that dates to the 1970s, one need only think of the Ku Klux Klan for another obvious example of a virulent social movement whose members were firmly convinced that they were resisting domination. In any case, the politics we have seen in recent decades have not led Pettit to modify his full-throated defense of contestatory rights to resist democratic outcomes. See Pettit, "Political realism meets civic republicanism," *Critical Review of International Social and Political Philosophy* 20, no. 3 (2017): 331–47, and "Democracy before, in, and after Schumpeter," *Critical Review* 24, no. 4 (2017): 492–504.

92. Pettit, *Republicanism,* p. 189.

93. Ibid., p. 188.

94. See also *State of Democratic Theory*, pp. 21–34.

95. Ibid., pp. 48–49.

96. Philip Pettit, "Democracy, electoral and contestatory," in *NOMOS XLII: Designing Democratic Institutions*, ed. Ian Shapiro and Stephen Macedo (New York: New York University Press, 2000), pp. 195–246.

97. See Nathaniel Popper, "Banks step up spending on lobbying to fight proposed stiffer regulations," *Los Angeles Times*, February 16, 2010, www.latimes.com/archives/la-xpm-2010-feb-16-la-fi-bank-lobbying16-2010feb16-story.html (accessed April 1, 2023).

98. The net effect of the lobbying and industry interventions in the comment period on the regulation led to the adoption of a vague, complex and highly discretionary proprietary trading framework. See "The Volcker Rule: Its past, present, and uncertain future," Americans for Financial Reform, October 2018, https://ourfinancialsecurity.org/wp-content/uploads/2018/10/AFR-Education-Fund-Volcker-Rule-Report-October-2018.pdf (accessed April 1, 2023). The rule was further weakened during the Trump Administration. See Erica Werner, "Trump signs law rolling back post-financial crisis banking rules," *Washington Post*, May 24, 2018, www.washingtonpost.com/business/economy/trump-signs-law-rolling-back-post-financial-crisis-banking-rules/2018/05/24/077e3aa8-5f6c-11e8-a4a4-c070ef53f315_story.html (accessed April 1, 2023).

99. Pettit, *Republicanism*, p. 150.

100. Pettit, "Democracy, electoral and contestatory," pp. 118–19; Brian Barry, *Political Argument* (New York: Routledge & Kegan Paul, 1965); and George Tsebelis, *Veto Players: How Political Institutions Work* (Princeton, NJ: Princeton University Press, 2002).

101. Pettit, *Republicanism*, p. 95.

102. Ibid., p. 56.

103. See Adam Przeworski et al., *Democracy and Development* (Cambridge: Cambridge University Press, 2000), pp. 78–186.

104. See *State of Democratic Theory*, pp. 86–103; and Ian Shapiro, "Tyranny and democracy: Reflections on some recent literature," *Government and Opposition* 43, no. 3 (Summer 2008): 486–97.

105. Judith Shklar, *Ordinary Vices* (Cambridge, MA: Harvard University Press, 1985); and Casiano Hacker-Cordón, "Global injustice and human malfare," PhD diss., Department of Political Science, Yale University, 2002.

106. Trolley-bus problems involve hypothetical examples of tragic choices, designed to provoke reflection on our moral intuitions. Typically they involve forced Hobson's

choices—as when the only way in which passengers in an out-of-control trolley bus can be saved is by diverting it in such a way that it will kill one or more pedestrians. The examples are sometimes contrived to the point that it is hard to see their relevance to the moral dilemmas that people actually confront. See Philippa Foot, *The Problem of Abortion and the Doctrine of the Double Effect in Virtues and Vices* (Oxford: Basil Blackwell, 1978); Judith Jarvis Thomson, "Killing, letting die, and the trolley problem," *The Monist* 59 (1976): 204–17, and "The trolley problem," *Yale Law Journal* 94 (1985): 1395–415; Peter Unger, *Living High and Letting Die* (Oxford: Oxford University Press, 1996); and Francis Kamm, "Harming some to save others", *Philosophical Studies*, no. 57 (1989): 227–60.

107. Albert O. Hirschman, *Exit, Voice, and Loyalty: Responses to Decline in Firms, Organizations, and States* (Cambridge, MA: Harvard University Press, 1970).

108. *Democratic Justice*, chaps. 5 and 6.

109. Ibid., chap. 2.

110. James Madison, "Majority government," *Letters and Other Writings of James Madison* IV (Philadelphia: J. P. Lippincott, 1865), p. 332. For additional discussion see Shapiro, *Real World of Democratic Theory*, pp. 38–67.

Chapter Four. The New Authoritarianism in Public Choice (with David Froomkin)

1. Steven Levitsky and Daniel Ziblatt, *How Democracies Die* (New York: Crown Publishing, 2018); David Runciman, *How Democracy Ends* (New York: Basic Books, 2018); Timothy Snyder, *The Road to Unfreedom: Russia, Europe, and America* (New York: Duggan Books, 2018).

2. Eric A. Posner and Adrian Vermeule, *The Executive Unbound* (Oxford: Oxford University Press, 2011); William G. Howell and Terry M. Moe, *Relic: How Our Constitution Undermines Effective Government, and Why We Need a More Powerful Presidency* (New York: Basic Books, 2016); Francis Fukuyama, *Political Order and Political Decay* (New York: Farrar, Straus and Giroux, 2014).

3. Kenneth Arrow, *Social Choice and Individual Values* (New York: Wiley & Sons, 1951); Charles R. Plott, "Axiomatic social choice theory," *American Journal of Political Science* 20, no. 3 (1976): 511–96; Allan Gibbard, "Manipulation of voting schemes," *Econometrica* 41, no. 4 (1973): 587–601.

4. The focus in this chapter is on the public choice movement but attempts to float defenses of alternative political institutions on the Arrovian incoherence of majority rule go considerably further afield. See Philip Pettit, "Popular sovereignty and constitutional democracy," *University of Toronto Law Journal* 27, no. 3 (2022): 278–80.

5. James Buchanan and Gordon Tullock, *The Calculus of Consent* (Ann Arbor: University of Michigan Press, 1962); William Riker, *Liberalism against Populism* (Longrove, IL: Waveland Press, 1982); William Riker and Barry Weingast, "Constitutional regulation of legislative choice: The political consequences of judicial deference to legislatures," Hoover Institution Working Paper Series, Stanford, CA, December 1986.

6. Jean-Jacques Rousseau, *The Social Contract*, trans. Maurice Cranston (Baltimore: Penguin Books. 1968 [1762]), p. 72.

7. Riker's canonical interpretation of Arrow as demonstrating the incoherence of democracy due to cycling has been subject to empirical critiques. See Donald P. Green and Ian Shapiro, *Pathologies of Rational Choice Theory* (New Haven: Yale University Press, 1994), chap. 6; Gerry Mackie, *Democracy Defended* (Cambridge: Cambridge University Press, 2003).

8. John Locke, *Two Treatises of Government and A Letter concerning Toleration*, ed. Ian Shapiro (New Haven: Yale University Press, 2003 [ca. 1680]); James Madison, "Majority government," in *Letters and Other Writings of James Madison* IV (Philadelphia: J. P. Lippincott, 1865), p. 332; Joseph Schumpeter, *Capitalism, Socialism, and Democracy* (New York: Harper & Brothers, 1942); Robert A. Dahl, *A Preface to Democratic Theory*, exp. ed. (Chicago: University of Chicago Press, 2006); Adam Przeworski, "Minimalist conception of democracy," in *Democracy's Value*, ed. Casiano Hacker-Cordon and Ian Shapiro (Cambridge: Cambridge University Press, 1999), pp. 23–55.

9. Charles E. Lindblom, *The Intelligence of Democracy* (New York: Free Press, 1965).

10. Ian Shapiro, *The State of Democratic Theory* (Princeton, NJ: Princeton University Press, 2003), pp. 192–207.

11. Adam Przeworski, "Minimalist conception of democracy," in *Democracy's Value*, ed. Casiano Hacker-Cordon and Ian Shapiro (Cambridge: Cambridge University Press, 1999), pp. 23–55.

12. Sean Ingham, *Rule by Multiple Majorities* (Cambridge: Cambridge University Press, 2019).

13. Nicholas Miller, "Pluralism and social choice," *American Political Science Review* 77, no. 3 (1983): 734–47.

14. James Buchanan and Gordon Tullock, *The Calculus of Consent* (Ann Arbor: University of Michigan Press, 1962).

15. George J. Stigler, "The theory of economic regulation," *Bell Journal of Economics and Management Science* 2, no. 1 (1971): 3–21.

16. Gordon Tullock, *The Politics of Bureaucracy* (Washington, DC: Public Affairs Press, 1965); William A. Niskanen, *Bureaucracy and Representative Government* (Chicago: Aldine-Atherton, 1971).

17. Jules Coleman and John Ferejohn, "Democracy and social choice," *Ethics* 97, no. 1 (1986): 6–25.

18. Robert Nozick, *Anarchy, State, and Utopia* (New York: Basic Books, 1974), p. 4.

19. Cf. Keith Dowding and Andrew Hindmoor, "The usual suspects," *New Political Economy* 2, no. 3 (1997): 451–63.

20. Donald P. Green and Ian Shapiro, *Pathologies of Rational Choice Theory* (New Haven: Yale University Press, 1994), pp. 1–12.

21. Ronald Reagan, Inaugural Address, January 20, 1981, www.presidency.ucsb.edu/node/246336 (accessed May 28, 2021).

22. Ronald Reagan, Address before a Joint Session of Congress on the State of the Union, February 4, 1986, www.presidency.ucsb.edu/node/254269 (accessed May 28, 2021).

23. *Clinton v. City of New York*, 524 U.S. 417 [1998].

24. Mueller added a chapter on dictatorship to the third edition of *Public Choice* that had not been featured in the prior 1989 edition, but it is notable that this chapter reviews almost exclusively literature from the intervening period. Dennis Mueller, *Public Choice III* (New York, NY: Cambridge University Press, 2003) pp. 406–26.

25. Hans-Hermann Hoppe, *Democracy* (New Brunswick, NJ: Transaction Publishers, 2001), pp. 17–33.

26. Mancur Olson, "Dictatorship, democracy, and development," *American Political Science Review* 87, no. 3 (1993): 567–76. We are grateful to an anonymous reviewer for this observation.

27. Gordon Tullock, Arthur Seldon, and Gordon L. Brady, *Government Failure* (Washington, DC: Cato Institute, 2002), p. 55.

28. Cf. Nozick, *Anarchy, State, and Utopia;* Jason Brennan, *Against Democracy* (Princeton, NJ: Princeton University Press, 2016).

29. Dowding and Hindmoor, "Usual suspects," p. 456.

30. Fukuyama, *Political Order and Political Decay,* p. 470.

31. Steven Calabresi, "Some normative arguments for the unitary executive," *Arkansas Law Review* 48, no. 1 (1995): 23–104.

32. Posner and Vermeule, *Executive Unbound,* p. 24.

33. Ibid., p. 44.

34. Ibid., p. 21.

35. Ibid., p. 24.

36. The chief examples cited are the Bush administration's enormous expansion of the national security apparatus in the wake of September 11, 2001, and the administration's implementation of the Troubled Asset Relief Program during the 2008 financial crisis.

37. Posner and Vermeule, *Executive Unbound*, p. 6.

38. As we point out below, the atrophying of legislative capacity was a conscious political choice made by congressional leaders during the 1980s and 1990s.

39. Posner and Vermeule, *Executive Unbound*, p. 205.

40. Ibid., p. 114.

41. Douglass North and Barry Weingast, "Constitutions and commitment," *Journal of Economic History* 49, no. 4 (1989): 803–32.

42. Brian Barry, *Political Argument* (London: Routledge & Kegan Paul, 1965), pp. 237–91; George Tsebelis, *Veto Players* (Princeton, NJ: Princeton University Press, 2002).

43. Douglas W. Rae, "The limits of consensual decision," *American Political Science Review* 29, no. 4 (1975): 1270–94; Jacob S. Hacker and Paul Pierson, *Winner-Take-All Politics* (New York: Simon & Schuster, 2010).

44. Graham Dodds, "The executive unbound: After the Madisonian republic," *Law and Politics Book Review* 22, no. 2 (2012): 75–79.

45. Posner and Vermeule, *Executive Unbound*, p. 5.

46. Ibid., p. 206.

47. Howell and Moe, *Relic*, p. xvii.

48. Ibid., pp. 52 and 57.

49. Ibid., p. 107.

50. Daniel Carpenter and David Moss, eds., *Preventing Regulatory Capture* (Cambridge: Cambridge University Press, 2013).

51. Howell and Moe, *Relic*, p. 187.

52. Ibid., p. 67.

53. Frances Rosenbluth and Ian Shapiro, *Responsible Parties* (New Haven: Yale University Press, 2018), p. 96.

54. Fukuyama, *Political Order and Political Decay*, p. 488.

55. Timothy Noah, "Obama's biggest health reform blunder," *Slate*, August 6, 2009, https://slate.com/news-and-politics/2009/08/how-big-pharma-s-billy-tauzin-conned-the-white-house-out-of-76-billion.html (accessed February 9, 2023); Ron Suskind, *Confidence Men: Wall Street, Washington, and the Education of a President* (New York: HarperCollins, 2011), pp. 292–96.

56. Carpenter and Moss, eds., *Preventing Regulatory Capture*, chap. 4.

57. Fukuyama, *Political Order and Political Decay*, p. 470.

58. Compare Jason Webb Yackee and Susan Webb Yackee, "Administrative procedures and bureaucratic performance," *Journal of Public Administration Research and Theory* 20, no. 2 (2009): 261–82; and Richard J. Pierce, "Rulemaking ossification is real," *George Washington Law Review* 80 (2012): 1493–503.

59. Elena Kagan, "Presidential administration," *Harvard Law Review* 114, no. 8 (2001): 2245–385.

60. Signals from OIRA about what regulations it will accept can, however, push agencies to regulate in particular ways, for instance, based on certain approaches to cost-benefit analysis.

61. Kagan, "Presidential administration," p. 2332.

62. John Ferejohn and Roderick Hills, *Blank Checks, Insufficient Balances,* unpublished ms. (2017). Ferejohn and Hills focus on possible changes in legal doctrine, such as reversing *INS v. Chadha* (eliminating legislative vetoes of administrative decisions), placing more stress on legislative history in statutory interpretation, and reversing *Franklin v. Massachusetts* (exempting the president from the Administrative Procedure Act). All of these would be desirable, but, as discussed below, salutary developments in separation of powers doctrine are unlikely to emanate from the courts in the near future.

63. Ira Katznelson, *Fear Itself: The New Deal and the Origins of Our Time* (New York: Liveright, 2014), pp. 403–66.

64. Lee Drutman and Steven Teles, "A new agenda for political reform," *Washington Monthly,* February 22, 2015, https://washingtonmonthly.com/magazine/maraprmay-2015/a-new-agenda-for-political-reform (accessed May 28, 2021).

65. Matthew Nussbaum and Elana Schor, "Trump signs Russia sanctions bill but blasts Congress," *Politico,* August 2, 2017, www.politico.com/story/2017/08/02/trump-signs-bipartisan-russia-sanctions-bill-241242 (accessed May 28, 2021).

66. Daryl J. Levinson and Richard H. Pildes, "Separation of parties, not powers," *Harvard Law Review* 119, no. 8 (2006): 2311–86; House Select Committee on the Modernization of Congress, "Final report," October 2020, https://modernizecongress.house.gov/final-repdort-116th (accessed February 9, 2023).

67. Ian Shapiro, *Democracy's Place* (Ithaca, NY: Cornell University Press, 1996), pp. 30–42.

68. James A. Robinson and Ragnar Torvik, "Endogenous presidentialism," *Journal of the European Economic Association* 14, no. 4 (2016): 907–42.

69. Linz offers other reasons why presidential systems tend to be more unstable than parliamentary democracies: presidentialism divides power between the independent

mandates of the president and the legislature, setting the system up for crises of authority. Juan Linz, "The perils of presidentialism," *Journal of Democracy* 1, no. 1 (1990): 51–69.

70. David J. Samuels and Matthew S. Shugart, *Presidents, Parties, and Prime Ministers* (Cambridge: Cambridge University Press, 2010).

71. William G. Howell and Terry M. Moe, "Why the president needs more power," *Boston Review,* July 2, 2018, https://bostonreview.net/politics/william-howell-terry-m-moe-why-president-needs-more-power (accessed February 9, 2023).

72. Archibald Foord, *His Majesty's Opposition, 1714–1830* (Oxford: Clarendon Press, 1964), p. 2.

73. Suskind, *Confidence Men,* p. 396.

74. Ibid., p. 153.

75. Ibid., p. 377.

76. Ian Shapiro, *Politics against Domination* (Cambridge, MA: Harvard University Press, 2016), pp. 91–93.

77. Sam Peltzman, "Toward a more general theory of regulation," *Journal of Law and Economics* 19, no. 2 (1976): 211–40; John C. Coffee, "The political economy of Dodd-Frank," *Cornell Law Review* 97, no. 5 (2012): 1020–82.

78. William F. West, "Presidential leadership and administrative coordination," *Presidential Studies Quarterly* 36, no. 3 (2006): 433–56; Bijal Shah, "Congress's agency coordination," *Minnesota Law Review* 103 (2019): 1961–2093.

79. James N. Druckman and Lawrence R. Jacobs, *Who Governs? Presidents, Public Opinion, and Manipulation* (Chicago: University of Chicago Press, 2015).

80. Posner and Vermeule, *Executive Unbound,* p. 208.

81. Eric Posner, "And if elected: What President Trump could or couldn't do," *New York Times,* June 3, 2016.

82. It is ironic that Posner's most plausible hope for preventing Trump's damage, that he might not be able to exercise effective control over the federal bureaucracy, also undermines the unitary executive theory. Nevertheless, administrative resistance to Trump proved effective in some cases. See, e.g., Christopher Flavelle and Benjamin Bain, "Washington bureaucrats are chipping away at Trump's agenda," *Bloomberg,* December 18, 2017, www.bloomberg.com/news/features/2017-12-18/washington-bureaucrats-are-chipping-away-at-trump-s-agenda (accessed May 28, 2021).

83. Fukuyama, *Political Order and Political Decay,* p. 471.

84. Rosenbluth and Shapiro, *Responsible Parties,* pp. 95–127.

85. Irving Janis, *Victims of Groupthink: A Psychological Study of Foreign-Policy Decisions and Fiascoes* (Boston: Houghton Mifflin, 1972).

86. Cass R. Sunstein and Reid Hastie, *Wiser: Getting beyond Groupthink to Make Groups Smarter* (Cambridge, MA: Harvard Business Review Press, 2014).

87. Conceived as a way to limit royal power, the unit veto rendered the Sejm hostage to conservative opponents of change who were often bribed to cast vetoes by foreign powers. See William Christian Bullitt, *The Great Globe Itself: A Preface to World Affairs* (New York: Charles Scribner's & Sons, 1946), pp. 42–43.

88. The Hastert Rule—an informal rule during Republican control—requires that legislation introduced in the House have the support of a majority of the members of the majority party in order to receive a vote, conceivably allowing 109 out of 435 House members to block legislation.

89. Alexander Kustov, Maikol A. Cerda, Akhil Rajan, Frances Rosenbluth, and Ian Shapiro, "The rise of safe seats and party indiscipline in the U.S. Congress," paper presented at the Midwest Political Science Association, Chicago, 2021.

90. John Aldrich, *Why Parties? The Origin and Transformation of Political Parties in America* (Chicago: University of Chicago Press, 1995).

91. Joel W. Simmons, *The Politics of Technological Progress* (Cambridge: Cambridge University Press, 2016), pp. 52–67.

92. Recent scholarship suggests that popular support for Jackson in 1824 has been exaggerated. Some states, notably New York, did not hold direct popular votes and indirect evidence suggests that Adams would have beaten him if they had done so. See Donald Ratcliffe, *The One-Party Presidential Contest: Adams, Jackson, and 1824's Five-Horse Race* (Lawrence: University of Kansas Press, 2015).

93. See, e.g., David Roberts, "Scott Pruitt is dismantling EPA in secret for the same reason the GOP health care bill was secret," *Vox*, August 14, 2017, www.vox.com/energy-and-environment/2017/8/14/16142150/scott-pruitt-epa-secrecy-republican (accessed May 28, 2021).

94. Damien Paletta, "Trump administration considers tax cut for the country's super-rich," *Independent*, July 31, 2018, www.independent.co.uk/news/world/americas/trump-tax-cut-superrich-billions-us-president-wealthy-washington-a8470736.html (accessed May 28, 2021); Bruce Ackerman, "No, Trump cannot declare an 'emergency' to build his wall," *New York Times*, January 5, 2019, www.nytimes.com/2019/01/05/opinion/no-trump-cannot-declare-an-emergency-to-build-his-wall.html (accessed May 28, 2021).

95. Ron Chernow, *Grant* (New York: Penguin Press, 2017), pp. 593–612.

96. *Myers v. United States*, 272 U.S. 71 [1926]; *Humphrey's Executor v. United States*, 295 U.S. 602 [1935].

97. Recent separation of powers jurisprudence has endorsed, at least partially, the unitary executive theory. In *Free Enterprise Fund*, 561 U.S. 477 (2010), the Court held that the existence of multiple layers of tenure protection in an agency leadership structure violates separation of powers, because it dilutes too much of the president's power to control executive officers.

98. See, e.g., *Trump v. Hawaii*, 138 S.Ct. 2392 (2018).

Chapter Five. Collusion in Restraint of Democracy

1. For example, see Jane J. Mansbridge, *Beyond Adversary Democracy*, 2nd ed. (Chicago: University of Chicago Press, 1983); Amy Gutmann and Dennis Thompson, *Democracy and Disagreement* (Cambridge, MA: Harvard University Press, 1996); Amy Gutmann and Dennis Thompson, *Why Deliberative Democracy?* (Princeton, NJ: Princeton University Press, 2009); James S. Fishkin, *The Voice of the People: Public Opinion and Democracy* (New Haven: Yale University Press, 1995); James S. Fishkin, *When the People Speak: Deliberative Democracy and Public Consultation* (Oxford: Oxford University Press, 2011); Hélène Landemore, *Democratic Reason: Politics, Collective Intelligence, and the Rule of the Many* (Princeton, NJ: Princeton University Press, 2012); Jürgen Habermas, *Communication and the Evolution of Society*, trans. Thomas McCarthy (Boston: Beacon Press, 1975); and Jürgen Habermas, *The Theory of Communicative Action*, trans. Thomas McCarthy (Boston: Beacon Press, 1984). There are, of course, major differences among these and other theorists of deliberative democracy that do not concern me here.

2. John Stuart Mill, *On Liberty*, ed. David Bromwich (New Haven: Yale University Press, 2003 [1859]), pp. 86–120.

3. See Anthony Downs, *An Economic Theory of Democracy* (New York: Harper and Row, 1957), pp. 244–46, 266–71.

4. Joseph Schumpeter, *Capitalism, Socialism, and Democracy* (London: George Allen & Unwin, 1942), p. 269.

5. Where there is substantial regional variation, by contrast, as in India, SMP systems can produce party proliferation.

6. Tocqueville described the Senate as peopled by America's "ablest citizens," men moved by "lofty thoughts and generous instincts." By contrast, the House of Representatives consisted of "village lawyers, tradesmen, or even men of the lowest class" who were of "vulgar demeanor," animated by "vices" and "petty passions." Alexis de Tocqueville, *Democracy in America*, ed. J. P. Mayer (New York: Anchor Books, 1969 [1835, 1840]), pp. 200–201.

7. Terence Samuel, *The Upper House: A Journey behind Closed Doors* (New York: Palgrave Macmillan, 2010), p. 68.

8. James Madison, Federalist no. 51, in *The Federalist Papers*, ed. Ian Shapiro (New Haven: Yale University Press, 2009 [1787–88]), p. 264.

9. Ibid.

10. Jane Mayer, *Dark Money: The Hidden History of the Billionaires behind the Rise of the Radical Right* (New York: Doubleday, 2016), pp. 198–225.

11. Walter Bagehot, *The English Constitution*, ed. Miles Taylor (Oxford: Oxford University Press, 2001 [1867]), p. 88.

12. Donald Shell, *House of Lords* (London: Paul Allan, 1988), pp. 152–74; and Meg Russell, *The Contemporary House of Lords: Westminster Bicameralism Revisited* (Oxford: Oxford University Press, 2013), pp. 45–46, 271–72. See also Vernon Bogdanor, *The New British Constitution* (London: Hart Publishing, 2009), pp. 16–18, 145–73, 222–25, 278–89.

13. The House of Lords Act of 1999 reduced the membership from 1,330 to 699 and got rid of all but ninety-two of the hereditary peers who were allowed to remain on an interim basis and ten who were made life peers. On the recent evolution, see Russell, *Contemporary House of Lords*, pp. 13–35, 258–84.

14. Ibid., pp. 138, 239–42.

15. Ibid., pp. 245, 254.

16. See Ian Shapiro, *The Real World of Democratic Theory* (Princeton, NJ: Princeton University Press, 2010), pp. 266–71.

17. Hélène Landemore describes the Irish example as "the jewel in the crown of deliberative democracy, having established that citizens' assemblies can be entrusted with complex, fraught, and profoundly divisive questions." *Open Democracy: Reinventing Popular Rule for the Twenty-First Century* (Princeton, NJ: Princeton University Press, 2022), p. 152.

18. Mayling Birney, Ian Shapiro, and Michael Graetz, "The political uses of public opinion: Lessons from the estate tax repeal," in *Divide and Deal: The Politics of Distribution in Democracies*, ed. Ian Shapiro, Peter Swenson, and Daniela Donno (New York: New York University Press, 2008), pp. 298–340.

19. Matteo Bonotti, "Conceptualising political parties: A normative framework," *Politics* 31, no. 1 (2011): 19–26, at pp. 20–22.

20. David Miliband, "The next leadership team needs to recognize the fundamental errors that made Labour unelectable," *The Guardian*, December 22, 2019.

21. BBC, "EU vote: Where the cabinet and other MPs stand," BBC News, June 22, 2016, www.bbc.com/news/uk-politics-eu-referendum-35616946 (accessed October 9, 2019).

22. Vernon Bogdanor, "Britain and the EU: In or out—one year on," Gresham College lecture, June 29, 2019, www.youtube.com/watch?v=Jqbc7yVnojE (accessed February 1, 2020).

23. Hovik Minasyan, "Brexit positions of MPs in the 2019 Parliament compared to the 2015 Parliament," mimeo, Leitner Program on Effective Democratic Governance, Yale University, 2020.

24. Charlie Cooper, "EU Referendum: Final polls show Remain with edge over Brexit," *The Independent,* June 23, 2016, www.independent.co.uk/news/uk/politics/eu-referendum-poll-brexit-remain-vote-leave-live-latest-who-will-win-results-popu lus-a7097261.html (accessed February 9, 2023); and Anushka Asthana, "Parliamentary fightback against Brexit on cards," *The Guardian,* June 26, 2016, www.theguardian.com/politics/2016/jun/26/fightback-against-brexit-on-cards-remain-eu-referendum-heseltine (accessed February 9, 2023).

25. Carlo Invernizzi-Accetti and Fabio Wolkenstein, "The crisis of party democracy, cognitive mobilization, and the case for making parties more deliberative," *American Political Science Review* 111, no. 1 (2017): 97–109, at p. 105.

26. Michael Graetz and Ian Shapiro, *The Wolf at the Door: The Menace of Economic Insecurity and How to Fight It* (Cambridge, MA: Harvard University Press, 2005), pp. 26–27.

27. Patrick McGuire, "Now it's Conservative, not Labour MPs who fear deselection," *New Statesman American,* June 12, 2018, www.newstatesman.com/politics/uk/2018/06/now-it-s-conservative-not-labour-mps-who-fear-deselection (accessed February 1, 2020).

28. Decisive evidence on why MPs switched positions is elusive. Some declared "respect for the Referendum result"; some responded to years of Brexit fatigue with Johnson's "Get Brexit done"; and some prevaricated. See Minasyan, "Brexit positions of MPs in the 2019 Parliament compared to the 2015 Parliament." As with studying the effects of primaries on position-taking by U.S. politicians, the possibility of deselection by "entryist" Brexiteers might have been sufficient, making an actual challenge unnecessary. Rob Merrick and Benjamin Kentish, "No-deal Brexit support and 'blatant entryism' surges among grassroots Conservatives and former Ukip voters," *The Independent,* June 29, 2019, www.independent.co.uk/news/uk/politics/conservative-leadership-news-latest-no-deal-brexit-boris-johnson-ukip-jeremy-hunt-a8978206.html (November 19, 2022).

29. In the event, Johnson turned out to be lucky that Labour was saddled with one of its most unpopular leaders ever who was touting a program that, as Miliband says, "came to be seen as more of a risk to the country than Brexit—even though every

study shows that it will cost the poorest communities the most" (Miliband, "Next leadership team needs to recognize the fundamental errors that made Labour unelectable").

30. Adam Bienkov and Thomas Colson, "Brexit deadlock: MPs reject all remaining alternatives to Theresa May's deal," *Business Insider,* April 1, 2019, www.businessinsider.com/brexit-indicative-votes-mps-reject-all-alternatives-to-theresa-mays-deal-2019-4 (accessed February 1, 2020).

31. Conservative Party, Conservative General Election Manifesto 1983, Thatcher Archive, www.margaretthatcher.org/document/110859 (accessed April 15, 2022).

32. The rebate agreement granted the UK 66 percent of the difference between its share of member states' VAT contributions and its share of EU spending in return. European Commission, "Commission working document," May 14, 2014, https://eur-lex.europa.eu/legal-content/EN/TXT/PDF/?uri=CELEX:52014DC0271&from=EN (accessed November 19, 2022).

33. Helene Von Bismarck, "Margaret Thatcher: The critical architect of European integration," The UK in a Changing Europe, https://ukandeu.ac.uk/margaret-thatcher-the-critical-architect-of-european-integration (accessed February 21, 2020).

34. Harold Wilson, *The Final Term: The Labour Government, 1974–76* (London: Weidenfeld & Nicholson, 1979), 109.

35. The Gang of Four who left were Roy Jenkins, David Owen, Shirley Williams, and Bill Rodgers. Had Tony Benn beaten moderate Denis Healey for the deputy leadership when Michael Foot became leader in November 1980, the defecting group would doubtless have been larger.

36. See Urfan Khaliq, "The EU and the European social charter: Never the twain shall meet?" *Cambridge Yearbook of European Social Studies* 15 (2017): 169–96.

37. Nyta Mann, "Foot's message of hope to left," BBC News, July 14, 2003, http://news.bbc.co.uk/1/hi/uk_politics/3059773.stm (accessed April 13, 2022); Riley Charlotte, "For Labour, the 2019 election echoes 'the longest suicide note in history,'" *Washington Post,* December 14, 2019, www.washingtonpost.com/outlook/2019/12/14/labour-election-echoes-longest-suicide-note-history (accessed December 19, 2019). In 1983 the party was harvesting the consequences rule changes adopted two years earlier, discussed more fully below, that strengthened the role of activists and unions in selecting its leaders at the expense of the Parliamentary Party, a change that came just as trade union membership began falling precipitously. This would render the party decreasingly representative of the British electorate, keeping Labour in the political wilderness until the party was fundamentally restructured a decade-and-a-half later.

38. Vernon Bogdanor, "The referendum on Europe—1975," Gresham College lecture, May 22, 2014, www.youtube.com/watch?v=U_4vNtSqahk (accessed February 9, 2023).

39. Kathleen Bawn and Frances Rosenbluth, "Short versus long coalitions: Electoral accountability and the size of the public sector," *American Journal of Political Science* 50, no. 2 (April 2006): 251–65.

40. James Buchanan and Gordon Tullock, *The Calculus of Consent: Logical Foundations of Constitutional Democracy* (Ann Arbor: University of Michigan Press, 1962). Robert Dahl flirted with the notion that attending to intensity might be desirable from the standpoint of political stability, though he was skeptical that it could be measured. Robert A. Dahl, *A Preface to Democratic Theory* (Chicago: University of Chicago Press, 1956), pp. 90–123.

41. For discussion of the dangers inherent in catering to intense preferences, see Ian Shapiro, *Politics against Domination* (Cambridge, MA: Harvard University Press, 2016), pp. 46–61.

42. See Mayer, *Dark Money*, pp. 120–58, 226–70, 354–87.

43. See *Buckley v. Valeo* 424 U.S. 1, 59 (1976); *Citizens United v. Federal Election Commission* 558 U.S. 310 (2010); and *SpeechNow.org v. Federal Election Commission* 599 F.3d 686, 689 (D.C. Cir. 2010).

Chapter Six. On Political Parties

1. Norberto Bobbio, *The Future of Democracy* (Minneapolis: University of Minnesota Press, 1987); Roberto Gargarella, "Full representation, deliberation, and impartiality," in *Deliberative Democracy*, ed. John Elster (Cambridge: Cambridge University Press, 1998); Nadia Urbinati and Mark E. Warren, "The concept of representation in contemporary democratic theory," *Annual Review of Political Science* 11 (2008): 389.

2. Recent scholarship suggests that popular support for Jackson in 1824 has been exaggerated. See p. 301 n.92 above. Also sagging is the conventional wisdom that House Speaker Henry Clay threw his support to Adams in a corrupt bargain in which Adams made Clay his secretary of state. Ratcliffe points out that Clay endorsed Adams before any chance of bargaining was in the cards, and others have noted that Clay was ideologically closer to Adams than to Jackson so that no corrupt bargain was needed. See Jeffrey Jenkins and Brian Sala, "The spatial theory of

voting and the Presidential election of 1824," *American Journal of Political Science* 42, no. 4 (1998): 1157–79.

3. Perry Anderson, *Lineages of the Absolutist State* (New York: New Left Books, 1974).

4. Bernard Manin, *The Principles of Representative Government* (Cambridge: Cambridge University Press, 1997); Nadia Urbinati, "Representation as advocacy: A study of democratic deliberation," *Political Theory* 28, no. 6 (2000): 758–86; Nadia Urbinati, *Representative Democracy: Principles of Genealogy* (Chicago: University of Chicago Press, 2006); Iris Marion Young, *Inclusion and Democracy* (Oxford: Oxford University Press, 2002); Jonathan White and Lea Ypi, *The Meaning of Partisanship* (Oxford: Oxford University Press, 2016); Daniel Weinstock, "On partisan compromise," *Political Theory* 47, no. 1 (2019): 90–96; Matteo Bonotti, *Partisanship and Political Liberalism in Diverse Societies* (Oxford: Oxford University Press, 2017).

5. Thomas Hobbes, *Leviathan, or the Matter, Forme & Power of a Commonwealth Ecclesiastical and Civill*, ed. Ian Shapiro (New Haven: Yale University Press, 2010 [1651]), p. 105.

6. Quentin Skinner, "Conquest and consent: Thomas Hobbes and the engagement controversy," in *The Interregnum: The Quest for Settlement, 1646–1660*, ed. G. E. Aylmer (London: Macmillan, 1972).

7. John Locke, *Two Treatises of Government and A Letter Concerning Toleration*, ed. Ian Shapiro (New Haven: Yale University Press, 2003 [1681]), 142–43.

8. Hobbes, *Leviathan*, pp. 100–101, 107–8. Of course, for Hobbes there are other ways of instituting commonwealths.

9. Kenneth Arrow, *Social Choice and Individual Values* (New Haven: Yale University Press, 1951); William Riker, *Liberalism against Populism: A Confrontation between the Theory of Democracy and the Theory of Social Choice* (New York: Waveland, 1988).

10. Robert Nozick, *Anarchy, State, and Utopia* (New York: Basic Books, 1974).

11. James Buchanan and Gordon Tullock, *The Calculus of Consent: Logical Foundations of Constitutional Democracy* (Ann Arbor: University of Michigan Press, 1962).

12. Jules Coleman and John Ferejohn, "Democracy and social choice," *Ethics* 97, no. 1 (1986): 6–25.

13. Brian Barry, *Political Argument*, 2nd ed. (Herefordshire: Harvester Wheatsheaf, 1990 [1965]); Douglas Rae, "The limits of consensual decision," *American Political Science Review* 69 (1975): 1270–94.

14. Hobbes, *Leviathan*, p. 100.

15. Francis Devine, "Absolute democracy or indefeasible right: Hobbes versus Locke," *Journal of Politics* 37, no. 3 (1975): 736–68, at p. 740.

16. Locke, *Two Treatises*, p. 163.

17. Jane Mansbridge, "Rethinking representation," *American Political Science Review* 94, no. 4 (2003): 515–28.

18. Benjamin Page, *Choices and Echoes in Presidential Elections: Rational Man and Electoral Democracy* (Chicago: University of Chicago Press, 1978), pp. 221–22.

19. Douglas Arnold, *The Logic of Congressional Action* (New Haven: Yale University Press, 1990), p. 17; Douglas Arnold, "Can inattentive citizens control their elected representatives?" in *Congress Reconsidered*, ed. Lawrence Dodd and Bruce Oppenheimer (Washington, DC: CQ Press, 1993), pp. 401–16, at p. 409; James Stimson, Michael Mackuen, and Robert Erikson, "Dynamic representation," *American Political Science Review* 89 (1995): 543–65, at p. 545.

20. Mansbridge, "Rethinking representation," p. 518; Lisa Disch, "Towards a mobilization conception of democratic representation," *American Political Science Review* 105, no. 1 (2011): 100–114, at pp. 101 and 113.

21. See Adam Przeworski, "Minimalist conception of democracy: A defense," in *Democracy's Value*, ed. Ian Shapiro and Casiano Hacker-Cordón (Cambridge: Cambridge University Press, 1999), pp. 23–55.

22. Edmund Burke, "Thoughts on the cause of the present discontents," in *Selected Works of Edmund Burke*, vol. 1, ed. E. J. Payne (Indianapolis, IN: Liberty Fund, 1999 [1770]), p. 150.

23. Joseph Schumpeter, *Capitalism, Socialism, and Democracy* (New York: George Allen & Unwin, 1976 [1943]), pp. 250–69.

24. Nozick, *Anarchy, State, and Utopia*; Riker, *Liberalism against Populism*.

25. Emilee Booth Chapman, "New challenges for a normative theory of parties and partisanship," *Journal of Representative Democracy* 57, no. 3 (2021): 385–400; Russell Muirhead and Nancy L. Rosenblum, "The political theory of parties and partisanship: Catching up," *Annual Review of Political Science* 23 (2020): 95–110; White and Ypi, *Meaning of Partisanship*.

26. This follows from Duverger's (1964) law, which holds that the number of parties is determined by district magnitude (the number of candidates elected per district) plus one. This will be true provided the districts are large and similarly diverse. If there is considerable regional variation, as in India, then there will be party proliferation even with single-member plurality districts.

27. Christopher J. Anderson, "Economic voting and political context: A comparative perspective," *Electoral Studies* 19, nos. 2–3 (2000): 155–56.

28. See Richard S. Katz, "No man can serve two masters: Party politicians, party members, citizens and principal-agent models of democracy," *Party Politics* 20, no. 2 (2014): 183–93, at pp. 187–88.

29. Anthony Atkinson, Lee Rainwater, and Timothy Smeeding, *Income Distribution in OECD Countries: Evidence from the Luxembourg Income Study* (Paris: Organisation for Economic Co-operation and Development, 1995), pp. 81–111; G. Bingham Powell, *Elections as Instruments of Democracy: Majoritarian and Proportional Visions* (New Haven: Yale University Press, 2000), pp. 159–232.

30. The effects of increasing fragmentation are hard to predict. Negotiations among three or more parties are inevitably more difficult than negotiations among two. On the other hand, a larger number of small parties might have to compete with one another to be part of the governing coalition—reducing the leverage of each in bargaining with the large parties. See Eric Browne and Mark Franklin, "Aspects of coalition payoffs in European parliamentary democracies," *American Political Science Review* 67, no. 2 (1973): 453–69; and Paul Warwick and James Druckman, "Portfolio salience and the proportionality of payoffs in coalition governments," *British Journal of Political Science* 31, no. 4 (2001): 627–49. Moreover, small parties are often single-issue parties with limited capacity to bargain, lest they undermine their raison d'être.

31. This might help explain why, when left-of-center parties are part of the government, unemployment increases by 1 percent. Christian Salas, Frances Rosenbluth, and Ian Shapiro, "Political parties and the new politics of insecurity," in *Who Gets What? The New Politics of Insecurity*, ed. Frances Rosenbluth and Margaret Weird (Cambridge: Cambridge University Press, 2021), pp. 237–58.

32. Frances Rosenbluth and Ian Shapiro, *Responsible Parties: Saving Democracy from Itself* (New Haven: Yale University Press, 2018), pp. 62–98; Emilee Booth Chapman, "New challenges for a normative theory of parties and partisanship," *Journal of Representative Democracy* 57, no. 3 (2021): 385–400.

33. Frances Rosenbluth and Kathleen Bawn, "Short versus long coalitions: Electoral accountability and the size of the public sector," *American Journal of Political Science* 50, no. 2 (2006): 251–65; Torsten Persson, Gerard Rland, and Guido Tabellini, "Electoral rules and government spending in parliamentary democracies," *Quarterly Journal of Political Science* 2, no. 2 (2007): 1–34; Bernard Caillaud and Jean Tirole, "Parties as political intermediaries," *Quarterly Journal of Economics* 117, no. 4 (2002): 1453–89.

34. The average number of parties represented in the legislatures of twenty-six OECD countries grew steadily from 5.5 to 8.5 from 1960 to 2018. The effective number of parties grew from 3 to 4.25 over the same period (Salas, Rosenbluth, and Shapiro, "Political parties and the new politics of insecurity").

35. Gary Cox, "Centripetal and centrifugal incentives in electoral systems," *American Journal of Political Science* 34, no. 4 (1990): 903–35; and *Making Votes Count: Strategic Coordination in the World's Electoral Systems* (Cambridge: Cambridge University Press, 1997), pp. 99–122.

36. Nancy Rosenblum, *On the Side of the Angels: An Appreciation of Parties and Partisanship* (Princeton, NJ: Princeton University Press, 2008), pp. 362–63; see also Russell Muirhead, *The Promise of Party in a Polarized Age* (Cambridge, MA: Harvard University Press, 2014), pp. 80–145.

37. William Notz and Frederick Starke, "Final-offer versus conventional arbitration as means of conflict management," *Journal of Conflict Resolution* 23, no. 2 (1978): 189–203; Henry S. Farber and Max Bazerman, "The general basis of arbitrator behavior: An empirical analysis of conventional and final-offer arbitration," *Econometrica* 54, no. 4 (1986): 819–44; Charles W. Adams, "Final offer arbitration: Time for serious consideration by the courts," *Nebraska Law Review* 66 (1987): 213–48.

38. Matteo Bonotti et al., "In defence of political parties: A symposium on Jonathan White and Lea Ypi's *The Meaning of Partisanship*," *Political Studies Review* 16, no. 4 (2018): 289–305, at pp. 296–98.

39. This is not to say that when parties converge in two-party systems they always converge on the median voter. Expectations of low turnout by younger and poorer voters can lead both parties to ignore their interests in favor of those of older and wealthier voters who turn out in higher numbers and contribute more money to parties. These are among the reasons why, even as the U.S. parties have become more polarized in recent years, both parties have moved to the right. See Nolan McCarty, Keith Poole, and Howard Rosenthal, *Polarized America: The Dance of Ideology and Unequal Riches* (Cambridge, MA: MIT Press, 2008).

40. Muirhead, *Promise of Party in a Polarized Age*, p. 176.

41. Jane Mansbridge, "A selection model of political representation," *Journal of Political Philosophy* 17, no. 4 (2009): 369–98.

42. Carlo Invernizzi-Accetti and Fabio Wolkenstein, "The crisis of party democracy, cognitive mobilization, and the case for making parties more deliberative," *American Political Science Review* 111, no. 1 (2017): 97–109, at p. 104.

43. Sunder Katwala, "The NHS: Even more cherished than the monarchy or the army," *New Statesman America*, January 14, 2013, www.newstatesman.com/politics/2013/01/nhs-even-more-cherished-monarchy-and-army (accessed September 22, 2019).

44. See Fabio Wolkenstein, "A deliberative model of intra-party democracy," *Journal of Political Philosophy*, 24, no. 3 (2016): 297–320; and "Intra-party democracy beyond aggregation," *Party Politics*, 24, no. 4 (2016): 323–34.

45. Joseph Schumpeter, *Capitalism, Socialism, and Democracy* (New York: George Allen & Unwin, 1976 [1943]), pp. 269–73.

46. Governance of public universities is also controversial, as was dramatically underscored by the battle between the Regents of the University of California and the faculty over the inclusion of loyalty pledges in employment contracts during the McCarthy era. See James F. Simon, *Eisenhower vs. Warren: The Battle for Civil Rights and Liberties* (New York: Norton Liveright, 2018), pp. 66–76. But at the end of the day, faculties at public universities are public employees, and the analog of a firm's residual claimants is taxpayers.

47. Labour List, "Number of voters in leadership contest revised down to 550,000," August 25, 2015, https://labourlist.org/2015/08/number-of-voters-in-leadership-contest-revised-down-to-550000 (accessed February 1, 2020); BBC, "Labour leadership results in full," BBC News, September 12, 2015, www.bbc.com/news/uk-politics-34221155 (accessed October 5, 2019).

48. Tim Bale, Monica Poletti, and Paul Webb, "Here's what we know about Labour's £3 supporters—and whether they'll pay £25 to help Corbyn again," *The Conversation*, July 14, 2016, https://theconversation.com/heres-what-we-know-about-labours-3-supporters-and-whether-theyll-pay-25-to-help-corbyn-again-62728 (accessed January 20, 2020).

49. Jenny Anderson, "How Theresa May blew a 20-point lead and saddled the UK with a hung Parliament," *Quartz*, June 9, 2017, https://qz.com/1002394/uk-election-how-theresa-may-blew-a-20-point-lead-and-gave-the-uk-a-hung-parliament (accessed December 19, 2019).

50. The scale of Labour's defeat forced the left to back down and agree to the election of the centrist Kier Starmer in 2020, but they still saddled him with a hard left deputy leader Angela Rayner, who lost little time in attacking him, leading to press speculation—fed by the prime minister's supporters—that she would mount a leadership challenge at the first opportunity.

51. Fernando Bizzarro et al., "Party strength and economic growth," *World Politics* 70, no. 2 (2018): 278.

52. Joel Simmons, *The Politics of Technological Progress: Parties, Time Horizons, and Long-Term Economic Development* (Cambridge: Cambridge University Press, 2016), pp. 7–8.

53. Joseph Postell, "The rise and fall of political parties in America," *First Principles* 70 (2018): 1–16, at p. 16.

54. Mike DeBonis, "Fuming over Ryan, some conservative voices turn on the Freedom Caucus," *Washington Post*, October 25, 2015, www.washingtonpost.com/politics/fuming-over-ryan-some-conservative-voices-turn-on-the-freedom-caucus/2015/10/25/8194f3ce-7999-11e5-a958-d889faf561dc_story.html (accessed December 16, 2019).

55. Jason Dick, "Paul Ryan runs through the tape as lame duck Congress limps to the finish line," *Roll Call*, December 19, 2018, www.rollcall.com/news/politics/paul-ryan-runs-through-the-tape-as-lame-duck-congress-limps-to-finish-line (accessed December 16, 2019).

56. National party leaders also have different incentives in this regard from local party leaders. See David Broockman et al., "Why local party leaders don't support nominating centrists," *British Journal of Political Science* (published online by Cambridge University Press, October 24, 2019), www.cambridge.org/core/journals/british-journal-of-political-science/article/abs/why-local-party-leaders-dont-support-nominating-centrists/1C6967FB44F7D3B5A7546BE02E20D32A (accessed April 1, 2023).

57. Stephen Gardbaum and Rick Pildes, "Populism and institutional design: Methods of selecting candidates for chief executive," *New York University Law Review* 93 (2018): 647–708.

58. Alan Abramowitz, Brad Alexander, and Matthew Gunning, "Incumbency, redistricting, and the decline of competition in U.S. House election," *Journal of Politics* 68, no. 1 (2006): 75–88; and Alexander Kustov, Maikol Cerda, Akhil Rajan, Frances Rosenbluth, and Ian Shapiro, "The rise of safe seats and party indiscipline in the U.S. Congress," presented at the Annual Meeting of the Midwest Political Science Association, Chicago, 2021.

59. Chris Riotta, "GOP aims to kill Obamacare yet again after failing 70 times," *Newsweek*, July 29, 2019, www.newsweek.com/gop-health-care-bill-repeal-and-replace-70-failed-attempts-643832 (accessed October 5, 2019).

60. James Curry and Frances Lee, "What is regular order worth? Partisan lawmaking and congressional processes," *Journal of Politics* 82, no. 2 (2020): 627–41.

61. Gary Cox and Matthew McCubbins, *Legislative Leviathan: Party Government in the House* (Berkeley: University of California Press, 1993).

62. Martin Gilens, *Affluence and Influence: Economic Inequality and Political Power in America* (Princeton, NJ: Princeton University Press, 2012).

63. Benjamin Page and Martin Gilens, *Democracy in America? What Has Gone Wrong and What We Can Do About It* (Chicago: University of Chicago Press, 2020); Michael Graetz and Ian Shapiro, *The Wolf at the Door: The Menace of Economic Inse-*

curity and How to Fight It (Cambridge, MA: Harvard University Press, 2020), pp. 1–36, 260–80.

64. Tucker Carlson, *Ship of Fools: How a Selfish Ruling Class Is Bringing America to the Brink of Revolution* (New York: Free Press, 2018), p. 3.

65. John Dewey, *The Public and Its Problems: An Essay in Political Inquiry*, ed. Melvin Rogers (University Park: Pennsylvania State University Press, 2012 [1927]), pp. 153–54.

66. E. E. Schattschneider, *Party Government* (New York: Holt, Reinhart and Winston, 1942), p. 1.

67. "Many forms of Government have been tried and will be tried in this world of sin and woe. No one pretends that democracy is perfect or all-wise. Indeed, it has been said that democracy is the worst form of Government except for all those other forms that have been tried from time to time." Winston S. Churchill, "Speech to the House of Commons, November 11, 1947." Reproduced in *Churchill by Himself: The Definitive Collection of Quotations,* ed. Richard Langworth (New York: Public Affairs, 2008 [1947]), p. 574.

Chapter Seven. Negative Liberty and the Cold War (with Alicia Steinmetz)

1. On the antecedents of Berlin's political theory, see Joshua Cherniss, *A Mind and Its Time: The Development of Isaiah Berlin's Political Thought* (Oxford: Oxford University Press, 2013), pp. 1–14.

2. J. G. A. Pocock, *Virtue, Commerce, and History: Essays on Political Thought and History, Chiefly in the Eighteenth Century* (Cambridge: Cambridge University Press, 1985), pp. 39–40; and "Virtues, rights, and manners: A model for historians of political thought," *Political Theory* 9, no. 3 (August 1981): 357–59.

3. On Pettit's third way view of freedom as "discursive control," see Philip Pettit, *A Theory of Freedom; From the Psychology to the Politics of Agency* (Oxford: Oxford University Press, 2001), 67ff.; *Republicanism: A Theory of Freedom and Government* (Oxford: Oxford University Press, 1997), pp. 17–79.

4. Quentin Skinner, *Hobbes and Republican Liberty* (Cambridge: Cambridge University Press, 2008), pp. 211–16; and "A third concept of liberty: Living in servitude," *London Review of Books,* April 4, 2002, pp. 16–18.

5. Leo Strauss, *Natural Right and History* (Chicago: University of Chicago Press, 1953), p. 323.

6. C. B. Macpherson, *The Political Theory of Possessive Individualism: Hobbes to Locke* (Oxford: Oxford University Press, 1962).

7. See, for instance, Karl Marx, *Capital: A Critique of Political Economy* I, trans. Ben Fowkes (London: Pelican Books, 1976), p. 492.

8. Herbert Marcuse, "Repressive tolerance," in *A Critique of Pure Tolerance*, ed. Robert Paul Wolff, Barrington Moore, Jr., and Herbert Marcuse (Boston: Beacon Press, 1965), pp. 81–117.

9. Gerard MacCallum, Jr., "Negative and positive freedom," *Philosophical Review* 76 (1967): 312–34.

10. See Ian Shapiro, "Gross concepts in political argument," *Political Theory* 17, no. 1 (February 1989): 73–76.

11. See John Lewis Gaddis, *George F. Kennan: An American Life* (New York: Penguin Press, 2011), p. 416.

12. In a note to Elizabeth Green, the director of the Mount Holyoke College News Bureau, Berlin said, "I must again beg you not permit any of this to appear in print under my name as the consequences to various persons in the U.S.S.R. would be very grave, & I should certainly decline to speak if I thought that there [was] any risk of my words appear in print anywhere." When Green replied that this would not be possible, Berlin apparently decided to speak anyway and agreed to meet briefly with the *New York Times* correspondent. From Isaiah Berlin, *Enlightening: Letters 1946–1960*, ed. Henry Hardy and Jennifer Holmes (London: Chatto & Windus, 2009), p. 98; Michael Ignatieff, *Isaiah Berlin: A Life* (New York: Henry Holt, 1998), p. 192; Isaiah Berlin to George Kennan on June 30, 1949, in *Enlightening*, p. 98n3.

13. Isaiah Berlin to the editor of the *New York Times*, June 30, 1949, *Enlightening*, p. 99.

14. Isaiah Berlin to Corinne Alsop, July 5, 1949, *Enlightening*, p. 101.

15. Ignatieff, *Isaiah Berlin: A Life*, p. 192; Isaiah Berlin, "Democracy, communism, and the individual," in *The Power of Ideas*, ed. Henry Hardy (Princeton, NJ: Princeton University Press, 2013), p. 277.

16. Isaiah Berlin, "Democracy, communism, and the individual," p. 277.

17. Ignatieff, *Isaiah Berlin: A Life*, p. 193.

18. Isaiah Berlin to Joseph Alsop, July 1, 1949, *Enlightening*, p. 100.

19. Isaiah Berlin to Corinne Alsop, July 5, 1949, *Enlightening*, p. 101.

20. "Address given by Ernest Bevin to the House of Commons (22 January 1948)," Parliamentary Debates, House of Commons, Official Report. Third session of the Thirty-Eighth Parliament of the United Kingdom of Great Britain and Northern Ireland, www.cvce.eu/content/publication/2002/9/9/7bc0ecbd-c50e-4035-8e36-ed-70bfbd204c/publishable_en.pdf (accessed April 3, 2023).

21. Isaiah Berlin to Alan Dudley, received March 17, 1948, *Enlightening*, p. 45.

22. Ibid., p. 46.
23. Ibid.
24. Isaiah Berlin, *Freedom and Its Betrayal; Six Enemies of Human Liberty*, ed. Henry Hardy (Princeton, NJ: Princeton University Press, 2003), p. 5.
25. Ibid., p. 9.
26. From "The fate of liberty" (December 6, 1952), *Enlightening*, p. 343.
27. "I even find myself in some sympathy with the wicked Hayek, although I think he is quite wrong in assuming that political liberty is indissolubly tied to economic private enterprise." Isaiah Berlin to Herbert Elliston, December 30, 1952, *Enlightening*, p. 350.
28. Ibid., pp. 350–51.
29. Ibid., p. 351.
30. Kennan's long-standing admiration for Berlin dates to their meeting in the Soviet Union in December 1945 when Berlin, who Kennan quickly identified as "undoubtedly the best informed and most intelligent foreigner in Moscow," was working for the British Information Services and Kennan was the State Department's deputy chief of mission. George F. Kennan, *The Kennan Dairies*, ed. Frank Costigliola (New York: W. W. Norton, 2014), p. 191.
31. Gaddis, *An American Life*, p. 417; Isaiah Berlin to Arthur Schlesinger, December March 17, 1954, *Enlightening*, p. 435. As it turned out Kennan never went into the Dulles State Department, though he did manage some foreign projects in the Eisenhower administration.
32. See Ian Shapiro, *Politics against Domination* (Cambridge, MA: Belknap Press of Harvard University Press, 2016), p. 139.
33. Gaddis, *An American Life*, p. 172.
34. Berlin to Morton White, March 4, 1953, *Enlightening*, p. 162; Berlin to Alice James, June 6, 1953, *Enlightening*, p. 378.
35. Berlin to Alice James, June 6, 1953, *Enlightening*, p. 37.
36. X [George Kennan], "The sources of Soviet conduct," *Foreign Affairs* (July 1947): 566–82. For discussion, see Shapiro, *Politics against Domination*, p. 138.
37. Aurelian Craiutu, *Faces of Moderation: The Art of Balance in an Age of Extremes* (Philadelphia: University of Pennsylvania Press, 2016), p. 87.
38. Cherniss, *A Mind and Its Time*, p. 67.
39. Isaiah Berlin to Herbert Elliston, December 30, 1952, *Enlightening*, p. 351.
40. Isaiah Berlin to Denis Paul, December 30, 1952, *Enlightening*, p. 352.
41. Ibid., p. 353.

42. Isaiah Berlin, "The intellectual life of American universities," in *Enlightening*, p. 760.

43. Isaiah Berlin, "Political ideas in the twentieth century," in *Four Essays on Liberty* (Oxford: Oxford University Press, 1990), p. 39.

44. Isaiah Berlin to Hamilton Fish Armstrong, May 25, 1950, *Enlightening*, p. 179.

45. Ibid.

46. Isaiah Berlin to John Hilton, received October 13, 1935, in *Isaiah Berlin: Letters 1928–1946*, ed. Henry Hardy (Cambridge: Cambridge University Press, 2004), p. 137.

47. It has often been noted that Berlin's interpretation of Rousseau seems to be one of his weakest treatments of a figure in the history of political thought. For some speculation on where Berlin may have gotten his peculiar reading of Rousseau see Christopher Brooke, "Isaiah Berlin and the origins of the 'totalitarian' Rousseau," *Isaiah Berlin and the Enlightenment*, ed. Laurence Brockliss and Ritchie Robertson (Oxford: Oxford University Press, 2016), pp. 89–96.

48. Isaiah Berlin to Jacob Talmon, December 30, 1952, *Enlightening*, p. 354.

49. Marilyn Berger, "Isaiah Berlin, philosopher and pluralist, is dead at 88," *New York Times*, November 7, 1997.

50. Henry Hardy, "Editor's Preface: A Tale of a Torso," in Isaiah Berlin, *Political Ideas in the Romantic Age*, ed. Henry Hardy (Princeton, NJ: Princeton University Press, 2006), p. ix.

51. From personal correspondence with Henry Hardy, "Editor's Preface: A Tale of a Torso," p. xix.

52. Isaiah Berlin to the president of Bryn Mawr College (Katherine McBride), June 13, 1950, *Enlightening*, pp. 182–83; Isaiah Berlin to Mrs. Samuel H. Paul (assistant to the president of Bryn Mawr College), November 20, 1951, *Enlightening*, pp. 257–58.

53. In a letter to Richard Crossman, dated February 11, 1963, he writes, "It seems to me that what happens is that advance, at least since the Renaissance, was always made by what must have seemed to be abstruse and technical in its own day—Descartes, Leibnitz, Kant, Hegel, and even Berkeley and Hume must have seemed so to the best-educated & clearest-headed 'practical politicians.' The revolutions occur by piecemeal advances by 'technicians' of this kind, and then are popularized by the Lockes and Voltaires, the Rousseaus, Carlyles, Laskis, etc., who may or may not be original themselves but certainly build on the comparatively abstruse writings of their predecessors or contemporaries." *Enlightening*, p. 145; Berlin, *Political Ideas in the Romantic Age*, p. 2.

54. Isaiah Berlin, *Isaiah Berlin: Building Letters, 1960–1975*, ed. Henry Hardy and Mark Pottle (London: Chatto & Windus, 2013), p. 512.
55. George Kennan to Isaiah Berlin, May 26, 1950, *Enlightening*, pp. 212–13.
56. Isaiah Berlin to George Kennan, February 13, 1951, *Enlightening*, pp. 213–14.
57. Ibid., p. 214.
58. Ibid., p. 216.
59. Ibid., p. 217.
60. Ibid.
61. Ibid., p. 219.
62. Commentators have noted that Berlin tended to slip from the plausible claim that positive libertarianism permits the endorsement of monistic conceptions of the good to the more debatable one that positive libertarianism requires such a commitment. On this subject, see Gina Gustavsson, "The psychological dangers of positive liberty: Reconstructing a neglected undercurrent in Isaiah Berlin's 'Two concepts of liberty,' " *Review of Politics* 76, no. 2 (2014): 276–91; George Crowder, "Why we need positive liberty," *Review of Politics* 77 (2015): 271–78; and Gina Gustavsson, "Reply to Crowder," *Review of Politics* 77 (2015): 279–84. We do not pursue the issue here, but we are inclined to think that Berlin might have conceded that positive liberty need not require a commitment to a monistic conception of the good, yet still have insisted that the variants of positive liberty that are likely to gain purchase in real politics would involve monistic conceptions. For the same reasons, discussed below, that he worried that negative freedom would prove insufficiently alluring to survive, particularly in times of great insecurity, he would also have been skeptical that pluralistic conceptions of positive freedom would endure.
63. In his introduction to *Political Ideas in the Romantic Age*, Joshua Cherniss remarks that this distinction, which he describes as "humanistic and non-humanistic conceptions of liberty," may have been the more crucial distinction for Berlin than the positive and negative conceptual divide which is more commonly and enduringly associated with his name. See Joshua L. Cherniss, "Isaiah Berlin's political ideas," in *Political Ideas in the Romantic Age*, p. xxxiv.
64. Berlin, *Political Ideas in the Romantic Age*, p. 114.
65. Ibid., p. 115.
66. Ibid., p. 116.
67. Ibid., p. 119.
68. For discussion of Berlin's attempt to blunt the tension that give rise to this paradox by distinguishing pluralism from relativism, see Steven Smith, "Isaiah Berlin on the Enlightenment and counter-Enlightenment," in *The Cambridge Companion*

to *Isaiah Berlin*, ed. Joshua Cherniss and Steven Smith (Cambridge: Cambridge University Press, 2021), pp. 132–48.

69. Berlin, *Political Ideas in the Romantic Age*, p. 148.

70. The rational universalism of Kant's thought and the ease with which it translated into the logic that propelled romantic nationalism does seem to have made Berlin wary about wholeheartedly endorsing him. For instance, responding to Noel Annan's drafted introductory essay to *Personal Impressions*, Berlin clarified his views on Kant as follows: "I am deeply pro-Kantian on certain issues, e.g. his obscure but epoch-making doctrine of freedom of the will, his concept of the moral autonomy of the individual, his doctrine of human beings as ends in themselves, and of moral values as constituted by human commitment to them. . . . So I am not to be taken as an opponent of Kantian morality *tout court*. . . . I think that if I am described as wanting to throw doubt on any moral or political system which is founded on, or includes, an unalterable hierarchy of values binding on all men at all times in all places, capable of providing an objective and unalterable solution to every moral and political (and aesthetic) problem, this would be true. But not much more than this." Isaiah Berlin to Noel Annan, October 2, 1978, *Affirming: Letters 1975–1997*, ed. Henry Hardy and Mark Pottle (London: Chatto & Windus, 2015), p. 89.

71. Isaiah Berlin to George Kennan, February 13, 1951, *Enlightening*, p. 214.

72. Isaiah Berlin to Stephen Spender, November 18, 1958, *Enlightening*, p. 656.

73. Isaiah Berlin to Karl Popper, March 16, 1959, *Enlightening*, p. 682.

74. Isaiah Berlin, "Freedom," in *Isaiah Berlin: Letters 1928–1946*, p. 637.

75. Karl Popper to Isaiah Berlin, February 17, 1959, *Enlightening*, p. 680.

76. Isaiah Berlin to Michael Walzer, October 17, 1995, *Affirming*, pp. 517–18.

77. Ibid., p. 518.

78. Ibid., p. 518n1; Aleksandr Herzen, *From the Other Shore*, trans. Moura Budberg (London: Weidenfeld and Nicolson, 1956), p. 133.

79. Isaiah Berlin to Dorothea Head, June 11, 1969, *Building*, p. 392.

80. Ian Shapiro, *Containment: Rebuilding a Strategy against Global Terror* (Princeton, NJ: Princeton University Press, 2007), pp. 32–36, 42–46.

81. Friedrich A. Hayek, *The Constitution of Liberty* (Chicago: University of Chicago Press, 1960), p. 160.

82. Gustavsson, "Psychological dangers of positive liberty," pp. 276–91. For discussion see note 62 above.

83. Isaiah Berlin and Steven Lukes, "Isaiah Berlin: In conversation with Steven Lukes," *Salmagundi*, no. 120 (1998): 52–134, at pp. 98 and 81.

Chapter Eight. Transforming Power Relations (with James Read)

1. Thomas Hobbes, *Leviathan, or the Matter, Forme & Power of a Commonwealth Ecclesiastical and Civill*, ed. Ian Shapiro (New Haven: Yale University Press, 2010 [1651]).

2. Courtney Jung, Ellen Lust-Okar, and Ian Shapiro, "Problems and prospects for democratic settlements: South Africa as a model for the Middle East and Northern Ireland?" in Ian Shapiro, *The Real World of Democratic Theory* (Princeton, NJ: Princeton University Press, 2011).

3. Robert Axelrod, *The Evolution of Cooperation* (New York: Basic Books, 1984), p. 13.

4. Ibid., p. 112.

5. Ibid., p. 138.

6. Axelrod explored the contrite and generous versions of TFT on the theory that we all know that people sometimes make mistakes and would not want to fall prey to an inadvertent error.

7. Robert Axelrod, *The Complexity of Cooperation: Agent-Based Models of Competition and Collaboration* (Princeton, NJ: Princeton University Press, 1997), pp. 33–39.

8. Axelrod, *Evolution of Cooperation*, pp. 88–105.

9. Ibid., pp. 73–87.

10. James D. Morrow, *Game Theory for Political Scientists* (Princeton, NJ: Princeton University Press, 1994), pp. 19–20, 34.

11. Axelrod, *Evolution of Cooperation*, pp. 85, 110–12.

12. One of this essay's coauthors (Read) heard this characterization of the 1990s—"everyone lost"—repeated by many contacts during study trips in 2003 and 2006 to the former Yugoslavia.

13. See Norman Frohlich, Joe A. Oppenheimer, and Oran R. Young, *Political Leadership and Collective Goods* (Princeton, NJ: Princeton University Press, 1971).

14. Nelson Mandela, *Long Walk to Freedom: The Autobiography of Nelson Mandela* (Boston: Little Brown, 1994), p. 457.

15. Jung, Lust-Okar, and Shapiro, "Problems and prospects," p. 94.

16. During the 1980s some forces within the South African government sought to paralyze the ANC by dividing its leadership, while others sought a political settlement. The catalyst for the "talks about talks" was a 1985 letter from Nelson Mandela to South African Justice Minister Kobie Coetsee. See Tom Lodge, *Mandela: A Critical Life* (Oxford: Oxford University Press, 2006), pp. 148–60.

17. Mandela, *Long Walk to Freedom*, pp. 457–59, 466–67; Lodge, *Mandela: A Critical Life*, pp. 158–60.

18. Lodge, *Mandela: A Critical Life*, pp. 165–66.

19. F. W. de Klerk, *The Last Trek—A New Beginning: The Autobiography* (London: Macmillan, 1998), p. 89.

20. Ibid., p. 158.

21. Jung, Lust-Okar, and Shapiro, "Problems and prospects," pp. 194–95; de Klerk, *Last Trek*, pp. 229–32.

22. For de Klerk's version of this dispute, see *Last Trek*, pp. 199–204, 258–67, 384–85; for Mandela's, see *Long Walk to Freedom*, pp. 509–15. Subsequent investigations established that some members of the South African security forces were involved in illegal and violent covert activities, though who authorized them is unknown.

23. South Africa's 1983 constitution had created a so-called "tricameral parliament" in which Coloured (mixed race) and Indian voters were permitted to vote for members of two separate and largely powerless chambers. Black South Africans, the vast majority of the population, remained wholly disenfranchised.

24. De Klerk, *Last Trek*, pp. 229–32.

25. Ibid., p. 232.

26. De Klerk, interview with Ian Shapiro, Cape Town, South Africa, December 9, 2003.

27. In an ironic illustration of how negotiations change the preferences of leaders, by 1996 de Klerk would abandon even the voluntary power-sharing model and lead the National Party out of the Government of National Unity proclaiming: "We believe that the development of a strong and vigilant opposition is essential for the maintenance and promotion of a genuine multi-party democracy." F. W. de Klerk, "Statement by Mr. F. W. de Klerk, leader of the National Party," National Party Media Release, May 9, 1996, South African Government Information, www.info.gov.za.speeches/1996/960513_0x824.htm (accessed March 3, 2023). Whether he had intended ever to get to that point remains unclear. In a December 2003 interview he cited unspecified others in the National Party negotiating team for abandoning entrenched power-sharing in the negotiations over the final constitution. Interview with Ian Shapiro, December 9, 2003.

28. De Klerk, *Last Trek*, pp. 103–6.

29. Ibid., p. 169.

30. Mandela, *Long Walk to Freedom*, p. 533.

31. Ibid., p. 457; de Klerk, *Last Trek*, p. 121.

32. De Klerk, *Last Trek*, p. 169; see also Mandela, *Long Walk to Freedom*, p. 503.

33. Timothy D. Sisk, *Bargaining with Bullets: International Mediation in Civil Wars* (London: Routledge, 2008), pp. 92–98.

34. Nicholas Sambanis, "What is civil war? Conceptual and empirical complexities of an operational definition," *Journal of Conflict Resolution* 48, no. 6 (2004): 814–58.

35. William H. Riker, *The Art of Political Manipulation* (New Haven: Yale University Press, 1986), p. 198; see also Torun Dewan and David P. Myatt, "On the rhetorical strategies of leaders: Speaking clearly, standing back, and stepping down," *Journal of Theoretical Politics* 24 (2012): 432.

36. James MacGregor Burns, *Leadership* (New York: Harper & Row, 1978); *Transforming Leadership: A New Pursuit of Happiness* (New York: Atlantic Monthly Press, 2003). See also Jay Conger, "Transforming and Visionary Leadership," in *Encyclopedia of Leadership*, ed. George R. Goethals, Georgia J. Sorenson, and James MacGregor Burns, vol. 4 (London: Sage Publications, 2004).

37. Thomas C. Schelling, *The Strategy of Conflict*, 2nd ed. (Cambridge, MA: Harvard University Press, 1981).

38. Ibid., p. 5.

39. Ibid., pp. 35, 70.

40. Mandela, *Long Walk to Freedom*, p. 533.

41. Schelling, *Strategy of Conflict*, p. 96.

42. Mandela, *Long Walk to Freedom*, pp. 506, 526.

43. De Klerk, *Last Trek*, pp. 316–19.

44. John L. Austin, *How to Do Things with Words*, 2nd ed. (Cambridge, MA: Harvard University Press, 1975).

45. Schelling, *Strategy of Conflict*, pp. 12, 43–44.

46. The military did not signal decisive support for the transition until March 1994, when they accepted an order from the Transitional Executive Council (by then the caretaker government) to put down a white separatist group that was supporting a local black leader in the Tswana homeland of Bophuthatswana who opposed the coming elections. Courtney Jung and Ian Shapiro, "South Africa's negotiated transition," in Ian Shapiro, *Democracy's Place* (Ithaca, NY: Cornell University Press, 1996), pp. 201–4.

47. Mandela, *Long Walk to Freedom*, p. 322; Kadar Asmal, ed., *Nelson Mandela: In His Own Words* (New York, NY: Little Brown & Company, 2003) pp. 59–62.

48. Josep M. Colomer, *Strategic Transitions: Game Theory and Democratization* (Baltimore: Johns Hopkins University Press, 2000).

49. Ibid., p. 49.

50. Ibid., pp. 51, 57–61.

51. Colomer also examines "mugging games," which resemble prisoner's dilemmas in some respects but, unlike the PD, give one actor a strategic advantage over the other. Ibid., pp. 53–57. For simplicity, our commentary focuses on Colomer's treatment of the PD.

52. Ibid., p. 51.

53. Ibid., p. 2.

54. Ibid., p. 52.

55. Ibid., pp. 57–58.

56. Daniel Kahneman, *Thinking, Fast and Slow* (New York: Farrar, Straus & Giroux, 2011), pp. 19–108, 259–376.

57. Colomer, *Strategic Transitions*, p. 41.

58. Ibid., p. 2.

59. In *Game Theory for Political Scientists*, Morrow nowhere mentions power. For the implicit presence of power in game theory, see Keith Dowding, introduction to Keith Dowding, ed., *Encyclopedia of Power* (London: Sage Publications, 2011), p. xxiv.

60. Steven Lukes, *Power: A Radical View*, 2nd ed. (New York: Palgrave Macmillan, 2005), pp. 14–38, 60–107.

61. Hobbes, *Leviathan*, p. 93.

62. Thomas Hobbes, *Elements of Law*, ed. Ferdinand Tönnies (Cambridge: Cambridge University Press, 1928 [1650]).

63. Robert Gilpin, *War and Change in World Politics* (Cambridge: Cambridge University Press, 1981), p. 94; John Mearsheimer, *The Tragedy of Great Power Politics* (New York: W. W. Norton, 2001), p. 2.

64. Quoted in Lukes, *Power: A Radical View*, p. 18.

65. See ibid. for that debate, including Lukes's recent revision of his original view, pp. 63–65.

66. For discussion and critique, see ibid., pp. 30–35; James H. Read, "Is power zero-sum or variable-sum? Old arguments and new beginnings," *Journal of Political Power* 5 (2012): 5–31.

67. For example, Anthony Giddens, *The Constitution of Society* (Berkeley: University of California Press, 1984); David A. Baldwin, "Power in international relations," in *Handbook of International Relations*, ed. Walter Carlsnaes, Thomas Risse, and Beth Simmons (Thousand Oaks, CA: Sage Publications, 2002), pp. 177–91; Dennis H. Wrong, *Power: Its Forms, Bases, and Uses* (New Brunswick, NJ: Transaction Publishers, 1995); for a more fully developed variable-sum argument incorporating both cooperation and conflict see Mark Haugaard, "Rethinking the four

dimensions of power: Domination and empowerment," *Journal of Political Power* 5 (2012): 33–54.

68. For example, John Gaventa, *Power and Powerlessness: Quiescence and Rebellion in an Appalachian Valley* (Champaign: University of Illinois Press, 1980).

69. For present purposes, we ignore the interactions between both sides and the then two million or so "Cape Coloureds" as well as the ethnic Zulu Inkatha Freedom Party. For discussion, see Jung and Shapiro, "South Africa's negotiated transition," pp. 185–99, 201–13; and Jung, Lust-Okar, and Shapiro, "Problems and prospects for democratic settlements," pp. 105, 122, 146–53.

70. In the 2010 Northern Ireland Life and Times survey only 13 percent of respondents found it "almost impossible to accept" if Northern Ireland were ultimately joined to the Republic of Ireland; 85 percent of respondents would either "happily accept" or "could live with" this result. Alternatively, if Northern Ireland were never to join the Republic of Ireland, only 2 percent found this "almost impossible to accept" while 93 percent would either "happily accept" or "could live with" this result. "Improving cross-community relations" and reducing unemployment were ranked as higher priorities than resolution of the national affiliation question. Northern Ireland Life and Times, www.ark.ac.uk/nilt/2010/Political_Attitudes/index.html (accessed March 3, 2023).

71. In the nine years preceding the 1998 Agreement (1989–1997) there were 509 political conflict–related deaths. For the period 1998 to 2006 there were 134, and numbers drop steeply after 1998. See John McGarry and Brendan O'Leary, "Power shared after the deaths of thousands," in *Consociational Theory: McGarry and O'Leary and the Northern Ireland Conflict*, ed. Rupert Taylor (London: Routledge, 2009), pp. 51–52.

72. George Mitchell, *Making Peace: The Inside Story of the Good Friday Agreement* (New York: Alfred A. Knopf, 1999), pp. 22–38.

73. Catherine McGlynn, Jonathan Tonge, and Jim McAuley, "The party politics of post-devolution identity in Northern Ireland," *British Journal of Politics and International Relations* 16, no. 2 (2014): 273–90; McGarry and O'Leary, "Power shared after the deaths of thousands," pp. 65–69.

74. McGarry and O'Leary, "Power shared after the deaths of thousands," p. 56.

75. Jonathan Powell, *Great Hatred, Little Room: Making Peace in Northern Ireland* (London: Bodley Head, 2008), pp. 54–55.

76. "Nationalist" refers broadly to all who seek to unite the North to the rest of Ireland, but is also employed to distinguish parties like John Hume's SDLP that work within the system and endorse only peaceful methods from "Republicans" like the

Irish Republican Army and its political affiliate Sinn Féin, who consider all existing Irish governments illegitimate and have in the past condoned the use of violence.

77. P. J. McLaughlin, *John Hume and the Revision of Irish Nationalism* (Manchester: Manchester University Press, 2010).

78. Powell, *Great Hatred, Little Room*, pp. 100, 147–48.

79. McLaughlin, *John Hume*, pp. 153–67. Hume also sought Sinn Féin's inclusion to strengthen the Nationalist bloc in any power-sharing settlement.

80. McGlynn, Tonge, and McAuley, "Party politics of post-devolution identity," pp. 10–14.

81. Powell, *Great Hatred, Little Room*, pp. 203–5.

82. Mitchell, *Making Peace*, pp. 108–17.

83. Landon E. Hancock, "There is no alternative: prospect theory, the yes campaign and selling the Good Friday agreement," *Irish Political Studies* 26 (2011): 95–116; esp. pp. 103, 111.

84. Bernadette C. Hayes and Ian McAllister, "Who voted for peace? Public support for the 1998 Northern Ireland Agreement," *Irish Political Studies* 16 (2001): 73–94.

85. The IRA defended its delay on decommissioning as a response to the UUP's stalling on reforming Northern Ireland's police force, a priority for Republicans. McGarry and O'Leary, "Power shared after the deaths of thousands," pp. 35, 45–47.

86. Jung, Lust-Okar, and Shapiro, "Problems and prospects for democratic settlements," pp. 107–14.

87. The Oslo Peace Index of Israeli public opinion rose from 46.9 in October 1995 to 58 on November 8, immediately following Rabin's assassination. "Peace Index, 1995," www.jewishvirtuallibrary.org/the-israel-peace-index#1995 (accessed April 3, 2023). In October 1995, 72.5 percent of Palestinians polled supported the peace process. "JMCC Public Opinion Poll #10," www.jmcc.org/documentsandmaps.aspx?id=501 (accessed April 3, 2023).

88. Barak went out on a limb under strong pressure from President Clinton, offering new concessions on Jerusalem that infuriated many in the Knesset and subsequently cost Barak his premiership. See Jung, Lust-Okar, and Shapiro, "Problems and prospects for democratic settlements," pp. 111–14.

Acknowledgments

The chapters in this book have all profited from discussion at workshops and conferences over the last decade. Colleagues, research assistants, students, and other friends have read many of them to good effect, as have editors and journal referees. Alicia Steinmetz deserves special mention for going well beyond the call of duty as a research assistant in helping me reconceive them as a book and then rework them into a whole that I hope and believe exceeds the sum of its parts. I am also grateful to her, to David Froomkin, and to James Read for their willingness to include our joint work here. Two anonymous readers for Yale University Press made constructive suggestions, as did my editor Bill Frucht. David Mayhew read the manuscript with his characteristic insight and thoroughness and sent pages of useful comments and suggestions. I am fortunate to be the beneficiary of all this generous help and am grateful for it. The usual caveats apply.

An earlier version of chapter 1 appeared in the *Journal of Politics* 78, no. 2 (April 2016): 467–80, and is drawn on with permission from the University of Chicago Press. An earlier version of chapter 2 appeared in the *Journal of Economic Literature* 49 (December 2011): 1251–63, and is drawn on with permission of the *Journal of Economic Literature*, © American Economic Association. An earlier version of chapter 3 was published in *University of Toronto Law Journal* 62, no. 3 (Summer 2012): 293–335, and is drawn on with permission from University of

ACKNOWLEDGMENTS

Toronto Press (https://utpjournals.press), https://doi.org/10.3138/utlj.62.3.293 © University of Toronto Press. An earlier version of chapter 4 (coauthored with David Froomkin) was published online by *Political Studies* on August 31, 2021, and is drawn on with permission from Sage Publications. An earlier version of chapter 5 appeared in *Daedalus* 146, no. 3 (Summer 2017): 77–84, and is drawn on with permission from the MIT Press. An earlier version of chapter 7 (coauthored with Alicia Steinmetz) appeared in *The Cambridge Companion to Isaiah Berlin,* ed. Joshua Cherniss and Steven Smith (Cambridge: Cambridge University Press, 2018), pp. 192–211, and is drawn on with permission from Cambridge University Press. An earlier version of chapter 8 (coauthored with James Read) appeared in the *American Political Science Review* 108, no. 1 (February 2014): 40–53, and is drawn on with permission from Cambridge University Press.

Index

Italicized page numbers indicate figures.

abolition of slave trade, 70–72, 285n62
abortion issue, 32–33, 45, 157–58, 276n16, 280n54
absolutism, 99
ACA (Affordable Care Act of 2010), 135–36, 190
accountability: argument enabling, 152; coalition governments and, 164–65; in cooperation to resolved communal conflict, 251–52; of legislators and politicians, 5, 69, 125–27, 141, 142, 146; power's monopoly character and, 176–77; of presidents, 135, 137–43, 150; referendums and, 164; two-party vs. multiparty systems, 183–84
Ackerman, Bruce, 279n46
Adams, Gerry, 265–66
Adams, John Quincy, 148, 170, 306n2
administrative agencies: congressional delegation to, 137, 139; congressional oversight of, 133, 136–37, 143, 149; consultation, reliance on, 143; era of administrative state, 132; interagency coordination legislation, benefits of, 143; pre-publication review of agency rules, 137–38; presidential control over, 137

Aesop, 40–41
Affordable Care Act (ACA, 2010), 135–36, 190
African National Congress (ANC), 21, 244–51; Freedom Charter (1955), 256
alternative facts and fake news, 3, 17–18
American Enterprise Institute, 9
Americans for Tax Reform, 160
Amin, Idi, 117
ANC. *See* African National Congress
antitax and antiregulatory movements, 17, 166, 232
anti-welfare agenda of New Right, 42
apartheid. *See* South Africa
Arab Spring, 270
Arafat, Yasser, 267–68
arbitration, 183
Archimedes, 5, 54
Arendt, Hannah, 218, 261
Aristotle, 6, 48, 50
arms races and reduction treaties, 21, 292n75
Armstrong, Hamilton Fish, Berlin letter to, 212
Arrow, Kenneth, 9, 125–26, 176, 295n4
Ashoka (Indian emperor), 55
Attlee, Clement, 184

INDEX

Austria, authoritarian nationalism in, 123
authoritarianism, 123–50; executive concentration and, 139–46; first wave, 125–30; judicial authority and, 45; misdiagnosis and prescription, 146–50; new authoritarianism, 130–39
authoritarian populism, 8, 17, 19, 123, 197
authorization for use of military force (AUMF), 148
autocracies, 130
autonomy, 82–83, 159, 201, 318n70
Axelrod, Robert, 236, 237–40, 253, 257, 270, 319n6
Ayyash, Yahva, 268

Bacon, Francis, 4
Bagehot, Walter, 156
ballot initiatives and referendums, 158–60; Brexit vote, 3, 159–64, 304nn28–29
banking regulation, 112, 142, 294n98
Barak, Ehud, 268, 324n88
bargaining, 110–11, 154–55, 165
Barry, Brian: on discrimination and tolerance, 32, 34–35, 47, 276n14, 277n18; equitableness test of, 33–34, 37–38, 47; on first- and second-order impartiality, 29–40; on good life, 31–34, 36; on harm principle, 35–36, 39; on inequality's growth in United States, 46–48; on judicial vs. legislative authority, 33–34, 37, 277n31; on justice as impartiality, 6, 29–30, 40–41, 65; *Justice as Impartiality*, 29–30; on majority rule, 30, 47; on media's role in democratic politics, 48; *Political Argument*, 47; on progressivity, 40; reaction to assault on British welfare state, 44; reasonableness test and, 31–33; Scanlonian test and, 31, 32, 35, 39, 276n14; Sen and, 51; on taxation and distributive regime, 39–40, 278n35; on unanimity rule and supermajority, 47; *Why Social Justice Matters*, 39–40, 41
basic interests and rights, 19, 29, 46, 74, 90–91, 97, 110, 116, 118. *See also* vulnerability to domination
Bawn, Kathleen, 182
Benn, Tony, 163, 305n35
Berlin, Isaiah, 16–17, 197–233; Armstrong letter, 212; on communism, 200–210, 217–18, 225–26; "Democracy, Communism, and the Individual" (speech), 202; on ease of mobilization in times of insecurity, 19; Elliston letter, 207–10; Flexner Lectures, 207, 215; *Four Essays on Liberty*, 197, 227; *Freedom and Its Betrayal* (BBC Lecture series), 206, 214, 222; on Hegel, 206–7, 217–19; Hilton letter, 213; on Hobbes, 215, 230; on insecurity of freedom, 219–28, 230–31, 233; James letter, 209; on Kant, 201, 217, 223–24, 318n70; Kennan and, 200, 201, 204, 208, 212, 216, 219, 223, 315n30; legacy of, 231–33; on Locke, 215; on Marx and Marxism, 202–3, 213, 217–19, 224, 229; McBride letter, 215; on McCarthyism, 209, 229; on morality, 218–19, 222–23; on negative freedom, 16–17, 197–98, 200–201, 204, 211, 226; Paul letter, 210–11; on pluralist democracy, 210, 225, 229; on political faith, 207–8;

Political Ideas in the Romantic Age, 207, 214–15, 222; "Political ideas in the twentieth century" (article), 211–12, 216; on positive libertarians, 100; on psychology of freedom, 213–19, 230; *The Roots of Romanticism*, 214, 215; on Rousseau, 203–4, 207, 213–16, 220–23, 225–26, 230, 316n47; Talmon letter, 213; "Two concepts of liberty" lecture, 197–98, 226, 232, 314n12
Bevin, Ernest, 205
bicameral system, 15, 113, 153
Bizzarro, Fernando, 188
Blackmun, Harry, 45
Blair, Tony, 40
Bob Jones University v. United States (1983), 34–35, 47, 278n31
Boehner, John, 189
Bogdanor, Vernon, 159, 163
Bohlen, Charles, 212
Botha, P. W., 244, 247
Bowers v. Hardwick (1986), 45, 279n52
Brady, Gordon, 130
Brazil, 70, 123
Brexit, 3, 159–64, 304nn28–29
Breyer, Stephen, 68
Britain: abolition of slave trade in, 70–71, 285n57, 285n62; Brexit vote, 3, 159–64, 304nn28–29; Collins reforms, 187; Commons, 153, 156; Dissenter MPs, 285n57, 285n62; Engagement Controversy, 175; House of Lords, 152, 156, 303n13; impeachment of Warren Hastings, 63; judicial review in, 45; Labour Party, 158–59, 161–63, 184, 187–88, 305n37, 311n50; Liberal Democrats, 163; Liberals, 163, 182; National Health Service, 184; New Labour, 40, 42; Northern Ireland, repression in, 265; Northern Ireland's peace agreement, role in, 264; Parliament Act (1911), 152; Parliamentary Labour Party (PLP), 187; Prime Minister's Questions, 153; railways in, 184; Tories, 159, 161–63, 285n62; trade union development in, 113–14; two-party system in, 154, 180
Brown v. Board of Education (1954), 45
Buchanan, James, 47, 125, 176; *Calculus of Consent* (with Tullock), 166
Buckley v. Valeo (1971), 168
Buddha and Buddhism, 54–55
Budget Sequestration Act (2011), 164–66
bureaucracy, 127, 130–31, 137–38, 142–43, 146. *See also* administrative agencies
Burger, Warren, 10, 44
Burger Court, 11
Burke, Edmund, 63, 178
Burns, James MacGregor, 252
Bush, George H. W., 108, 160, 293n83
Bush, George W., 108, 129, 136, 284n52, 298n36
Buthelezi, Mangosuthu, 247

Calabresi, Steven, 131
California, Proposition 13, 109, 159–60
campaign contributions, 46, 147, 168
Canada, 107
capabilities-based theory of justice, 61–62
capitalism, 39, 199, 284n50; communism vs., 209; socialism vs., 58, 83
Capitol riot (January 6, 2021), 18
Carolene Products Co., United States v. (1938), 39

INDEX

Carpenter, Daniel, 135
categorical imperative, 5, 57, 76, 82
Catholicism, 34, 285n62
Cato Institute, 9
Charles II (English king), 175
checks and balances, 124, 132–33, 136–37, 145–47, 154. *See also* separation of powers
Cherniss, Joshua, 210, 317n63
Churchill, Winston, 43, 193, 278n43, 313n67
Citizens United v. Federal Election Commission (2010), 168
civic humanism, 198–99, 230
civil rights, 10
Civil Rights Cases (1883), 44, 279n48
Civil War Amendments, 44
Clay, Henry, 306n2
clientelism, 12, 30, 125, 140, 165, 167, 179, 185, 191
climate change denial, 17
Clinton, Bill, 129, 268, 324n88
coalition governments: accountability and, 164–65; parliamentary, 69–72; proportional representation and, 154, 155; two-party structure in analogy to, 180, 182. *See also* multiparty systems
Cohen, G. A., 78, 80–81
Cohen, Joshua, 111
Cold War: ANC receiving Soviet support, 244–45; Berlin and, 16–17, 197–213; end of, 9, 20, 21, 197; geopolitical stability of, 42; intellectual implications of, 200, 202–13; Kennan and, 229; psychology of freedom in, 201, 213–19. *See also* Berlin, Isaiah; communism
collective action, 126, 128–29, 131, 173, 176, 240

Collins, Lord, 187
Collins, Michael, 265
collusion in restraint of democracy, 151–68; accountability and, 152, 164–65; ballot initiatives and referenduma, 158–64; deliberation and, 12, 151–58; median voter and, 165–66; negotiations and, 161–62; proportional representation and, 153–54, 164; single member plurality (SMP) electoral system and, 153, 164; supermajorities and, 153, 155
Colomer, Josep M., 236, 253, 256–58, 270, 322n51; *Strategic Transitions: Game Theory and Democratization*, 256–57
communism: Berlin on, 200–210, 217–18, 225–26; negative freedom as repudiation of, 200–201; one right way to live and, 203; Stalinist form of, 200. *See also* Cold War
competition: accountability enhanced by, 165; deliberative vs. competitive institutions, 152–57; essential in democratic politics, 12, 167; partisan parties and, 173, 179–84; Schumpeter's model of, 173
compromise, 29, 131, 153–54, 172–73, 183, 266. *See also* strategically hopeful action
Condorcet, Nicolas de, 222
congressional power: accountability and, 4–5, 141, 146; arguments to strengthen, 146–48; Barry on, 33–34; collective-action problems of, 126, 128–29, 131; complexity of legislation produced by, 134; delegation to administrative agencies, 137, 139; executive power vs., 10–11, 124–31, 141; first wave authoritarianism on,

INDEX

125–30; impeachment, 149; information gathering and, 145–46; judicial power as curb on, 10, 125; lack of coordination hampering, 132, 134; new authoritarianism on, 130–31; oversight of federal agencies, 133, 136–37, 143, 149; reasons for dysfunction of, 146–50; regulatory capture of, 127, 135, 136, 139, 168; Republicans criticizing for out-of-control spending, 128; responsiveness to electorate opinion, 144; school desegregation ended by, 45; slowness of legislative process, 145; as weakest branch of government, 16. *See also* Senate, U.S.
congressional primaries, 190
Constitution, U.S.: Article I, 70; Presentment Clause, 129. See also *Federalist Papers;* founders
constitutional courts, 38, 46, 116, 278n33
constitutional law and Sen's impartiality, 68
Consumer Financial Protection Bureau, 184–85
Corbyn, Jeremy, 158, 163, 187–88
corruption: in authoritarian presidencies, 124–25; injustice as result of, 29; in South Africa, 22–23
Council of Europe's Social Charter, 163
Cover, Robert, 29
Covid-19 pandemic, hostility to public health measures during, 17, 271n5
Cox, Gary, 190
Craiutu, Aurelian, 210
cross-cutting cleavages, theory of, 15–16, 140

Cuba, 70, 107
Curry, James, 190

Dahl, Robert: on constitutional courts' role in democracies, 46; on intensity of popular views, 306n40; on majority rule, 126; on protection of rights under democratic politics, 43; on theory of cross-cutting cleavages, 15–16
death penalty, 66
deconstructionists, 2
de Klerk, F. W.: compromises with ANC, 249–51, 320n27; democratic transition, role in, 22, 236, 270; as political manipulator, 252–53; relations with Mandela, 248, 253–54, 260–62; snap referendum called by, 248–49; strategically hopeful leadership of, 243–44, 247–51; support of constituency for, 235–36; Trimble compared to, 266; variable-sum approach of, 261–62
delegation of powers: legislative to executive, 137, 139; from voters, 13, 171
deliberation, 12, 151–58; argument distinguished from, 151–52; bargaining resulting from, 110–11, 154–55; benefits of, 151; coalition government and, 154; competitive vs. deliberative institutions, 152–57; democracy and, 8, 157–66; easy to abuse rules designed to promote, 152; goal of agreement, 153; good faith required by, 155; institutionalizing as elusive endeavor, 157; participatory democratic theorists and, 12; proportional representation and, 153–54; referendums and, 157–64

INDEX

democracy and democracies: Churchill on, 43, 278n43; communism vs., 203; countering domination, 4, 23–24, 32, 43, 104, 118, 120, 171–72; courts undermining, 47; deliberation and, 8, 157–66; dissatisfaction with, 8–10, 23, 123, 272n12; economic development as key to survival of, 116; expansion after Cold War's end, 20–21; fairness required in, 235; famine and, 68–69; as "government by discussion," 68; impartiality and, 40–48; judicial review and, 45; justice linked to, 4–5, 8–9, 73, 104; Lincoln on, 174; Nietzsche on, 289n35; public choice theorists' criticism of, 123–27, 150; reasons for embracing, 4–5, 8–9; rich and powerful subverting, 49; Sen's defense of, 67–71; South Africa becoming, 21–22, 246, 251, 256, 262. *See also* collusion in restraint of; nondomination

Democratic Party, 171, 190

deregulation, 137. *See also* antitax and antiregulatory movements

Descartes, René, 2

determinism, 91

Devlin, Lord, 45

Dewey, John, 192

discrimination and tolerance: Barry on, 32, 34–35, 47, 276n14; Marcuse's repressive tolerance, 199

distributive justice, 39, 78, 82, 84–85

Dodd-Frank Act (2010), 143, 185

Dodds, Graham, 134

domination: Barry's impartiality and, 6; basic interests involved in, 97; as capacity to interfere with someone, 104–5, 107; conceptions of, 8, 18, 28, 75, 87–92; democratizing as best path to mitigate, 4, 23–24, 32, 43, 104, 118, 120, 171–72; hostility to, 27; as illicit use of power, 8, 28–29, 89–90, 96–97, 101, 118; justice and, 73, 75–77; knowledge used for, 4; moral arbitrariness and, 77–82; negatives of, 3; Pettit on, 91–92, 104–5, 107, 292nn69–70; rooted in human collective arrangements, 91; as unfreedom, 89–92; vulnerability to, 48, 74, 115, 118, 120, 286n3. *See also* nondomination; power

Don Quixote, 219

Dowding, Keith, 130

Downs, Anthony, 152

downward mobility, 19

Dred Scott v. Sandford (1857), 44, 279n48

Druckman, James N., 144

Dudley, Alan, 205–6

Dulles, John Foster, 209, 315n31

Dunn, John, 8–9

Duverger's law, 308n26

Dworkin, Ronald, 10, 39, 44, 78–81, 279n46, 287n17, 293n79

efficacy of ideological arguments, 9, 24

efficiency in governance, 12, 124, 130–32, 135, 142–43, 150

egalitarianism, 50, 61, 74–86, 92, 98, 105–6, 116–18

Eisenhower, Dwight, 44

Electoral College, 11, 170

Elliot, W. Y., 212

Elliston, Herbert, Berlin's letter to, 207–10

INDEX

Ely, John Hart, 10, 39, 44, 279n46
empathy: gaps in, 47, 79; leadership employing, 237
employment insecurity, 19, 20, 22, 180, 233
enabling conditions of freedom, 18
Enlightenment and Enlightenment Project: Foucault and, 95; Habermas and, 94; Marx and, 213; modern critics of, 1–3; post-World War II era and, 41; promise in politics, 13, 23; reworking of, 232; values in post–Cold War triumphalism, 18
equality: moral, 7, 117; as neutrality, 85–87; nondomination and, 75–76, 88, 116–20; Rawls's theory of justice and, 7; Sen on, 7
executive power: accountability and, 135, 137–43, 150; appointment and removal powers, 149; concentration of, 124, 131, 139–46; credibility of president and, 133; efficiency and speed of, 132, 135; growth of, 16, 124, 132–33, 139; information-gathering problems of, 143; limits to, 142–43; personalized politics and, 139–40; plebiscitary presidency and, 133; presidential decision making, 145–46; presidential responsiveness, limits of, 143–45; principal-agent dynamics and, 142–43; public opinion and, 143–44, 301n92; as remedy to congressional power, 10–11, 124–31, 141; unitary structure of, 11, 131, 138, 140, 142–43, 145, 302n97; weak political parties and, 141, 147, 169. *See also* clientelism
experts: impugning of, 3, 271n5; knowledge of, 2–4

fairness: in democracy, 235; justice as (Rawls), 77, 85–87
fairness doctrine in media, 48
famine, 68–69
Faulkner, Brian, 264
Federal Communications Commission (FCC), 48
The Federalist Papers: Federalist 10 (Madison), 49, 282n12; Federalist 47 (Madison), 133; Federalist 51 (Madison), 14–15
Ferejohn, John, 138, 299n62
Fichte, Johann, 17, 207
financial crisis (2008), 112, 298n36
Fishkin, James, 288n34
Foord, Archibald, 141
Foot, Michael, 162–63, 305n35
Foucault, Michael, 8, 95–97, 119
founders: intentions of, 15, 110, 115, 131; political parties and, 178, 193; Senate, intentions for, 154; structuring of government, flaws in, 16. *See also The Federalist Papers;* Madison, James
France, Anatole, 18, 103, 292n68
Fraser, Nancy, 84
freedom: as antithesis of slavery, 100; choice vs., 224; debate over kinds of, 18, 74, 99, 103, 199, 214, 219–20, 226–27, 232; enabling conditions of, 18; individual liberty as, 99; insecurity of, 219–28; neo-Roman conception of (Skinner), 98–104; nondomination and, 88, 116; psychology of, 201, 213–19; restraints on, 18, 101–2; Sen as advocate for, 50. *See also* liberty; negative freedom; positive freedom
freedom of religion, 32–34, 86, 277n21
Free Enterprise Fund (2010), 302n97

INDEX

free-riding, 132
Froomkin, David, 8–9, 123
fugitive slave laws, 29
Fukuyama, Francis: on checks and balances, 136–37; on congressional power, 10, 130–31; on executive concentration of power, 124, 131, 145; on liberal-democratic end to history, 9, 272n11
Fuller Court, 44

Gaddafi, Muammar, 108
gag rules, 109, 113
game theory, 240. *See also* prisoner's dilemma
gay marriage, 109
Geithner, Tim, 142
general will, Rousseau on, 9, 12, 100, 125–26, 221
Germany, multiparty system in, 180, 182
gerrymandering, 86, 147, 167
Gibbard, Allan, 125
Gingrich, Newt, 160
globalization, 19
Godwin, William, 30, 276n6
Good Friday (or Belfast) Agreement (1998), 264–65
good life, conception of, 31–34, 36, 49, 76, 85, 100, 220, 288n34, 293n79
Gorbachev, Mikhail, 258
Gove, Michael, 3
Government Accountability Office, 138
Great Depression, 20
Great Society, 10, 20, 39, 184
Greece, multiparties in, 182
gun lobby, 17
Gustavsson, Gina, 230

Habermas, Jürgen: on legitimacy, 289n43; on nondomination, 8, 93–95, 119; Pettit and, 111; on triumph of reasoned persuasion, 156
Hacker-Cordón, Casiano, 116
Hamas, 268
Hardy, Henry, 213–14, 227
harm principle. *See* positive harm principle
Harris, Ian, 214
Harsanyi, John, 77
Hastert Rule, 147–48, 301n88
Hastie, Reid, 146
Hastings, Warren, 63, 283n32
Havel, Vaclav, 258
Hayek, Friedrich, 200–201, 207, 229, 315n27
Healey, Denis, 163, 305n35
Heath, Edward, 162
Hegel, Georg: Berlin on, 206–7, 217–19; as positive libertarian, 17, 99
Heidegger, Martin, 91
Helvetius, Claude Adrien, 207, 222
Herder, Johann Gottfried von, 201, 223–24
Heritage Foundation, 9
Herzen, Alexander, 213; *From the Other Shore*, 227; *My Past and Thoughts*, 227
Hills, Roderick, 138, 299n62
Hilton, John, Berlin letter to, 213
Hindmoor, Andrew, 130
Hirschman, Albert, 21, 23, 118
Hobbes, Thomas: Berlin on, 215, 230; on civil peace, 234; on hypothetical state of nature, 234; *Leviathan*, 99, 198; on liberty, 98–103, 198; on majority rule, 14, 172, 175–76; on monopoly character of power,

INDEX

176–77; as negative libertarian, 17, 103, 119; on power, 259–60; Rousseau's critique of, 51; Skinner and, 98–101, 230; on social contract, 13–14; on sovereignty of the people, 174–75
Hobson's choices, 294–95n106
Hochschild, Arlie, 20
Holmes, Oliver Wendell, 286n13
Holocaust, 20, 217, 222, 223
homosexuality, 45, 279n52
hope: performative dimension of, 23; refusal to give up, 21, 202. *See also* strategically hopeful action
Hoppe, Hans-Hermann, 130
Howell, William, and Terry Moe: on congressional power, 10, 130–31, 146; on executive concentration of power, 124, 134–35, 140, 146; responses to positions of, 146–48
Hume, John, 264–66, 323n76, 324n79
Hungary, 123
Hurley, Susan, 82, 287n20
Hurricane Katrina, G. W. Bush administration's response to, 284n52
Hussein, Saddam, 108

identity politics, 17, 22
Ignatieff, Michael, 202
impartiality, 27–49; Barry on first- and second-order impartiality, 6–7, 29–40, 277n21; dangers of ignoring, 30; democracy and, 40–48; Godwin on, 30; inability to settle disagreements about justice of political arrangements, 27, 29; resourcism and, 36, 43; Smith's impartial spectator, 65–67
impeachment powers, 149
imperialism, 30

impossibility theorem, 9
India, 123, 308n26
individualism, 289n35
inequality: in access to courts, 46; Barry on, 46–48; growth of, in United States since 1970s, 46; in South Africa economy, 22
information gathering, 142–46
Ingham, Sean, 126
injustice, chronic nature of problems of, 69
Inkatha Freedom Party (IFP), 247, 251
insecurity: endemic to human condition, 17; of freedom, 219–28; susceptability to populist appeals, 19–20, 233. *See also* employment insecurity
institutional constraints, 135–36
Iran-Contra affair (1985–1987), 142
Iraq war (2003–2011), 63, 108, 129, 145, 166, 283n32
Ireland, Republic of: Northern Ireland's peace agreement, role in, 264; referendums on abortion and equal marriage, 158, 303n17
Israel, political parties in, 180, 182
Israeli-Palestinian conflict, 234–36, 239, 263, 266–67, 269
Iustitia (goddess of justice), 27

Jackson, Andrew, 301n92, 306n2
Jacobs, Lawrence R., 144
James, Alice, Berlin letter to, 209
Jameson, Frederick, 2
Janis, Irving, 146
Japan, 21
Japanese internment during World War II, 44
Jefferson, Thomas, 154
Jenkins, Roy, 163, 305n35

335

INDEX

jobs, loss of. *See* employment insecurity
Johnson, Andrew, 149, 304nn28–29
Johnson, Boris, 159
judges as conservatives, 11, 45
judicial power: Barry on, 33–34, 38–39; congressional power curbed by, 10, 125; inequality in access to, 46, 49, 114; as least dangerous branch of government, 16, 49; reluctance to check presidential discretion, 150; as veto method, 147. *See also* Supreme Court
judicial review: administrative efficacy and, 137; Pettit on, 113; as prevention to domination, 45; public choice theorists and, 124
Judt, Tony, 41–43
juries and unanimity requirements, 154–55
justice: as blind, 27, 275n1; capabilities-based theory of, 61–62; as constraint on democracy, 49; democratizing as best path to, 4–5, 8–9, 73, 104; domination and, 73, 75–77; equality as bedrock of, 7, 76–77, 85; as fairness (Rawls), 77, 85–87; freedom and, 50; impartiality and, 6–8, 27, 30, 40–41, 277n21; no general principle of, 3; nondomination as bedrock of, 73–75, 88, 116, 120; resourcist camp on, 36; Sen on, 6–7, 50–72, 74–75

Kagan, Elena, 137–38
Kane, John, 76, 286n5
Kant, Immanuel: on autonomy, 82; Berlin on, 201, 217, 223–24, 318n70; ethics of, 5, 272n8; Habermas's Kantian interpretation of nondomination, 94; on knowledge, 2; on people as ends in themselves, 198, 217; as positive libertarian, 17; rational universalism of, 318n70; Rawls's Kantian interpretation of nondomination, 76, 82–85; Rawls's Kantian interpretation of social contract tradition, 52; on welfare, 287n23
Kaufman, Gerald, 163
Kennan, George: Berlin and, 200, 201, 204, 208, 212, 216, 219, 223, 315n30; as Cold War liberal, 17, 229; on Dissenters' share of electorate, 285n57; as political realist, 229
Keynes, John Maynard, 123
knowledge, 2–4
Koch, Charles and David, 166
Koh, Harold, 68
Ku Klux Klan, 293n91
Kuwait, 1990 war in, 108

laissez-faire, 118, 286n13
Landemore, Hélène, 303n17
Larmore, Charles, 288–89n34
last-best-offer arbitration, 183
Lawrence v. Texas (2003), 279n52
leadership role in transforming power relations, 237–44, 251–58; foresight and, 258; moral dimension of, 255; transactional vs. transformative leaders, 252. *See also* de Klerk, F. W.; Mandela, Nelson; strategically hopeful action
League of Nations, 21
Lebanon, 268
Lee, Francis, 190
legislative power. *See* clientelism; congressional power; parliamentary systems

INDEX

liberals and liberalism: Berlin as, 210, 212, 229; Cold War liberals, 17, 229; fear of majority tyranny, 284n50; freedom and, 220; of post-war generations seeking impartial rationale for welfare states, 42; Warren era as "heroic age" for, 11
libertarians: attacks on democracy, 130, 176; collective-action regime and, 177; MacCallum on, 101; negative, 17–18, 103, 119; Nozick arguing as, 282n26; positive, 17–18, 99, 200, 201, 317n62; Sen on, 61; social contract metaphor and, 127–28; suspicious of all governments, 130
liberty: basic human liberty vs. liberty as political value, 227; Hobbes on, 98–103, 198; republican liberty, 102. *See also* freedom; negative freedom; positive freedom
Lieberman, Joseph, 136
Lincoln, Abraham, 174
Line Item Veto Act (1996), 129
Linz, Juan, 140, 299–300n69
"live and let live" ethic, 239
local values, 51, 65
Lochner era, 10, 44
Locke, John: Berlin on, 215; on domination, 29; on government to be a single collective entity, 191; *Letter Concerning Toleration*, 198; on liberty of conscience, 198; on majority rule, 14, 126, 172, 175; on monopoly character of power, 176–77; as negative libertarian, 17; on political institutions based on natural rights, 52; on social contract, 13–14; on sovereignty of the people, 174–75

loss of confidence in democracy, 8–10, 23, 123, 272n12
loyal opposition, 5, 141, 153, 183

MacCallum, Gerald, Jr., 18, 101–3, 199–200, 232
Machiavelli, Niccolo, 100, 215
MacIntyre, Alasdair, 1, 50, 90
Macpherson, C. B., 199
Madison, James: on bicameral system, 15; on checks and balances, 154; fear of majority factions, 49; on necessity of government, 155; on political parties, 178; reversing his thinking on republican institutions, 120, 126; on separation of powers, 15–16, 132; on tyranny, 15; vetocracy and, 136. See also *The Federalist Papers*
Maistre, Joseph de, 207
majority rule: as absolute democracy, 177; attacks on, 8–10, 125–27; Barry on, 30, 47; democracy and, 172; disappointments on both the left and the right with, 11; general will and, 9; Hobbes on, 14, 172, 175–76; Locke on, 14, 126, 172, 175; Pettit on, 108–9, 112–13; power best exercised under, 173; public choice theorists on, 10, 127; reasons to embrace, 9–10, 14; social welfare and, 126; veto power and, 147
Mandela, Nelson: compromises with de Klerk government, 250–51; democratic transition, role in, 22, 236, 270; as political manipulator, 252–53; relations with de Klerk, 248, 253–54, 260–62; release from prison, 247; strategically hopeful leadership of, 22, 243–46, 319n16; variable-sum approach of, 261–62

337

INDEX

Mansbridge, Jane J., 177–78
Marcuse, Herbert, 199
marital rape, 98, 291n54
Marshall, T. H., 42, 278n41
Marshall, Thurgood, 66
Marshall Plan, 21, 42
Marx, Karl, and Marxism: Berlin on, 202–3, 213, 217–19, 224, 229; *Das Capital*, 199; on exploitation, 84–85; Hegel and, 206; on majoritarian politics and parliamentary road to politics, 284n50; Mill and, 199; as positive libertarian, 17; rational choice Marxism, 128; Rousseau and, 213; on "withering away of the state," 56. *See also* Cold War; communism
May, Theresa, 159, 161, 188
McBride, Katherine, Berlin letter to, 215
McCarran Act (1950), 208
McCarthy, Joseph, and McCarthy era, 107, 208–9, 229, 311n46
McCubbins, Matthew, 190
McGovern-Fraser Reforms (1970s), 190
means/ends dichotomies, 49
median voter, 165–66, 180, 189, 284n50, 310n39
media's role in democratic politics, 48
medical care, entitlement to, 37–38, 66
Medicare, 160, 184; Part D, 129, 136
Mexico, 107
Miliband, David, 158, 304n29
Mill, John Stuart: on benefits of argument, 151–52, 167; on competition over ideas, 12; fear of tyranny of majority, 284n50; harm principle of, 35; on knowledge, 2, 12; Marx vs., 199; as negative libertarian, 17; *On Liberty*, 151, 198
Miller, Nicholas, 126
Missouri Compromise (1820), 70
Moe, Terry. *See* Howell, William, and Terry Moe
monistic conceptions of human purposes, 220, 230, 317n62
moral arbitrariness, 38, 77–82, 277n30
moral equality, 7, 117
morality, 218–19, 222–23, 318n70
Moss, David, 135
Mother Theresa, 36
multiparty systems, 13, 164, 167, 172–73, 180–86, 309n34
Munchausen syndrome, 36

NAFTA replacement bill including big pharma, 136
Nagel, Tom, 2
national security, 138, 298n36
natural law, 52–53, 199
natural rights theorists, 43, 199
Nazis, 218
negative freedom: Berlin on, 16–17, 197–98, 200–201, 204, 211, 220, 228, 317n62; critics of, 198–99; in debates within political theory, 214; Hobbes on, 198; longevity of concept, 228; MacCallum on, 199–200; in post-Cold War era, 231–33
negative libertarians. *See* libertarians
negotiations, 21–22, 161–62, 183–84, 309n30. *See also* compromise
neoclassical economists, 71
neo-Kantians, 5–6, 51
neo-Rousseauists, 12, 126
Netanyahu, Benjamin, 268
Netherlands, 45, 123

INDEX

neutrality: equality as, 85–87; Larmore's defense of, 288n34; as nonexistent in politics, 3, 5; Rawls on, 65, 76, 85–87, 283n37
new authoritarianism, 130–39
New Deal, 10, 39, 44, 184, 231
New Right, 42
Newton, Isaac, 207
Nietzsche, Friedrich, 1, 3, 90, 289n35
nondomination, 7–8, 73–120; Barry and, 48; as bedrock of justice, 73–75, 88, 116, 120; conceptions of, 92–116; equality and, 75–76, 88, 116–20; Foucault on, 95–97, 119; freedom and, 88; Habermas on, 8, 93–95, 119; Kantian interpretation, 82–85; link to distributive considerations, 82–85; Pettit on, 8, 85, 104–16, 119–20, 289n40; as political freedom, 118; as primary good, 107; Rawls on, 8, 76–87; Skinner on, 98–104, 119; Walzer on, 97–98. *See also* domination
nonprofits, 186
Norquist, Grover, 160
North, Douglass, 133
North, Oliver, 142
Northern Ireland: British violent repression in, 265; conflict resolution in, 234, 239, 257, 263–64; Democratic Unionist Party (DUP), 265; Good Friday (or Belfast) Agreement (1998), 264–65; Irish Republican Army (IRA), 265–66, 324n76, 324n85; option of joining Republic of Ireland, 264, 323n70; Sinn Féin, 265–66, 324n76, 324n79; Ulster Unionist Party (UUP), 265, 324n85
Norway, judicial review in, 45

Nozick, Robert, 14, 61, 74, 80, 128, 176, 179, 282n26

Obama, Barack: banking regulation, 112, 142, 294n98; cap-and-trade policy for toxic emissions, 155; drug prices and, 136; Libya and, 108; stimulus plan, 142; Tea Party opposition to, 109–10, 155, 188
Office of Information and Regulatory Affairs (OIRA), 137–38, 299n60
Office of Technology Assessment, 138
old-age poverty, 20
Olson, Mancur, 130
O'Neill, Terence, 264
Oslo Accords (1993), 267–68, 324n87
ossification thesis, 137
Owen, David, 305n35

PAC (Pan Africanist Congress), 247
Page, Benjamin I., 178
Paine, Tom: *American Crisis*, 23; *Common Sense*, 23; *Rights of Man*, 23–24
Paisley, Ian, 264–65
Palestinian-Israeli conflict. *See* Israeli-Palestinian conflict
Palestinian Liberation Organization (PLO), 267
Pape, Robert, 285n57
Paperwork Reduction Act (1980), 137
parliamentary systems: advantages of, 16, 116, 139, 141, 148, 149, 299–300n69; in Britain, 152–53; coalitions in, 69–72
Parsons, Talcott, 261
participatory democratic theory, 8, 11–12
parties. *See* political parties
partition, 235

INDEX

Paul, Denis, 210–11
PD. *See* prisoner's dilemma
Pelosi, Nancy, 141, 189
pension systems, fears for, 19–20
Peres, Shimon, 267–68
Pettit, Philip: advocating for constraints on majoritarian politics, 112–13; on bargaining as inferior to deliberative contestatory forums, 110–11; on domination as capacity to interfere with someone, 104–5, 107, 292nn69–70; on domination as political mechanism, 91–92; on egalitarianism, 105–6; on freedom, 198; on gag rules, 109, 113; on government as malevolent actor, 112; on majority rule, 108–9, 112–13; on nondomination, 8, 85, 104–16, 119–20, 289n40; on reciprocal power, 113; on redistributive policies, 91, 105; on republican institutions, 104, 120; *Republicanism: A Theory of Freedom and Government*, 104, 110, 293n91; on social movements' role, 108–9, 293n91; on veto powers, 113
Philippines, 123
Pitt, William, 285n62
Plekhanov, Georgi, 213
Plessy v. Ferguson (1896), 44, 45, 279n48
PLO (Palestinian Liberation Organization), 267
Plott, Charles, 125
pluralist democracy: Berlin prizing, 210, 225, 229; criticism of, 126; Madison on, 15
Pocock, J. G. A., 198, 291n62
Poland, authoritarian presidentialism in, 123

Polish-Lithuanian Commonwealth, 147, 301n87
political parties, 169–93; backbenchers, effect of, 148, 167, 188–90; benefits of two strong, disciplined parties, 13, 164, 167, 181, 188, 193; campaign contributions, effect of, 46, 147, 168; competition among, 173, 179–84; discipline by leaders, 174; governance of, 186–87; internal bickering of, 169; loyal opposition, role of, 5, 141, 153, 183; platforms of, 158; principal-agent dynamics of, 170–74, 190–91; public interest and, 169, 172–74, 178–79, 184, 193; retrospective voting and, 173, 177–79; Schumpeter's analogy to corporations, 186, 191; similarities between parties, 173, 184–86, 310n39; in single member plurality (SMP) electoral system, 153–54, 164, 302n5; small parties, 155, 165, 180, 309n30; strength and purpose of, 147, 170, 188–90; unpopularity of, 169; voter ignorance and, 192; weakness exacerbated by presidentialism, 141, 147, 169. *See also* multiparty systems; two-party system
politics: money's role in, 46, 147, 168; neutrality as nonexistent in, 3, 5; political legitimacy, 1, 14, 172; political philosophy, 5, 53, 73; power as focus of, 13
Polsby, Nelson, 260
Popper, Karl: Berlin and, 207, 211, 225–26; as Cold War liberal, 17, 229; on negative freedom, 200–201
populism: exploiting fears of working class, 20; negative liberty and, 232;

INDEX

Trump and, 192. *See also* authoritarian populism
pork-barrel politics, 10, 131, 140, 167
positive freedom, 17, 99, 198, 200, 214, 219–20, 226, 229–30, 317n62
positive harm principle, 35–36, 39, 48
positive libertarians. *See* libertarians
positive-sum conflict, 236, 240, 246, 269
Posner, Eric, and Adrian Vermeule: on checks and balances, 133; on collective-action problems of legislatures, 131; on congressional power, 10, 131, 133, 149; on executive concentration of power, 124, 132–33, 138, 143–44; *The Executive Unbound*, 144; ossification thesis of, 137; on parliamentary model, 148; on separation of powers, 132, 144; on unitary structure of the executive, 143, 300n82
post-Marxists, 2
postmodernists, 2
poststructuralists, 2
post-World War II prosperity and peace, 20, 41
poverty: in old age, 20; in South Africa, 22; in unequal democracies, 47–48
power: definition of, 259–60, 261; domination as illicit use of, 8, 28–29, 89–90, 96–97, 101, 118; as focus of politics, 13, 155; Foucault on, 96; Hobbes and Locke on, 176–77, 259–60; knowledge as, 4; as natural monopoly, 13, 14, 172, 173, 176; in prisoner's dilemma, 259; of strategically hopeful leaders, 242. *See also* domination; variable-sum conflict; zero-sum conflict

pragmatists, 285n62
presidential elections: accountability and, 143–44, 301n92; primaries, 189–90
presidential power. *See* executive power
principal-agent dynamics, 142–43, 170–74; negatives of, 190–91; presidential primaries and, 189–90; rejection of, 174–77, 191; superficial appeal of, 191
prisoner's dilemma (PD), 234, 237–38, 240–41, 246, 257–59
progressivity, 40
proportional representation (PR), 153–54, 164, 180
PR (proportional representation), 153–54, 164, 180
Przeworski, Adam, 126
public choice theorists, 123–31, 295n4; on bureaucratic growth, 130; on checks and balances, 133; constitutionalizing protection of property and contracts, 136–37; damage to democracy, 123–27, 150; on majority rule, 10, 127; market-oriented bias of, 124, 135; principal-agent dynamics and, 142
public interest: partisan conceptions of, 179–86, *185*; political parties and, 169, 172–74, 178–79, 184, 193; president in best position to address, 135

Rabin, Yitzhak, 267–68, 324n87
racial discrimination, 34–35
Ratcliffe, Donald, 306n2
rational choice theory, 128, 243, 252, 255
rationalism, 128, 203

341

Rawls, John, 50–61; Barry and, 31, 48; on basic structure of political institutions, 5–6, 56; commitment to ideal theory, 54–58; comparative reasoning used by, 58; difference principle and, 58, 288n34; on equality as bedrock of justice, 7, 76–77, 85; established church eschewed by, 86; on the good, 36; Habermas compared to, 93–94; on helping the least advantaged, 58, 60; on impartiality's relationship with justice, 40; on justice, 54–58, 286n10; on moderate scarcity, 57, 76, 281n6; on moral arbitrariness, 38, 76, 78–82, 277n30; neo-Kantians and, 51; on neutrality, 65, 76, 85–87, 283n37; on nondomination, 8, 76–87; on overlapping consensus, 63–64; partial orderings by, 57–58; resourcism and, 43, 293n79; on self-interest, 55, 58, 77; Sen's critique of, 7, 51, 52–58; *A Theory of Justice*, 5, 57, 271–72n7, 281n6; universalizability and, 53; veil of ignorance and, 52, 54, 56, 57, 76–77, 86
Rayner, Angela, 311n50
Read, James, 22, 234, 319n12
Reagan, Ronald, 20, 42, 128–29, 137, 142
realist school of international relations theory, 260
reasonableness, 31–33, 36, 37, 41
Reconstruction: abandonment of, 166; Andrew Johnson and, 149; Supreme Court undermining of, 44
redistributive policies, 46, 81, 83, 85, 105, 180, 284n50
Reeve, Andrew, 36

referendums, 157–64, 179, 264. See also ballot initiatives and referendums
regulatory capture, 127, 135, 136, 139, 168
Rehnquist Court, 11, 44
religious liberty, 32–34, 86, 277n21
rent-seeking, 10, 127, 130, 131, 135, 140, 165
republican institutions: democracy and, 8; Madison on, 15, 120; Pettit and, 104, 120; self-defeating nature of, 16, 116
Republican Party: bottom-up model for candidate selection and platform writing, 190; on Congress's out-of-control spending, 128; structural advantage in Senate and Electoral College, 11; Supreme Court appointments by, 11; Trump's takeover, 190
resourcism, 36, 43, 48, 74–75, 89, 97, 118, 279n45, 293n79
restraints, freedom described by referencing, 18, 101–2
retrospective voting, 173, 177–79
Riker, William, 125, 179, 252, 296n7
Roberts Court, 11, 44
Rodgers, Bill, 305n35
Roe v. Wade (1973), 45
Roemer, John E., 36
Romanticism and Romantic Age, 207, 213–15, 219–20, 222–23
Roosevelt, Eleanor, 202, 204
Rorty, Richard, 1–2
Rosenblum, Nancy, 182
Rosenbluth, Frances, 182
Rousseau, Jean-Jacques: Berlin on, 203–4, 207, 213–16, 220–23, 225–26, 230, 316n47; challenging democratic government, 125; on freedom,

220–22, 226–27; on general will, 9, 12, 100, 125–26, 221; Hirschman's construction of, 21, 274n40; Hobbes critiqued by, 51; Marx and, 213; on nature, 222; as positive libertarian, 17, 99; Schumpeter on, 178
Russell, Meg, 156
Russia: corruption of authoritarian presidency in, 125; sanctions on, 139, 148
Ryan, Paul, 189

Saint-Simon, Henri de, 207
Scanlon, T. M., 31, 32, 35, 39, 40, 51, 276n14
Schattschneider, E. E., 193
Schelling, Thomas, 236, 253–57, 270; *Strategy of Conflict*, 253, 256
school desegregation, 45
Schumpeter, Joseph, 126, 152–53, 173, 178, 186, 191
secret ballots, 63
Seldon, Arthur, 130
self-interest, 55, 58, 77
Sen, Amartya: alternative theory to neo-Kantians, 6; American constitutional law appealing to impartiality of, 68; antipathy for domination and, 51; on Ashoka, 55; Barry compared to, 6; on behavioral adaptation, 56; on Buddha, 54; capabilities-based theory of justice and, 61–62; comparative theory of, 51, 56–57, 59–63, 65; on democracy, 52, 67–71; on equality, 7, 74–75; flute trilemma example of, 60–63; on human rights, 66; *The Idea of Justice*, 6–7, 51, 67; on immunity of democracies from famine, 68–69;

on incommensurable values providing insights, 60–61; on justice, 6–7, 50–72, 74–75; on local parochialism of values, 51, 65; partial orderings by, 64; on plural grounds, 63–64, 283n32; Rawls's transcendental theory rejected by, 7, 51, 52–58; resourcism and, 293n79; on slavery's injustice, 70; Smith's impartial spectator and, 51, 65–67; Sunstein and, 283n32
Senate, U.S.: filibuster, 147–48, 155; founders' intentions for, 154; Republican advantage in, 11, 147; Tocqueville's praise of, 302n6; Webster's praise of, 154
separation of powers, 15–16, 113, 116, 132, 144, 299n62, 302n97
sexual orientation, right to, 32–33
Shakespeare, William: *Hamlet*, 36
Shapiro, Ian: *Democracy's Place*, 287n17; *Democratic Justice*, 106; *The Evolution of Rights in Liberal Theory*, 36
Shklar, Judith, 116
Simmons, Joel, 188
Single European Act, 162
single member plurality (SMP) electoral system, 153–54, 164, 302n5
Skinner, Quentin: civic humanism of, 198, 230; Hobbes and, 98–101, 230; *Hobbes and Republican Liberty*, 99, 102; on nondomination, 8, 98–104, 119
Slaughter-House Cases (1873), 44, 279n48
slavery and slave trade, 70–72, 82–83, 100, 102, 287n22. *See also* abolition of slave trade

343

INDEX

Smith, Adam: impartial spectator and, 65–67; Sen and, 51; *The Theory of Moral Sentiments,* 65
Smith, John, 40
SMP (single member plurality) electoral system, 153–54, 164, 302n5
social choice theorists, 125–26
social contract theorists, 13–14, 52, 127–29, 172, 221
social democratic welfare states, 30, 41–42, 44, 279n46
social movements, role of, 108–9, 293n91
Social Security, 19, 160, 184
social wage regime, 106, 118
South Africa, 21–23, 234–35, 244–62; apartheid, 21–22, 45, 83, 117, 234–35; Conservative Party, 248; Constitutional Court on right to medical treatment for renal failure, 38, 278n33; corruption in, 22–23; democracy in, 21–22, 246, 251, 256, 262; economic inequality in, 22; "Homelands" policy, 235; Israeli-Palestinian conflict compared to, 268; leadership role in settling conflict in, 239, 270; military role in transition, 256, 320n46; National Party, 117, 244, 248–50, 255; Pan Africanist Congress (PAC), 247; political flux in, 236, 237, 242; political violence in, 251; poverty in, 21–22; voting rights under 1983 constitution, 320n23. *See also* de Klerk, F. W.; Mandela, Nelson
South African Communist Party, 247
Soviets. *See* Cold War; communism
Spencer, Herbert, 17
Stalin, Josef, 7, 200
Starmer, Kier, 311n50

Steinmetz, Alicia, 16, 197
Stigler, George J., 127
strategically hopeful action, 236–44, 269–70; assassination risks, 239, 265, 267; Axelrod's approach, 237–40; community cooperation initiatives, 239–40; compromise seen as weakness, 245–46, 253–54, 266; "live and let live" ethic, 239; mutual cooperation outcome, 240–41, 259; preference for peace over war, 258; prisoner's dilemma (PD), 237–38, 240–41, 246, 257–59; rational choice analyses and, 243–44; "tit for tat" (TFT) strategy, 238–39, 319n6; trust problem, 241, 259, 262; variable-sum conflict, 236, 240, 242, 246, 250, 253–54; zero-sum conflict, 235–36, 239–40, 253, 269. *See also* de Klerk, F. W.; Mandela, Nelson; Northern Ireland
Strauss, Leo, 1; *Natural Right and History,* 199
Summers, Larry, 142
Sunstein, Cass, 63–64, 146, 283n32
supermajorities, 14, 47, 113, 153, 155, 170
Supreme Court, U.S.: on Line Item Veto Act, 129; money's role in politics expanded by, 46, 168; on socially divisive issues, 45; Trump and, 150. *See also specific Court by chief justice's name*
Suskind, Ron, 142
Sweden, judicial review in, 45

Taft Court, 44
Taft-Hartley Act (1947), 184
Talmon, Jacob, Berlin letter to, 213
Taney Court, 44

INDEX

Tawney, R. H., 47
taxation and distributive regime: Barry on, 39–40, 278n35; Hobbes on, 177; majority rule on, 284n50; repeal of federal estate tax, 109; Republican pledge not to raise taxes, 160; Trump tax cuts, 129, 149; on the wealthy, 39–40, 158
Taylor, Charles, 99
Tea Party movement, 109–10, 155, 167, 188, 293n91
Tenure of Office Act (1867), 149
Thatcher, Margaret, 42, 162, 184
Thompson, Judy, 276n16
"tit for tat" (TFT) strategy, 238–39, 319n6
Tocqueville, Alexis de, 49, 154, 284n50, 302n6
tolerance. *See* discrimination and tolerance
totalitarianism, 216. *See also* authoritarianism
trade union movement, 113–14, 180, 184
Tribe, Laurence, 10, 44
Trimble, David, 244, 265–66
Troubled Asset Relief Program, 298n36
Truman, Harry, 138, 184
Trump, Donald: administrative resistance to, 300n82; ambitions of, 79; banking regulation, 294n98; circumventing Congress, 139, 149; drug prices and, 136; federal spending hikes and tax cuts, 129, 149; line-item vetoes and, 129; populist agenda of, 192; Posner's reaction to, 144–45; Republican Party and, 190; rogue exploits, 142, 145; Supreme Court and, 150

Tullock, Gordon, 47, 125, 130, 176; *Calculus of Consent* (with Buchanan), 166
Turkey, 123
two-party system: accountability in, 183; advantages of competition in, 173, 179–84; birth of, 171; longevity of parties in, 182; median voter and, 165–66, 180, 189, 310n39; winner-take-all dynamic of, 5, 179, 181, 186
tyranny, 14–15, 49, 133. *See also* domination

uMkhonto we Sizwe, 21, 244
unanimity rule, 47, 162, 176–77
United Kingdom. *See* Britain
United Nations, 21
universalizability, 53, 83
utilitarianism, 30, 50, 57, 61, 77, 166, 219
utility drift, 133
Utley, Thomas, 207

vanguardist politics, 42, 49
Van Parijs, Philippe, 37
variable-sum conflict, 236, 240, 242, 246, 250, 253–55, 257, 261–62
Venezuela, 125
Vermeule, Adrian. *See* Posner, Eric, and Adrian Vermeule
veto powers, 113, 120, 128–29, 147, 153
Vietnam war, 145
vulnerability to domination, 48, 74, 115, 118, 120, 286n3
Vyshinsky, Andrey Tanuar'evich, 204

wages: social wage regime, 106, 118; stagnation, 19
Wagner Act (1935), 114, 184
Waite Court, 44

INDEX

Walzer, Michael: Berlin and, 226; on inequality, 35, 84; on nondomination, 8, 97–98; on values guiding human social practices, 90
War Powers Resolution (2019), 149
Warren, Earl, 10, 44
Warren Court, 10–11; as aberration in Supreme Court history, 11, 44, 279n46
wealth: democracy subverted by, 49; distribution of, 22, 39; domination and corruption as uses of, 84; growth of, 20; taxation on, 39–40, 158. *See also* clientelism
Weber, Max, 2, 92, 129, 142
Webster, Daniel, 154
Weingast, Barry, 125, 133

West India–based slave traders, 71
Westminster model. *See* Britain
Whigs (American party), 182
White Court, 44
Williams, Shirley, 163, 305n35
Wilson, Harold, 162–63
Wittgenstein, Ludwig, 28
Working Party on Spiritual Aspects of Western Union, 205

Young, Iris Marion, 84
Yugoslavia, atrocities after partition, 235, 242, 270, 319n12

zero-sum conflict, 235–36, 239–40, 246, 250, 253–54, 256, 259–63, 269